JOHN PERRY

THE DETROITING OF AMERICA

WHAT HAPPENED TO THE MOTOR CITY

WHY OTHER CITIES FOLLOWED

HOW DETROIT IS COMING BACK

FIDELIS
PUBLISHING

FIDELIS PUBLISHING ®

ISBN: 9781956454512
ISBN (eBook): 9781956454529

The Detroiting of America:
What Happened to the Motor City
Why Other Cities Followed
How Detroit Is Coming Back

Cover Design by Diana Lawrence
Interior Layout Design by Lisa Parnell
Edited by Amanda Varian

Order at www.faithfultext.com for a significant discount. Email info@fidelispublishing.com to inquire about bulk purchase discounts.

Fidelis Publishing, LLC • Winchester, VA / Nashville, TN • fidelispublishing.com

Manufactured in the United States of America

10 9 8 7 6 5 4 3 2 1

TO ALL THE DETROITERS WHO NEVER GAVE UP

Contents

"It has been said that each generation must rewrite history in order to understand it. The opposite is true. Moderns revise history to make it palatable, not to understand it. Those who edit 'history' to popular taste each decade will never understand the past—neither the horrors nor the glories of which the human race is equally capable—and for that reason, they will fail to understand themselves."

—*T. R. Fehrenbach*

"Everyone is entitled to his own opinion, but not his own facts."

—*Daniel Patrick Moynihan*

"There is nothing new under the sun."

—*Ecclesiastes 1:9*

■ ■ ■

Introduction

"The longer you can look back, the farther you can look forward."
—Winston Churchill

■ ■ ■

THIS IS not another book about Detroit-bashing. There have been enough of those already.

This is the story of a great city that lost its way but now shows promising signs of renewal. It is also a powerful cautionary tale for other cities that today face the same challenges Detroit once faced. As Winston Churchill noted, "The longer you can look back, the farther you can look forward." The only thing better than learning from our own mistakes is learning from someone else's. Understanding the decisions Detroit's leaders made and the results that followed gives the rest of us valuable insights absolutely risk-free.

Knowing history, we can predict the future. Leaders who make the same choices Detroit once made will get the same results. The proof of this truth is in today's headlines. Some cities in 2020s America are thriving, growing, and healthy while others are hemorrhaging population, jobs, tax revenues, and hope. The failing cities fail because they follow Detroit's old playbook. The growing cities succeed because their leaders have chosen a different path.

An essential part of understanding Detroit's rise, fall, and future prospects is to realize the popular history of the city is tantalizingly

1

incomplete. History cannot teach us if history is distorted. Long-established assumptions about Detroit's problems collapse under the weight of information either overlooked or suppressed for decades. In these cases, the objective is not to thumb a revisionist nose at past narratives but to offer important historical accounts, especially those from trailblazing minority reporters and journalists who present key chapters of the city's history in an entirely new light.

Theirs is a city worth understanding. Worth learning from. Worth saving.

For more than fifty years "Detroit" has been shorthand for all that is wrong with urban America: crime, corruption, decay, racial tension, struggling businesses, failing schools, a declining tax base, and dismal public services. Since 1950 Detroit has lost more than two-thirds of its residents, falling from fifth place in the U.S. census (just behind Los Angeles) to twenty-ninth (just behind Memphis, Tennessee), a drop unmatched in American history. Between 2000 and 2021 alone, its population fell 32 percent, more than any other major U.S. city. A third of its land now lies vacant or dotted with empty, derelict houses.

The good news is there are unmistakable signs of renewal in Detroit. Given a fresh start—courtesy of the largest municipal bankruptcy in history, followed by heroic commitments to the community from visionary local entrepreneurs and business leaders—Detroit has slowed its rate of population decline, stabilized its finances, and set out to prove to the world it is once again open for business. Even longstanding symbols of Detroit on the ropes such as the old railroad station and the infamous remains of the Packard automobile plant have moved off the "urban blight" tours. The former has new life as a state-of-the-art transportation technology research center for Ford while the latter was mercifully felled at last by the wrecker's ball.

The bad news is how the very decisions and choices that led to Detroit's devastating collapse are being duplicated today in city councils and state legislatures across the country. Rather than learning from Detroit's missteps, far too many community leaders and politicians are on a path to repeating them. The consequences of their misguided policies are all around them: soaring street crime, declining public services, taxpayers squeezed ever tighter to fund ballooning entitlements, erosion of community support for law enforcement favoring criminals over law-abiding residents and business owners, and the paralyzing effect of political correctness that confuses racism and other "isms" with accountability and the rule of law.

How did it happen? How did the mighty Motor City where once half the cars in the world were built become the poster child for urban failure? Why did other Industrial Belt cities such as Columbus, Indianapolis, and Pittsburgh survive the urbanization of the '50s, racial unrest of the '60s, oil crisis of the '70s, and globalization of the '80s while Detroit foundered?

Why does Chicago have the same population it had a hundred years ago while Houston has grown 1,675 percent in the same period? Phoenix and Albuquerque were both pinpoints in the desert in 1950. Why is Phoenix three times the size of Albuquerque today?

On a state level, why have an estimated 15,000 businesses left California in recent years? Why have so many of them moved to Texas? When the American automobile industry revived in the 1970s and '80s, why did manufacturers build their new plants in Alabama, Georgia, Tennessee, and South Carolina instead of Michigan where purpose-built factories and an established knowledge base were already in place?

The answers to all these questions are found in the choices city and state leaders are making today. Time and again when those leaders decide to follow policies that Detroit's example has shown to be disastrous, the results are just as bleak: another once-great city begins the downward spiral into urban decay. Detroit suffered terribly for its poor decisions. Yet instead of learning from them, too many metropolitan leaders are blindly following the same fatal path. This is the Detroiting of America.

Along with making decisions resulting in negative outcomes, Detroit's leaders consistently cast blame for the city's ills onto someone or something else. From their perspective, the problem was never their fault. This may be one reason why its history is so distorted. It is only human nature to conceal mistakes and point the finger in another direction. However, by obscuring their true causes, this tendency prevents issues from being resolved.

The problems and pitfalls that pinned Detroit to the mat were the city's own doing, just as current crises in Los Angeles, San Francisco, Chicago, Seattle, and other foundering urban centers are direct results of decisions made by city leaders and the voters who elected them. Federal policies, Covid, the national economy, or any other outside influence are convenient excuses for local failures. While these cities have struggled, San Antonio, subject to the same headwinds, grew by more than 30 percent in the past twenty years. Phoenix, with a larger population than San Francisco or Seattle and the same potential for big-city problems, has grown more than 25 percent since 2000.

Phoenix, Charlotte, and Houston are booming these days while St. Louis, New Orleans, and (still) Detroit see residents streaming for the exits. People are not merely moving to a warmer climate. While warmer weather is a plus, Columbus, Ohio, not known for its balmy temperatures, has grown a healthy 25 percent in the past twenty years. (Chilly Toronto is the fourth largest city in North America after Mexico City, New York, and Los Angeles.)

Nor are people necessarily moving to cities specifically because of their political leanings. Though many of America's most troubled cities are politically liberal, successful cities embrace a range of political viewpoints. Austin, the state capital and home to the University of Texas, is proud of its liberal culture in a conservative state as expressed in its unofficial motto, "Keep Austin Weird." Yet despite a spike in crime due to its short-lived "defund the police" movement of 2020, Austin's population has exploded more than 45 percent since 2000, primed by the relocation of dozens of major corporate headquarters including Oracle, Tesla, and Hewlett-Packard.

The Detroiting of America has transformed our nation by embracing policies that drive out the middle class, small businesses, families looking for good schools and safe neighborhoods, and productive citizens who give back to their communities. Those people vote with their feet, pulling up stakes and starting new lives in places where they are nurtured, protected, and encouraged.

This trend is clear on a small scale when families and businesses move from the city of Detroit to suburban jurisdictions just outside of town for lower taxes, better schools, safer streets, and more opportunity. Stepping across the city limits is stepping into another world.

For a large-scale example, the states of New York and Florida provide a dramatic lesson. The Empire State and the Sunshine State have comparable populations—about 22 million for Florida and about 19 million for New York according to U.S. census 2022 estimates. But because Florida's political and regulatory climate embraces the middle class, small business, homeowners, and all the rest while New York's, in the old Detroiting mode, does not, the relative economic health and living environments of these two states are very different.

For the 2022–23 fiscal year Florida's state budget was $117 billion, including a $20 billion surplus. For New York, with three million fewer residents, the 2022–23 budget was $229 billion, nearly twice the Florida figure. That money comes ultimately from only one source: the pockets of each state's residents. When people see their income siphoned off to support a huge bureaucracy and entitlement system (even for illegal migrants) while public services are failing, they tend to move to a place where the burdens are lower, freedoms greater, and opportunities higher. Populations and their pocketbooks go where they're welcome.

Florida has no personal income tax. New York State has a personal income tax rate of between 4 and almost 9 percent. On top of that, New York City residents pay another 3 percent city income tax; city employees have to pay the tax whether they live within the city limits or not.

The result? In the two years between 2020 and 2022 Florida's population grew 17 percent while New York posted a net loss of 1 percent. This difference is predictable, explainable, and inevitable.

The lessons of Detroit's rise and fall are there for anyone willing to see them. And so is the source of its renewal. The story of Detroit encompasses all the courage, adventure, pitfalls, and triumphs of the human experience. From the rubble of a once-great community, green shoots of life are springing up today thanks to a return of the can-do spirit and freedom of opportunity that made Detroit a world-class city the first time around. Failing cities, take note.

Is it too late to stop the Detroiting of America? That's up to America. Up to you. ■

Chapter 1

Coming of Age

". . . an interminable swamp . . ."
—Government surveyors' report
on Michigan, c.1812

■ ■ ■

SWAMPS. FIRE. Cholera. Cannibals. Detroit spent its first tenuous years struggling for survival, all in the name of fashion.

By the turn of the eighteenth century, Louis XIV, the Sun King of France, had been on the throne more than fifty years. He and his court were not only one of the most powerful political and military forces in Europe, they also set fashion trends throughout the Western world. Essential to the well-dressed Frenchman of the day was fur. Portraits of the time often show wealthy subjects covered in ermine and other luxurious pelts.

The French and their fashion followers particularly loved beaver hats, so much so that by the beginning of the 1700s the beaver population in Europe was trapped out. Eager for other sources, traders looked to the vast, unsettled expanse of Canada, which was already legendary for its furs.

French merchants tried, with mixed results, to control commercial exchange between French trappers and the native North Americans. An ongoing war between the Huron and Iroquois tribes made trapping a dangerous business. Furthermore, because French traders earned a reputation as cheats in their dealings with the Indians, many frontiersmen and natives set up their own local bartering systems, completely bypassing official French oversight. To counter this trend, the French government declared all fur trade had to pass through a central office in Montreal.

To sort out the trade network and establish a permanent base for French control in the region, the king assigned an explorer with wide experience in North America to build a fort that would supply and protect trappers and represent the power of the Sun King in the Canadian wilderness. This seasoned vanguard, Antoine Laumet de la Mothe Cadillac, had been in Canada since 1683, gaining experience as an Indian fighter, military leader, and civilian administrator.

Previous French settlements in Canada remained small, struggling villages. Cadillac suggested a site farther south in order to block British access to the fur trade and shore up French defenses against future British encroachment. He also recommended bringing farmers and craftsmen to set up a self-sustaining economy where families could eventually live.

On July 24, 1701, Cadillac and a small armada of birchbark canoes carrying soldiers, farmers, traders, craftsmen, and priests landed at the foot of a bluff on the shore of a river running between Lake St. Clair and Lake Erie. The high terrain formed a good strategic position, and from the north bank of a bend in the river, defenders could see both up and downstream from the same spot. This river acted as a strait connecting the two lakes and so was known as the *detroit*, the French word for *strait*. Combining that feature with a title honoring King Louis's chief counselor, Louis Phélypeaux, Count Pontchartrain, Cadillac christened his settlement Fort Pontchartrain du Detroit.

Within a year Cadillac reported more than two thousand Indian fur traders in the area, with others coming from as far as Lake Superior. Within five years several women, including Cadillac's wife, and families joined the settlement. The founder's careful planning paid off in that Detroit thrived as the center of the region's fur trade. Cadillac left to become governor of Louisiana Territory in 1711, and eventually returned to France where he died in 1730 at the age of seventy-two.

As part of the settlement of the French and Indian War, Detroit was ceded to the British in 1760. Relations with the native trappers, which blossomed under Cadillac to the benefit of both sides, soured under British rule as the new government gained a reputation for dishonesty and price gouging. Three years later, Indians ended a period of growing tension by attacking local families, indiscriminately scalping women and children. Further attacks led the British to retaliate by scalping the nephew of a chief. Natives then turned on Captain Donald Campbell, second-in-command of the Detroit garrison and a prisoner of war at the time, who was cut up and eaten by his captors. His heart was reserved for the chief, who ate it raw, symbolically taking on the courage of the enemy. Eventually the Ottawa chief Pontiac proposed peace terms suspending the hostilities even though there was never any official treaty put in place.

Murderous encounters resumed during the American Revolutionary War, when British partisans used Detroit as a base for leading Indian raids against American settlers in Kentucky, Pennsylvania, and New York. More than two thousand pioneers—men, women, and children—were killed, many of them scalped.

Detroit was still in British hands when the war ended. Even though the final peace treaty, signed in 1783, ceded all the new Northwest Territory to the United States, Britain kept control of Detroit and its rich fur trade by claiming America had not yet met all its treaty obligations.

Britain's position meant the American government was technically sovereign in Detroit but the British maintained practical control. A British military garrison held the city, and its residents used British courts across the river in Canada until 1796 when, as part of a trade agreement, Detroit was turned over to the United States at last.

The settlement was home to around 500 residents at the time, with another 2,000 or so in outlying areas. Those who wanted to keep their British citizenship moved to Canada. Citizens who owned slaves under colonial rule were allowed to keep them. There were about

175 slaves in town, half of them Indian and the other half of African descent. Besides residual French and British residents, there were a handful of German, Dutch, Scottish, and Irish, giving the town what one historian called "a cosmopolitan flavor that it has always retained."

On January 18, 1802, Detroit was incorporated as a city. One of the new board of trustees' first steps was to issue ordinances for fire protection. Detroit was full of narrow streets lined with wooden houses jammed close together. Any fire would spread like the wind to neighboring structures. The law required each property owner to have a ladder on the roof, fire buckets at hand, and to cover his hearth every night.

But the precautions were all in vain. On the morning of June 11, 1805, embers from a pipe ignited the straw in a barn. Within minutes the barn was destroyed and townspeople formed bucket brigades to save what they could. The town fire engine was hauled into position but proved useless when the cistern suppling it with water was clogged with felt scraps from a hatmaker's shop. In three hours Detroit was burned to the ground.

Miraculously, no one was killed. Surveying the smoldering devastation all around him, Father Gabriel Richard of St. Anne's Catholic Church quietly declared, *"Speramus meliora; resurget cineribus."* ("We hope for better things; they will arise from the ashes.")

Instead of rebuilding Detroit as it had been, members of the Michigan Territory governing board, especially Governor William Hull and board member Judge Augustus B. Woodward, envisioned a far grander city with wide boulevards connecting spacious open areas modeled after Washington, D.C. Woodward, who once lived in Washington, drew up a detailed new plan featuring circular plazas or "circuses" connected by grand boulevards two hundred feet wide, all overlaid with a complex system of interconnected secondary streets and plazas. Each adult resident, including free blacks, would receive a free lot in the new town with lots assigned by random drawing.

Rebuilding began according to Judge Woodward's ambitious plan, though after a few years the city reverted to the more traditional urban grid layout. The main thoroughfare was named Woodward Avenue in honor of the judge, and even today Campus Martius, Grand Circus Park, and a number of downtown streets radiating from central points like spokes of a wheel are historic reminders of Woodward's grand vision.

As it rebuilt and expanded, Detroit held its place as a principal center for the fur trade. Trappers and merchants prospered but continued their conflict with native Americans who chafed at dishonest treatment from white settlers and encroachment on their traditional hunting grounds. The Shawnee chief Tecumseh organized his forces against the Americans and asked British Canadians for help. By 1812 Britain and the United States were at war again.

That year the British invaded Detroit. With his supply lines cut off and fearing the Indians would slaughter the city's residents, Governor Hull surrendered without firing a shot, making Detroit the only significant American city in history to surrender to a foreign army. British soldiers occupied Detroit for more than a year, during which they allowed their native allies free access to take what they wanted from shopkeepers in hopes it would keep the tribes on their side. It was only after the British navy was defeated by American Commodore Oliver Hazard Perry on Lake Erie, in September 1813, that the redcoats finally abandoned Detroit and the city reverted to United States control for good.

Up until this time Detroit grew modestly, from about 500 to around 850 residents during the previous century. One reason for the slow growth was Michigan Territory's reputation in the East as a trackless swamp, inhospitable and dangerous, suitable for trapping but not for farming or building a life on the frontier. Another was the long history of conflict with native tribes around the Great Lakes whose savagery, especially scalping women and children, made would-be settlers afraid to stake their future within reach of such deadly raids. A third handicap for Detroit was its distance from population centers on the Eastern seaboard. To get there from New York City, Boston, or Philadelphia, travelers had to go by land to Buffalo, New York, and either sail west from there or go overland through the swamps of Canada or Ohio, north or south of Lake Erie. Travel by ship was expensive and in winter when the lakes were iced over, land was the only choice. During the season when ships were unavailable, the trip took more than two punishing months.

Into this mix of obstacles stepped the man who would become Detroit's first great visionary leader. Lewis Cass, a colonel of Ohio volunteers in the War of 1812, was appointed territorial governor of Michigan by President James Madison in 1813 in the wake of Governor Hull's humiliating surrender. By the time Cass left office in 1831, he had played a key role in transforming Detroit into one of the first major manufacturing centers in the West. Cass went on to serve as Secretary of War, Minister to France, senator from Michigan, and U.S. Secretary of State. He died in Detroit in 1866 at the age of eighty-three.

Cass's first order of business as governor was to counteract Michigan's negative public image. A government survey described the territory as "an interminable swamp." Cass wrote glowing articles about Michigan for Eastern publications and encouraged Detroit residents to write to friends and family promoting the city.

Another crucial step was reaching a peace accord with the native tribes, who liked the portly governor and called him Big Belly. Tensions relaxed following the War of 1812. Beginning in 1820, a series of treaties negotiated by Cass ceded vast tracts of land to the United States government, who then sold it to settlers in eighty-acre lots for $1.25 per acre. Not only did the raids stop, now new arrivals were guaranteed plenty of land for their homesteads.

Meanwhile, a revolution in transportation made Detroit accessible as never before. In 1811 Robert Fulton built the first successful steamboat. Seven years later the first steamer built on the Great Lakes, *Walk-in-the-Water*, was launched near Buffalo and made its maiden voyage to Detroit. The 135-foot side-wheeler carried one hundred passengers in heretofore unimagined comfort in a fraction of the time it took sailing ships to make the trip.

Then in 1825 the Erie Canal opened, connecting Buffalo to the Hudson River near Albany, 363 miles across the state of New York. Now passengers and freight could steam from New York City up the Hudson, through the canal to Lake Erie and directly to Detroit—in five and a half days! By 1830 a steamer docked in Detroit an average of once a day during ice-free months. On a single day in May 1836, more than 2,400 settlers arrived in town.

Though some of these families put down roots in or near Detroit, most of them used the city as a jumping-off point for destinations west and south. For decades Detroit's geographical position was a handicap. Now the new transportation network made it a nexus for travel between the East and America's vast central and western plains. Detroit merchants and manufacturers catered to the needs of these transient visitors and shipped their surplus production to newly accessible markets on the Atlantic seaboard. The same ships bringing frontier settlers returned with Michigan crops, pork, salted fish, cider, ice, and other goods. By the time of the 1830 census the population of Detroit had grown to 2,222. In 1840 the number was over 9,000 with no end in sight.

The one tragic chapter in the city's history during these years was a series of cholera epidemics, terrifying the residents and sickening hundreds. The first wave began with cholera-infected soldiers who arrived by ship on Independence Day 1832. The disease spread quickly, carried through the population by drinking water and exposure to farm animals. The second and most serious episode was two years later when 122 people—7 percent of the population—died. After more epidemics in 1849 and 1854, the city was mercifully spared any further outbreaks.

Otherwise, Detroit was unstoppable. Michigan joined the Union as the twenty-sixth state in 1837, with Detroit as its capital until replaced by Lansing in 1847 to move the government closer to the middle of the state. With lake transportation booming, the city's main challenge was moving goods in the winter when ice brought all shipping to a halt. Then in 1854, the Great Western Railroad extended its western terminus to Windsor, Ontario, just across the Detroit River. With that, Detroit was open to the fastest available transportation year-round. Between 1830 and 1850, the city grew tenfold.

Detroit businessmen who had seen the potential in supplying settlers passing through now saw even bigger opportunities in serving the shipping and railroad industries. This led to expansion of local copper and iron ore mining, limestone quarrying, timber production, and other industries. The growing mining and logging companies needed more engines and equipment, which Detroit turned out as well.

The city thrived as a manufacturing center and transportation hub. In 1869 the first refrigerated rail car rolled out of Detroit, its cargo chilled by ice and insulated with straw. That same year, George Pullman consolidated manufacturing operations for his Pullman sleepers in Detroit. These popular railroad cars had fold-down beds and privacy curtains so train passengers could sleep in comfort through the night.

One of the most curious and interesting products invented in Detroit during these years was the McCoy automatic lubricating cup. Railroad locomotives had to be lubricated frequently, which required stopping the train. Elijah McCoy, a free black man and U.S. citizen originally from Ontario, invented a device that dripped oil onto moving parts as the engine ran, meaning engineers no longer had to stop their trains to oil them. Though other companies tried to copy McCoy's design, the original was far superior in quality and performance—hence the term "the real McCoy." McCoy went on to patent more than fifty inventions before his death at the age of eighty-five.

McCoy's parents were slaves in Kentucky who escaped to Canada and freedom by way of the Underground Railroad, a network of way stations, routes, safe houses, and volunteers who secretly escorted escaped slaves to freedom. Michigan's state constitution outlawed slavery from the beginning, and Detroit's location between slaveholding states and the Canadian border made it a key destination for runaways.

Scarcely a month after Abraham Lincoln became president, the Civil War began and the men of Michigan were quick to answer the call to arms. About 6,000 Detroiters fought in the conflict, including the Twenty-Fourth Michigan Infantry and the First Michigan Colored Infantry.

After the war, the soldiers came home and Detroit resumed its upward trajectory. The population that more than doubled between 1840 and 1850 doubled again over the next ten years to 45,619. Postwar prosperity further increased the number to almost 80,000 in 1870. Metalworking, mining, logging, railroad equipment manufacturing, and shipbuilding thrived, surging past the fur trade in value, ending the trappers' two-hundred-year run as Detroit's most important industry. But the new star in the city's manufacturing crown was an unlikely product: the humble kitchen stove.

Cast iron kitchen stoves were a fixture in homes across America. Many of them were made at factories in Albany and Troy, New York. Replacement parts for customers in Detroit and points south or west were expensive and slow to arrive. As the market grew, a local iron works started making replacement parts. Seeing strong demand for their products, the company began manufacturing complete stoves. Thanks to the city's existing manufacturing infrastructure, all the necessary materials and skills were near at hand, making it easy for businesses to add capacity. By the 1860s there were numerous competitors in the field, with some companies attracting large capital investments. Stove manufacturing became Detroit's leading industry for more than fifty years.

The economy soared, new residents poured in, and the city continued its phenomenal growth. By 1880 the population topped 116,000, including large neighborhoods of Germans and Poles—the former (one-seventh of the population in 1880) often arriving with education and capital to start a business, the latter recruited to satisfy an insatiable demand for workers in stove factories, shipyards, and railroad industries. There was also a large Irish population, fleeing famine and political troubles at home.

In 1880 fewer than 3 percent of Detroit residents were of African descent. Some were born free in the United States, some came from Canada, and the rest were former slaves. At the close of the Civil War this population owned businesses serving primarily a white clientele, including barber shops, tailors, dry cleaners, and delivery services. By 1880 the local economy shifted so that blacks catered mostly to black customers. Moving companies, coal companies, lumber yards, drug stores, newsstands, restaurants, and funeral homes were some of the most popular of these businesses.

Its exciting growth, access to transportation, and thriving manufacturing base made Detroit a magnet for other businesses, all of which seemed to prosper at the turn of the twentieth century. Local tobacco companies employed an army of women to hand-roll cigars by the millions. By 1905 half the shipping tonnage on the Great Lakes was launched from the city's shipyards.

Two hundred years earlier Detroit was a struggling frontier settlement threatened by marauding natives, isolated by trackless swamps, and devastated by fire. Hit with one challenge after another its citizens rallied not only to preserve their city but, after every setback, to make it more prosperous than before. The 1900 census reported Detroit was home to 285,000 people—more than the nation's capital city and good for thirteenth place overall, one spot behind New Orleans.

City streets teemed with people going about their business, and factories hummed with activity. New arrivals streamed down the gangplanks from eastern ports to start fresh in the great American Midwest. Detroit retained its international flavor with large blocs of Germans, Poles, and Irish, each with their own neighborhoods, politics, newspapers, and traditions.

Into this fertile stew of energy, innovation, and ideas a revolutionary new invention appeared that would soon take the country by storm. And it would make Detroit one of the most famous cities in the world. ■

Chapter 2

Setting the Template

"The darn thing ran!"
—Henry Ford after driving
his first automobile, 1896

■ ■ ■

"THE FIRST horseless carriage seen in the city was out on the streets last night. The apparatus seemed to work all right, and it went at the rate of five or six miles an hour at an even rate of speed." This short article on the back page of the *Detroit Free Press* on March 7, 1896, scarcely hinted at what was in store for Detroit and the American automobile industry over the next thirty years. During that time cars went from a rare and expensive curiosity to a staple of American life, transforming the nation physically, socially, and economically. Over those same years, the auto industry put Detroit on the world map to the extent its name became one-word shorthand for the whole business the way "Hollywood" meant "motion pictures."

The world's first self-propelled vehicle was an 8,000-pound steam-powered monstrosity built in 1769 to pull French artillery pieces. The first machines recognizable as ancestors of modern-day cars were built in Germany in the 1880s by Karl Benz, Gottlieb Wilhelm Daimler, and Wilhelm Maybach. Two bicycle mechanics from Springfield, Massachusetts, Frank and Charles Duryea, designed and constructed the first American "horseless carriage" in 1893. Five years later, Cleveland bicycle maker Alexander Winton formed the first company in America to make and sell cars to the public. His first year in business he sold his entire annual output of four cars for $1,000 each, a profit of $400 per car.

The driver of Detroit's first car that late winter night in 1896 was Charles B. King, who built it in a machine shop on St. Antoine Street. The first run was only a few blocks to Cadillac Square, where the engine died. A few months afterward, a night shift engineer at the municipal electric company, Henry Ford, took his own homemade "quadricycle" for its first spin. On June 4, 1896, he was ready to drive it out of its shed behind his house on Bagley Avenue when he realized the finished machine wouldn't fit through the door. After widening the doorway by demolishing part of the shed wall, Ford got it out, turned the starting crank, and to his pleasant surprise as he said years later, "The darn thing ran!"

Ford incorporated the Ford Motor Company in 1903. That same year the Ohio Automobile Company, begun in 1899, moved to Detroit from Warren, Ohio, and renamed itself the Packard Motor Car Company in honor of its founders, brothers James and William Doud Packard. James started the business after buying a Winton. When he complained about problems with the car, Alexander Winton suggested he build a better one himself. In meeting that challenge, Packard launched what would become one of the most storied brands in the business.

The first company to build automobiles in Detroit was the Olds Motor Works, founded by Ransom E. Olds in 1899. After a fire destroyed his factory in 1901, Olds started over, this time using sub-contractors to make various components. Many of them would go on to be important players in the automotive industry. Henry Leland's company built engines; bicycle makers (and former stove component manufacturers) John and Horace Dodge supplied transmissions; Fred Fisher designed bodies. This new outsourcing system dropped the price of an Olds car from $2,382 to $625. Within a year, 25 percent of cars sold in the United States were Oldsmobiles.

In 1905 Leland, a college-educated businessman and skilled tool-maker from Vermont, launched the Cadillac Motor Car Company, for which Fred Fisher built the first ever fully enclosed car bodies. (Up to that time cars were open to the weather, the same as the carriages they replaced.) By 1910 there were over two hundred companies building cars in the United States.

Within only a few years—the blink of an eye in historical terms—the car industry sparked demand for thousands of workers and huge factories to satisfy America's massive automotive appetite. The showpiece of car plants was the Packard factory on East Grand Avenue, opened in 1903. Designed by noted Detroit architect Albert Kahn, the complex eventually totaled five million square feet.

Ford Motor Company started making cars in a factory on Mack Avenue, moved to larger quarters on Piquette Avenue in 1906, then in 1910 opened a new purpose-built factory in Highland Park also designed by Albert Kahn and known as the Crystal Palace for its skylights and open space. At first, workers assembled the popular Model T one by one as they had since production of the T type began in 1908: each chassis sat on a sawhorse and workers swarmed around it putting on components until a car was complete. In 1913 Ford introduced the moving assembly line, which carried a chassis along a path past assembly workers, with each one adding the same part or performing the same task to each car in succession. Production soared from 7.5 to 146 an hour. The retail price per car dropped from $850 to $260. As a result, during the 1920s half the automobiles in the world were Fords. Fifteen million Model Ts were built before production ended in 1927.

Standard pay for a factory worker in the automotive industry was around $2.75 a day for a ten-hour day. In 1914, explaining how workers who built his cars should be able to afford them, Henry Ford announced a new wage of $5.00 a day for an eight-hour shift. Men poured into Detroit to apply for work at Ford and at other plants. By 1917 there were 23 car manufacturers in the city along with 132 outside suppliers, employing a total of more than 135,000 workers.

In 1904 Ford had 31 employees; by 1920 the company payroll numbered 56,000.

When the United States joined World War I in 1917, the automobile industry answered the call to supply military equipment. Though they never stopped making cars for the retail market, Detroit's auto factories turned out everything from infantry helmets to aircraft engines, tanks, trucks, and ambulances. Ford even built a fleet of sixty 200-foot-long submarine chasers.

Though auto production was far and away the biggest industry in town, the local economy was still diversified and growing in every direction. Between 1915 and 1919, industrial production rose 50 percent, from $600 million to $900 million, with stoves, marine equipment, and other industries all showing healthy increases.

A city leading the nation in efficient, modern manufacturing also needed an efficient, modern government. Detroit's path to good city government was a long, steep climb. As far back as 1890 city leaders were mired in corruption, self-dealing, and monopoly control. Having grown so fast, Detroit outpaced a frontier-era government structure and political playbook still operating according to shoot-from-the-hip methods of the past. As Lewis Cass cast a bold vision for a bigger, better Detroit after the devastating fire of 1805, a visionary new leader now appeared to rescue the city from a political morass bred of graft and backroom dealing and recast its government for modern times. He took hold of the longstanding corruption and incompetence in local affairs and refused to let go until they were resolved.

Hazen S. Pingree was born in Maine in 1840 and enlisted in the Civil War as a Massachusetts artilleryman. Captured and interred at the infamous Andersonville prisoner of war camp in Georgia, he met other prisoners from Detroit who couldn't stop talking about how wonderful and full of opportunity the city was. Pingree later escaped, returned to the battlefield, and witnessed the Confederate surrender at Appomattox. Mustered out in August 1865, he got a job in Detroit as a cobbler, his trade in Maine before the war, then became a shoe salesman.

When his employer announced he was going out of business a year later, Pingree and a partner bought him out and opened their own factory with eight workers. By 1886 Pingree and Smith was the second largest shoe company in America, its 700 employees turning out nearly half a million pairs of shoes a year. Hazen Pingree became one of Detroit's most respected business leaders, successful, generous, and always impeccably dressed. His friends encouraged him to run for mayor in 1889. They believed the city was poorly positioned to take full advantage of its economic potential because of a corrupt and unaccountable political structure. These friends were convinced that Pingree, a Republican, could take on the entrenched Democratic Party machine impeding Detroit's progress, and they refused to take "no" for an answer. Pingree agreed to run.

Assessing the situation, Pingree must scarcely have known where to start. Only 20 percent of Detroit's residents were born to American citizens; the rest were foreign-born or the children of immigrants. Polish, Irish, and German populations formed large constituencies competing for influence and political power. (The city had eight German-language newspapers.) Intimidation and assault were common. Political bosses nominated the two Common Council (i.e., city council) aldermen from each of sixteen wards, largely away from the public spotlight. As one historian explained, the city leaders' "only concerns were with city contracts, rewarding allies with jobs, and hammering enemies."

Two of the many practical problems candidate Pingree surveyed were the city streets and streetcars. Detroit had some of the worst roads and public transportation in the country. The *Detroit Journal* described city streets as "150 miles of rotting, rutted, lumpy, dilapidated paving." Four streets had brick or asphalt surfaces, some of them inferior work by contractors who bribed aldermen for the jobs with a kickback or "boodle." In summer the asphalt melted and sometimes caught fire. The rest of the streets were surfaced with cedar blocks, the oldest dating to the 1830s. Since property owners along paved roads had their taxes raised—because good roads made their land more valuable—they fought against any improvements.

The streetcars were no better. While other cities were converting their systems to electricity, Detroit retained horse-drawn cars on out-dated iron rails, a combination unchanged since the 1840s. Private owners of the streetcar concession refused to spend money to modern-ize, and their contract with the city left it powerless to force a change.

Pingree threw himself into campaigning with as much enthusi-asm as he put into making shoes. He spoke in Polish neighborhoods through an interpreter, drank whiskey with the Irish to disprove rumors he was opposed to alcohol, and bought a German-language newspaper, installing a new editor who gave him full-throated support.

The day a victorious Pingree assumed office, seven aldermen were indicted for bribery.

Mayor Pingree immediately began tackling the problems before him, building consensus when he could and moving boldly ahead on his own when he met resistance. He took aldermen and reporters on a tour of city streets to point out their flaws. He hosted another group on a visit to the city's ineffective sewers, where suppliers who had paid boodle to win contracts used soft, weak, poor quality concrete. When contractors threatened to sue, Pingree set up a testing lab in his office to demonstrate how bad their concrete was. He also pressured Detroit's unscrupulous utilities to lower their rates; electricity was nearly twice as expensive in Detroit as in Toledo, Cleveland, or Grand Rapids.

When the school board illegally blocked his efforts to end their longstanding practice of bribery, he had them arrested. One member was acquitted, two went to prison, one jumped bail, and one commit-ted suicide.

The Republicans who had encouraged Pingree to run for office were furious at him for dismantling one money-making scheme of theirs after another. Democrats despised him even more. He was forced off the board of a local bank and even his church turned against him and his family. But the people loved him. As the *Free Press* reported in

1894, "There are thousands of plain, thoughtful citizens of Michigan who love Mayor Pingree for the enemies he has made."

When unemployment spiked during a nationwide depression in 1894, Pingree convinced bakeries to lower the price of bread and replaced construction site vehicles with wheelbarrows in order to employ more workers. But his most successful project was to turn vacant city land into vegetable gardens so destitute citizens could raise their own food. The local press mocked him and the churches, where Pingree turned for partnership with his idea, raised a grand total of thirteen dollars.

Pingree sold a prize horse to fund the garden project himself. Within two years there were 1,700 gardens producing $30,000 worth of food (over a million dollars in current value). "Ping's potato patch" was copied from Boston to Seattle and made Pingree a national figure.

In 1896 Pingree was elected governor of Michigan. After completing his second term he took a long vacation to Africa and Europe, and he died in London in 1901. In 1904 a statue of the popular mayor was unveiled in downtown Detroit. Many of the 5,000 contributions to build it came from families who survived the depression by farming the land he made available.

Mayor Hazen Pingree laid the groundwork for Detroit's incredible growth and prosperity as the Roaring Twenties roared and America fell in love with the automobile. Another great leader during this era was John C. Lodge, a Detroit native who became the city's mayor three times in ten years. A former newspaper reporter, Lodge was kind, courteous, and conscientious. He replaced Mayor James Couzens in 1922 when Couzens became a U.S. Senator, then won election in 1924 over acting mayor Joseph Martin, who took office after Frank Doremus resigned due to ill health. In 1927 Lodge ran against incumbent John W. Smith and won without doing any campaigning whatever while also refusing to let his supporters criticize his opponent. By the time he left office in 1929, Detroit's level of prosperity was at a historic high.

The main driver of Detroit's success remained the auto industry. In 1920, 1.5 million cars were built in the United States. By 1929 that figure surged to 5.3 million. Ford and upstart Swiss engineer Louis Chevrolet each sold more than a million autos that year. Ford alone employed more than 100,000 workers.

Another important business in Detroit during the 1920s was importing illegal alcohol from Canada. By the time liquor was banned nationwide in 1920 after passage of the Eighteenth Amendment, alcohol had already been outlawed in Michigan for a year and a half. This was plenty of time to set up an illicit network of importers of booze from Ohio. After America went dry, merchants switched their source of supply to Canada. The city of Windsor, Ontario, just across the river from downtown Detroit, was only a short boat ride away. Estimates were that 85 percent of the illegal liquor smuggled into the United States from Canada came through Detroit—up to 500,000 cases a month. As one commentator put it, the Windsor-Detroit Tunnel became the "Windsor-Detroit Funnel" until Prohibition was repealed in 1933.

The Detroit skyline was remade during the 1920s with skyscrapers that still impress today: the new headquarters for General Motors (1923), then the second-largest office building in the world; the elegant Book-Cadillac Hotel (1924); the Fisher Building (1928), featuring lavish stonework, exuberant gilding, and soaring barrel vaults; a collection of spectacular movie theaters; and the Penobscot Building (1928), with its distinctive fusion of Native American and Art Deco styles, for almost fifty years the tallest building in town.

Like other cities across the country, Detroit was devastated by the Great Depression. Car sales took a nosedive as millions lost their jobs and savings. From a peak of 5.3 million sales in 1929, auto manufacturers—most of them in or around Detroit—moved only 1.3 million units during the darkest days of the downturn. General Motors laid off more than a third of its workers. Ford shed two-thirds of its workers with the rest going on shorter hours. By the end of 1931, Detroit had 223,000 unemployed.

On the heels of John Lodge as mayor, Charles Bowles proved how quickly corrupt and incompetent leadership could undo years of good government. Bowles was a spectacular failure from the moment he assumed office in January 1930. He enjoyed wide support from the Ku Klux Klan, particularly Klan members who came north to join the Detroit police force. When the police commissioner repeatedly raided gangs that were active in town at the time, Bowles fired him. Bowles was so corrupt and beholden to criminal elements that he became the first mayor of a major American city to be recalled. Barely eight months into his term, Charles Bowles was turned out of office by the voters of Detroit. Unbowed and unrepentant, he ran in the special election to replace himself but lost to former court judge Frank Murphy.

Following Hazen Pingree's example from previous hard times, Mayor Murphy promoted individual vegetable gardens and pressured public utilities to lower their rates. He steered a careful course in the Depression economy, offering help to struggling families with temporary assistance while placating those who opposed "welfare" or "handouts" on principle. City treasurer (and future mayor) Albert E. Cobo came up with a novel plan to help strapped homeowners avoid tax foreclosure by stretching payment of delinquent property taxes over seven years.

Hazen Pingree, John Lodge, and Frank Murphy made heroic strides in transforming Detroit's political machinery from a corrupt, small-town operation to one capable of leading a world-class industrial power. Unfortunately, there was no great reformer of comparable skill and dedication to lead the charge for Detroit's school system during these years. While at first glance a school system seems like a relatively small component part of a city's historical progression, in this case the chronic difficulties of public education in Detroit have had a continuing impact on its fortunes. Decisions made and priorities set between the World Wars put Detroit schools on a downward path from which they have never fully recovered.

By the beginning of Detroit's post-World War I boom, its schools had been racing to catch up with population growth for decades.

Enrollment in kindergarten through twelfth grade was up fourfold between 1900 and 1920 with nearly half the students foreign-born or the children of immigrants. Despite Mayor Hazen Pingree's dramatic housecleaning in 1894, some citizens insisted he hadn't gone far enough. There were claims that the school board, a large group with representatives from each of the city's wards, paid too much for textbooks and that men with financial interests in saloons were among those responsible for students' education.

More to the point, Detroit schools suffered a chronic shortage of school buildings, overcrowded classrooms, and an acute shortage of teachers. The old board produced disastrous results. There never seemed to be enough room or enough instructors for the student population.

A newly constituted seven-member board elected at-large in 1917 set out with reformers' zeal to improve the system. They raised teacher salaries, recruited more teachers, and launched an ambitious building program. To mitigate overcrowding, they set up programs to rotate classrooms of children through what they called a "platoon" system, ensuring every educational space was used most efficiently and no resources were wasted. Their success brought broad public support for the schools that saw them recognized by 1929 as "one of the preeminent school systems in the nation."

In spite of the school board's progress, the system remained overcrowded as the economy began to fall. In 1931, twenty thousand schoolchildren still attended class in buildings constructed in the nineteenth century. Thousands still attended half-day sessions (a longstanding stopgap measure for lack of classroom space) though far fewer than in the past.

When the Depression put the brakes on Detroit's economic expansion, unemployment in the auto industry and in other trades introduced two new difficulties to the school system. First, as the economy shrank, assessed property values declined, which reduced Detroit's tax base. Second, as hundreds of thousands of workers lost their jobs, tax delinquencies skyrocketed, meaning the city could not collect payments from newly destitute homeowners even if assessments were lower. As the number of students in the city continued to grow, the tax revenues used to pay for their education withered.

Municipal projects launched during the prosperous 1920s required the same debt service in bad times as in good, which now meant borrowing from banks to keep up payments. Meanwhile the city department of welfare redirected millions of dollars from schools to the poor and unemployed. By 1931 Detroit was spending more than $10 million per year on interest payments and almost $14 million on relief, the two figures together far overshadowing the $18 million available to the school district.

This unprecedented financial strain divided Detroit along class lines. In previous years, schools sparked little real controversy over organization or curriculum. But in a time of drastically shrinking budgets, two opposing philosophies emerged, with organized labor and other liberal groups in favor of higher taxes and more spending for public schools, while businessmen and conservatives promoted lower taxes and reduced budgets. This was also when educational controversies morphed from issues directly related to curriculum and policy into larger battles over political and financial control. School management became enmeshed in the larger political arena.

These changes affected the Detroit school system in ways that marked the turning point from "one of the preeminent school systems in the nation" to a hopelessly dysfunctional bureaucracy that became a key driver of the middle-class exodus from the city sooner than many people would imagine possible.

As the Depression deepened, teacher salaries were reduced repeatedly, the school year shortened, building construction and remodeling virtually halted, and supplemental programs slashed even as student enrollment continued to grow. Some months teachers received no salaries at all and other months they were paid in scrip (a form of IOU). Both teachers' savings and school district deposits vanished when banks failed. Teachers were forced to join the breadlines along with other municipal employees.

Budget reductions, though unavoidable under the circumstances, meant that as the nation shook off its economic malaise and its factories geared up to supply a war economy in the early 1940s, Detroit schools were totally unprepared for the flood of new residents coming to run the city's production lines. As they had during the '20s, schools played a frantic game of catch-up, recruiting teachers, building classrooms, and putting thousands of children on half-day schedules because of the shortage of space.

Troublesome as these practical shortages were, another Depression-era change was even more responsible for the district's fading reputation: revisions to the school curriculum producing graduates in 1940 with only a fraction of the education of those who graduated in 1928.

During the boom years of the 1920s, as many as half of all fourteen- to eighteen-year-olds in Detroit left high school before graduating, most of them to go to work. When the job market dried up in the '30s, these students stayed in class; between 1930 and 1940, the number of high school graduates doubled.

Many of these children were from poor or middle-class families. Educators assumed they could not learn as well as students from wealthier families who traditionally could afford to stay in school. Both conservative and liberal political camps supported lowering academic standards as a solution to keep these "underachievers" from dropping out. The business owners didn't need more workers because thousands of skilled and experienced people were unemployed, instantly available, and eager to take any job at any wage. (Metal finishers, the most highly skilled and best-paid auto industry assembly line workers, saw their wages drop from $1.10 an hour to 15 cents.) Socialists, labor leaders in the city's rising union movement, and other liberals wanted to keep classrooms full to reduce competition in the shrunken labor market.

Beginning in 1920, Detroit students were divided into groups based on IQ tests given to first-graders. The highest-performing students entered the academic track, while others were assigned to commercial, technical, or general tracks, with "general" being for the lowest performing students. Wisdom of the day held that by sorting young learners this way, each could be helped to achieve maximum potential. The result, unfortunately, was a new curriculum that was vastly inferior to the old and drastically reduced educational equity. This was especially true for students in the general track.

In summarizing this moment in the history of Detroit schools, professor and educational expert Jeffrey Mirel wrote: "By 1940, high schools in Detroit were relegating a substantial number of students to a second-rate education primarily to keep them out of the shrunken labor market. In other words, during the depression, Detroit's high schools went from institutions largely concerned with academic and vocational education for most students to institutions in which only some students received such an education while increasing numbers received custodial care."

Within a few years employers were complaining regularly about the inadequate skills of Detroit's high school graduates. The apparent failure of the Detroit school system to fulfill its most important obligation—educating its students—along with the consequences of years of deferred building and maintenance, low teacher salaries, and the politicization of school policy, simmered uneasily while the city and the nation turned their attentions to national defense as European nations ground relentlessly toward another world war.

More obvious and newsworthy were the incredible expansion of Detroit industry during the war years and the rise of the labor movement that would go on to shape so much of the city's story in the years ahead. ▨

Chapter 3

Crucible of Conflict

*"Too many people of Detroit are confused, embittered
and distracted by factional groups that are fighting each
other harder than they are willing to fight Hitler."*
—*Life* magazine, 1942

■ ■ ■

FOR TWENTY-FIRST-CENTURY Americans whose world is defined by innovation and change, it is difficult to imagine the impact the auto industry had on the national economy, and on the economy of Detroit in particular. By 1926 Ford Motor Company alone employed 100,000 workers, many of them in its massive River Rouge complex, which became the largest factory in the world. The resulting demand for housing, schooling, and all the other needs of a surging population transformed the Motor City. In 1900 Detroit was the nation's thirteenth largest city with a population just over 285,000. Thirty years later on the eve of the Depression, the city was home to more than one and a half million residents and ranked fourth in population, leapfrogging over St. Louis, Boston, and Pittsburgh among others.

> *"The complacency of fools will destroy them."*
> —Proverbs 1:32

As the city struggled through the 1930s, two forces solidified their positions as chief influencers in directing Detroit's future: the car companies and their workers' unions.

Detroiters could be wary in the matter of unions. Faced with repeated pay cuts, ballooning class sizes, and deteriorating buildings, the city's teachers nevertheless hesitated to support unionization, both because any job was better than no job and because union organizers were often tagged as "socialist" or "communist" sympathizers. Though the Detroit Federation of Teachers was organized in 1931, it was more than three years before they took the risk of announcing themselves publicly.

As the auto industry grew rapidly in the first years of the twentieth century, trade unions made little effort to organize its workers. Generally, union members had a particular skill—making shoes, rolling cigars—and worked for low wages. A typical worker at General Motors was relatively well-paid and did unskilled tasks anyone could learn in a few days. Henry Ford's five-dollar-a-day wage was more than twice the average for factory work. A further complication for union organizers was the auto industry mix of languages and cultures. Many thousands of employees came from the South where unions were rare. Workers also knew union organizing, or even talking about it, could put them out on the street, easily replaced from a ready pool of applicants.

Depression-era legislation tipped the bargaining scale in the unions' favor. The National Industrial Recovery Act and the National Labor Relations Act gave workers the right to organize and required employers to bargain collectively. In 1935 the United Automobile Workers union was formed. Determined to keep unions out of their factories, employers sent spies to the assembly line to report anyone who talked about a union. Wearing a pro-union button or passing out pro-union literature could get a worker beaten. Companies formed their own "unions" and pressured employees to join. The sheer size of auto manufacturers made opposing them a daunting task. In 1936

General Motors was the largest private employer in the world, its sixty-nine plants employing 172,000 hourly workers.

On December 30, 1936, about fifty workers at a Fisher Body plant in Flint, Michigan, that made bodies for Buick refused to work. They sat down, some of them in the car seats they were making and demanded union representation. A plant in Detroit building bodies for Cadillac did the same. Leaving the factory or picketing outside would subject the strikers to attacks by company "security" forces. By staying inside they protected themselves, since management did not want to risk damaging buildings or equipment by attacking the workers there. Strikers set up committees to deliver food, watch for fires, and police themselves—no liquor, no guns, no damage to company property. Eventually, fifty plants went on strike or stopped production due to lack of parts.

After more than three weeks of stalemate, management turned off the heat in sixteen-degree weather. An unsuccessful charge by police left thirteen people shot and wounded. On February 11, 1937, General Motors agreed to national union representation in all its plants. In March ten thousand workers staged a sit-down strike at the Chrysler Corporation's Dodge plant in suburban Hamtramck; a month later Chrysler agreed to let its employees join the union. By July there were 200,000 United Automobile Workers members in Detroit.

The big holdout was Henry Ford, who swore he would never negotiate with a union and hired an army of private security men to make good on his word. This standoff led to an incident that turned public opinion against Ford and forced him to rethink his position. On May 26, three months after the General Motors–UAW agreement, a group of union officials headed for Ford's mammoth River Rouge plant to hand out pro-union leaflets. On an overpass in front of the plant, dozens of security men intercepted them and beat them bloody. A photograph of two of them, Walter Reuther (later president of the union) and Richard Frankensteen, their faces battered and white dress shirts covered in blood, appeared in newspapers the next day. After losing a string of court cases accusing the company of unfairly firing union members and following a strike at River Rouge, Ford reversed course and agreed to deal with the UAW. In May 1941, the union became the sole bargaining representative for Ford employees.

The UAW was suddenly a force to be reckoned with, opening what the union called "a new era in human rights." Auto sales were still far below their pre-Depression levels but were on an upward trend. Yet according to union reports, as the economy stabilized the workers' share of industry income fell. The Congress of Industrial Organizations reported the percentage of national income going to wages and salaries fell from over 77 percent in 1932 to 60 percent in 1936. The union insisted the share of workers' pay should remain proportional as the national economy recovered. Otherwise, they argued, workers would become less and less able to purchase the goods they produced.

World War II began on September 1, 1939, when Nazi Germany invaded Poland. In the summer of 1941, Detroit auto plants started ramping down their production of cars and trucks to build military vehicles and weapons. After Pearl Harbor and America's entry to the war, civilian production halted completely in order to concentrate Detroit's manufacturing output exclusively on the war effort. Detroit transitioned from the Motor City to the "Arsenal of Democracy" as its assembly lines switched from sedans and convertibles to airplanes, tanks, machine guns, ammunition, bombs, and other implements of war.

Detroit had vast manufacturing capacity to dedicate to the cause. Raw materials were readily available and the transportation network was excellent. What Detroit needed were workers. Women by the thousands stepped into manufacturing jobs when men left to go to war. The lure of good-paying work fulfilling government war contracts brought hundreds of thousands of newcomers from the South—200,000 whites and 150,000 blacks who pulled up stakes and migrated to Detroit in hopes of a better future.

Detroit and the UAW took their lumps in the national press for fighting turf wars while the fate of Western Civilization was at stake.

In a long feature in its August 17, 1942, issue, at which time America had been at war just over nine months and was still very much on the defensive, *Life* magazine looked upon the Arsenal of Democracy with a critical eye.

"Detroit workers," the story reported, "led by the lusty U.A.W., seem to hate and suspect their bosses more than ever" with "a morale situation which is perhaps the worst in the U.S." On July 31, the UAW called a strike at three plants in Pontiac, Michigan, converted from building cars to making anti-aircraft guns. Union grocery store clerks were on strike and set up picket lines at the factories that sympathetic UAW members refused to cross. Another strike broke out when workers at a tank plant were denied permission to smoke during their shift. The mood was too often belligerent and confrontational. One worker in a bomber plant told a reporter he punched holes in a plane's gas line after finding out he had been called in the military draft.

The article declared the city "which gave the nation its first miracles of production has worked no miracles in this war. . . . too many of the people of Detroit are confused, embittered and distracted by factional groups that are fighting each other harder than they are willing to fight Hitler."

City leaders reverted to some of the antics that Hazen Pingree and Frank Murphy previously cleared out of city hall: "Detroit's politicians have shamefully plundered the city in the past. The last mayor, Richard W. Reading, is appealing a jail sentence for graft." Five-foot-three-inch Richard "Little Dick" Reading, who served from 1938 to 1940, was convicted of accepting hundreds of thousands of dollars in bribes to protect illegal gambling in the city and eventually spent three years in prison.

According to *Life*, more than half the city's population arrived in the previous twenty years. "They have no great love for their city and they give their loyalty to their own group, creed, or union." The largest bloc of workers, more than half of UAW members, was Polish Catholics, numbering 260,000. After that were white Southerners followed by Southern blacks. Even within the UAW, these and other groups, including communists, fought for "influence and control."

Housing for the hundreds of thousands of new war workers was a constant headache for employers, workers, and city government alike. The war economy meant building materials were in short supply and many former carpenters, plumbers, and electricians exchanged their hammers and wrenches for guns on the battlefield. By the summer of 1942, it was, according to *Life*, "impossible to rent a decent house within 50 miles of the city."

Around Ford's huge Willow Run plant where more than 8,000 B-24 bombers would be built before the war ended, "hundreds of tents, trailers and shacks have sprung up in woods, fields and barnyards." There were impromptu grocery stores, restaurants, and bars built in the same wood-scraps-and-tar-paper style as the houses. Many homes had no running water, forcing residents to use communal bathhouses. Single workers jammed into shared quarters and families made do with whatever they could find.

The housing crisis was especially severe for the 150,000 black Southerners streaming into town. They were crowded into traditionally black neighborhoods already bursting at the seams and often charged two or three times the market price for rent because landlords knew these families had no other choice.

New minority employees fared relatively well on the assembly line. Detroit automakers had a history of hiring black workers. As far back as 1926, 10 percent of Ford's workforce was black, more than twice the 4.1 percent of the population they represented at the time. The UAW and its parent Congress of Industrial Organizations (CIO) made a point of reaching out to black prospective members. In a newsletter article titled "No Jim Crow in the CIO," the union affirmed its constitution protected workers "regardless of race, creed, color, or nationality . . . the CIO gives the Negro the full rights he deserves as an American and as a fellow worker."

Struggling to keep pace with the surge of newcomers, the Detroit Housing Commission approved two sites for new federal housing projects, one for whites and one for blacks. When the Sojourner Truth Homes, the black development named in honor of a former slave and Emancipation spokeswoman, was sited in a Polish Catholic neighborhood, local residents complained and federal underwriters refused to back mortgages in the area. The Federal Housing Administration then decided to reserve the Sojourner Truth project for whites only.

Pressure from Mayor Edward Jeffries, Detroit housing officials, and other groups convinced federal authorities to reverse their decision and designate Sojourner Truth as a residence for blacks. White protesters kept their new neighbors away for two months until, at the end of April 1942, police and National Guard troops escorted the first six black households into the project. Eventually 168 families lived there.

While there were many white families who objected to having black neighbors, there were also reports that racial tension around the issue of housing was stirred up at least in part by outside agitators. The National Workers League, a Nazi front group with a significant presence in Detroit, was reportedly "heavily involved in agitating for violence." Hoping to influence the UAW, which welcomed and supported black members, outsiders from the Ku Klux Klan tried to create dissension within the organization.

Was violence—not discord and disagreement but violence— caused by local residents who were parties to the issue or by outsiders taking advantage of the situation to advance their own agendas? The question of who fanned the flames of race-related conflict would recur in years ahead. The urban upheavals and bitter divisions that later left indelible scars on the city were blamed on one group of likely suspects at the time. Yet new information brought to light decades after the fact once again would raise the prospect of outside instigators infiltrating a situation to serve their own ends, then disappearing as stealthily as they had come.

In wartime Detroit, authorities knew all about the housing crisis, especially for black workers, but no one seemed to be able to get control of the situation. A statement from the director-secretary of the

Detroit Housing Commission underscored the reality that whatever remedies were available required white families to accept black neighbors. While the city could legislate this, they could not rush a change in public perception.

Black residents were right in objecting to the hypocrisy of whites who said black neighbors were all right in their place, but that place was a slum or railroad yard. As the commission statement acknowledged, "This Negro resentment is honest and justified and can be corrected only when the majority of Detroit's citizens recognize the problem and so plan the future growth of the city that the Negro can live in a home in a clean and decent environment." Black families did not insist on mixing with whites, the statement continued, only that they have a good place to live their lives and raise their families. The director-secretary explained the commission was threading a careful path between "bigots who refuse to recognize the Negro's just demands" and the "well-meaning and honest idealist who refuses to recognize that his philosophies are several years ahead of the average citizen and cannot be accepted at this time."

A campaign flyer from Mayor Jeffries exemplified the convoluted logic politicians and civic leaders invoked for supporting equal rights on one hand and slow-walking the process on the other: "I have tried to safeguard your neighborhoods in the character which you, the residents, have developed them. . . . There is much that the Negro people have a right to hope for and to aspire to. Those things, however, cannot be accomplished by the edict of a mayor, no matter who he may be."

Detroit's black population aspired to and hoped for better housing for a long time. Deed covenants in Detroit and elsewhere in America prohibited homeowners from selling to black buyers (and often to Jewish buyers as well). Mortgage lenders and insurance underwriters steered black buyers to neighborhoods designated for them.

The main neighborhood for people of African descent in Detroit was Black Bottom, sixty blocks on the east side of the city along the Detroit River. The Savoyard River once flowed directly through the area, depositing rich, dark-colored soil that gave the neighborhood its name. The river was directed underground in the 1820s as the city grew. Overlapping Black Bottom was Paradise Valley, a commercial center crowded with restaurants, nightclubs, drug stores, grocery stores, beauty salons, and other businesses owned by and catering to the black population.

Blacks were less than 10 percent of Detroit's population on the eve of World War II, yet the housing shortage for them was already acute. In 1910 there were fewer than six thousand blacks in the city, just over 1 percent of the population. By 1920 that number grew to 40,000, still only 4 percent of the total but a 700 percent increase in ten years with no corresponding increase in available housing. Black newcomers were shoehorned into the increasingly crowded and unhealthy Black Bottom neighborhood. New arrivals who wanted to live elsewhere in the city risked retaliation at the hands of angry residents.

There were some east-side neighborhoods outside Black Bottom where a sprinkling of middle-class black families lived quietly among whites. In one of them, late in the summer of 1925, a black gynecologist named Ossian Sweet bought a two-story brick house at the corner of Garland and Charlevoix. Sweet graduated from Howard University and later attended lectures in France by Madame Marie Curie, famous for her early work with radioactivity and a two-time recipient of the Nobel Prize. Dr. Sweet had his office behind the Palace Drug Company in Black Bottom but wanted a nice home in a better area for his wife and young daughter.

After whites in Dr. Sweet's new neighborhood heard the family was moving in, they threatened him to the degree that when his belongings arrived on September 8, the moving van had a police escort. Angry neighbors milled around day and night while a squad of ten policemen held the crowd back. Fearing attack, Sweet invited several friends and relatives to stay in the house until matters quieted down.

By the night of September 9, the crowd had grown to hundreds, some of them throwing rocks and bottles. When it looked like the crowd was surging to storm the embattled residents, defenders inside fired gunshots into the mob. One rabble-rouser was wounded. An innocent white neighbor sitting on his porch was shot and killed. The police arrested everyone in the house and charged them all with first-degree murder.

To help defend Dr. Sweet and the others, the National Association for the Advancement of Colored People retained legendary defense lawyer Clarence Darrow. A lengthy trial before an all-white jury resulted in a hung jury. Prosecutors retried the case, this time charging defendants one at a time. When the first one up, Ossian's brother Henry, was acquitted by another all-white jury, the defense dropped all charges against the rest of the parties involved. Sweet eventually moved back into the house where he lived for another thirty years.

In the wake of Sweet's experience, Mayor John Smith appointed an interracial committee, the first in the city's history, to find jobs and housing for blacks. Mayor Smith's committee evidently made no headway in achieving its goals. By 1943 Detroit's enormous manufacturing might, focused on churning out armaments for defense, depended on black newcomers to fill positions on assembly lines but the city still had no place for them to live.

Despite continued discrimination, racially motivated violence such as Dr. Sweet and his family experienced remained rare. Unfortunately, the next flashpoint was far more damaging and more deadly than the attack on Sweet. And it left both a legacy and a mystery that would mark the city of Detroit from then to the present time.

Sunday, June 20, 1943, was a sultry summer day, a great day to visit Belle Isle. This island in the Detroit River featured an amusement park that locals had enjoyed for generations. Formerly accessed by ferry, the island was now connected with the city by a bridge. That night a fight broke out between whites and blacks on the bridge, soon spilling over onto Belle Isle and along East Jefferson on the landward end.

One account reported the initial conflict was between black residents and two hundred sailors at the Brodhead Naval Armory. At about the same time, other separate fights broke out on Detroit's east side. Before the night was over, 5,000 people were fighting in the streets and at the request of Governor Harry Kelly and Mayor Edward Jeffries, 6,000 army troops and tanks were deployed to restore order.

Over two days of rioting thirty-four people died, twenty-five of them black, sixty-seven were injured, and almost 2,000 arrested. Among the fatalities was Dr. Joseph De Horatiis, an Italian immigrant, who was beaten to death while making house calls in a black neighborhood. The *Detroit News* later reported, "Many of those killed died of blunt trauma wounds or multiple stabbings, a testament to the anger and hatred unleashed on the streets."

Though this tragic incident has gone down in history as a "race riot," solid facts are scarce and elusive. Detroit historian Arthur M. Woodford writes of that bloody night, "No one knows what incident touched it off." Wild rumors inflamed blacks and whites alike, setting them against each other without justification and giving parties on both sides cover for looting and fighting that might have been sparked by anything, or nothing.

Black patrons of the Forest Social Club circulated a rumor about whites throwing a black woman and her baby off the Belle Isle Bridge. A white crowd heard that a white woman was raped by blacks near the bridge. Neither of these actually happened or was supported by a shred of evidence.

Reporting for the *Detroit News* four days after the riot began, Philip A. Adler questioned whether the events were "a spontaneous outbreak of race resentment or a carefully planned affair?" Authorities insisted it was spontaneous but Adler reported, according to "intelligent spokesmen" both black and white, the Belle Isle riot "was a carefully staged affair, planned over a long period of time."

Adler insisted fights breaking out simultaneously in different parts of the city "indicate something besides spontaneity." He also noted the timing and location of the disturbance, taking place in "the arsenal of democracy on the very eve of the Allies' invasion of Europe." The clear implication is that outside forces, not Detroit residents, initiated the fighting and reports of racial conflict were a smoke screen to throw off suspicion from true instigators whose real objective was to embarrass Detroit and the nation as they were going on the offensive against Hitler.

In fact, over Nazi-controlled Vichy Radio in Europe, the Nazi propaganda machine hailed the Detroit riot in what it described as a country "torn by social injustice, race hatreds, regional disputes, the violence of an irritated proletariat and gangsterism of a capitalistic police."

In the eight decades since the Belle Isle riot, the narrative that this event was sparked by racial injustice and discontent has been set in stone as irrefutable fact. Certainly, blacks were treated as second-class citizens and were absolutely justified in resenting the system and working to change it. But defining the Belle Isle fight in 1943 as a race riot requires making assumptions and jumping to conclusions not supported by facts. Philip Adler, a professional reporter writing in the immediate aftermath of the disturbance, challenges this character-ization of events. The best we can say, looking back from our historical vantage point, is that the true and complete story of those tragic days is not yet known. ▪

Chapter 4

Shifting Gears

*"This is a great, rich city. It has never
defaulted upon a debt—and it never will."*
—Frank Murphy, Mayor of Detroit, 1930

■ ■ ■

THE END of World War II ushered in a wave of economic prosperity for Detroit and the rest of the country. To be sure, there were still problems to address in the city, particularly the acute housing shortage, postwar inflation, and chronically underperforming schools. But for two decades beginning in 1945, the Arsenal of Democracy—Motor City USA—appeared to be thriving.

Census figures in 1920–1940 ranked Detroit the fourth largest city in America by population. Though in 1950 the city slipped to fifth place behind upstart Los Angeles, the population that year reached an all-time high of 1,849,568. Pent-up demand for cars was a driving force behind the surging economy. Not only was civilian auto production suspended during the war, gasoline and rubber rationing also limited driving for anyone lucky enough to have a car. Now, as manufacturers struggled to meet demand, Detroit sat at the pinnacle of the industry. Half the cars built in the world and nine out of ten cars sold in America in 1950 were made in Detroit. Mighty General Motors held its place as the world's largest employer.

The United Auto Workers union was quick to claim a share of postwar prosperity for its members. The union agreed not to strike during the war. In November 1945, the union's chief negotiator with General Motors, Walter Reuther (one of those bloodied by Ford security when trying to organize that company's workers), proposed a raise for GM employees. General Motors refused, claiming they could not pay workers more without raising car prices above competitive levels.

Reuther challenged General Motors, insisting they could pay workers more without raising prices and demanding they open their books to prove they could not. When GM resisted, the UAW called a strike. Both sides settled in for a long siege. After a 113-day walkout by 320,000 GM workers around the country, the union got some of the raise it wanted but GM did not open its books. The next year, Walter Reuther became president of the United Auto Workers.

In 1955 General Motors became the first company in history to earn a billion dollars in a single year. That same year the U.S. automotive industry built more than nine million cars and trucks for the first time. Though the auto industry continued fueling Detroit's growth and prosperity, it went through a series of changes that had an impact on the city's economy. The minor players in America's car business shrank to nearly nothing and were gone within a few years. Packard, once a world standard of luxury, made an ill-advised merger with Studebaker, a legendary builder of covered wagons in the pioneer era. The iconic Packard plant—a vanguard of innovation when it opened in 1903—was closed in 1956, and Studebaker shut down its American operations entirely in 1963. Nash, Hudson, Kaiser, Frazer, and Willys were other makes that disappeared, closing plants on Detroit's east side and eliminating 70,000 jobs.

City residents faced other historic changes as well. In the mid-1950s the federal government began building a nationwide system of limited-access highways. This interstate system, modeled after the autobahn highways President Eisenhower saw and admired in Germany, enabled motorists to go between and around major cities without an intersection or a traffic light. One effect of the new system was to further stimulate the demand for cars. Another was improving access to Detroit as a manufacturing and transportation center. Detroit also benefitted from the opening of the St. Lawrence Seaway in 1959, allowing ocean-going vessels direct access to Detroit and other Great Lakes ports for the first time.

To take maximum advantage of the new interstate highway system, Detroit and other cities planned their own local freeways to supplement the national network. In the 1950s Detroit was completely reshaped by urban renewal. Even before the end of the war, landlords and the city bureaucracy began large-scale eviction proceedings against mostly low-income residents in anticipation of vast new federal building programs. In what turned out to be a disaster on an unprecedented scale, entire neighborhoods were cleared away to make room for a new network of express highways.

More than 20,000 homes and 2,000 businesses were eventually demolished on the way to building more than 200 miles of freeway in and around Detroit. Poor, run-down neighborhoods near the city center where proposed freeways would converge were prime candidates for demolition. Those were also the neighborhoods that had been the home of black residents and businesses for generations, their populations swollen in recent years by the immigration of newcomers to work in the factories. In these established neighborhoods they were welcome and some of them flourished. Many would struggle to afford housing elsewhere. Moreover, by practice if not by law, they were still excluded because of their race.

Federal urban renewal programs targeted the most important black neighborhoods in the city, Black Bottom and Paradise Valley, for demolition. They also set their sights on traditionally Mexican and Polish neighborhoods, as well as Corktown, Chinatown, and other ethnic strongholds.

As buildings began to fall before the bulldozers and wrecking balls, other neighborhoods resisted having these uprooted families on their streets. Further frustrating the process was the fact that after a block was razed, it might sit empty for months or years, caught up in bureaucratic red tape.

Yet another consequence of the new freeway system was that it made it easy for residents and businesses to move to the suburbs where land was plentiful and cheap and children could have their own yard to play in. Auto companies began migrating to expansive new factory sites outside the city. Modern assembly lines were best built on a single level in a low-rise factory with a huge footprint, not the old multi-story downtown buildings of the past. Between 1950 and 1960, Detroit's population declined slightly by about 180,000 while the surrounding suburbs grew by more than 900,000.

Public transportation, once a key component to the city's growth, shriveled during the 1950s, further contributing to residents' moving to the suburbs. Electric streetcars introduced at the end of the nineteenth century with such fanfare grew to a network of 534 miles by the time of World War II. The busiest lines had a streetcar running every sixty seconds. Yet in 1956 the last car was taken out of service. Busses took over some of the routes, but much of the old network and its riders were abandoned for good.

The prosperous postwar economy obscured decisions by Detroit's leaders during these years that marked the city's first tentative steps— seemingly inconsequential at the time—on the path to ruin. As the population leveled off and dipped slightly, city revenues declined. Instead of reducing expenses by a similar amount to keep the balance sheet in order, the city government not only maintained previous levels of spending but spent more than before.

Municipal employees, police officers, firemen, and other city workers negotiated generous legally guaranteed health and retirement benefits to be paid regardless of any changes in the city's income. School teachers, whose wages had been crimped first by the Depression and then by war, eventually negotiated substantial raises as well.

City schools were funded by property taxes, but as the urban population leveled off and began to decline, there were fewer homeowners to pay them. Remaining residents not only resisted higher rates, they, along with many other Detroiters, saw the school system as a disaster undeserving of their hard-earned dollars. Students were getting a second-rate education in outdated and unsafe buildings. The policy of lowering standards to keep students from dropping out was widely condemned, yet it continued as before.

By the mid-1950s, local employers complained that Detroit high school graduates could not perform jobs requiring basic reading, language, and math skills. Allowing students to choose cafeteria-style from a long list of electives including photography, family living, jewelry making, and stage crew, or to get credit for working in the school office or library, diluted academic standards to a critical degree. A 1958 investigation by the *Detroit Free Press* found that over the previous two years, about 90 percent of Detroit high school graduates who took the Wayne County Civil Service Commission exam failed the test. These graduates could not answer questions about "simple arithmetic, arithmetical reasoning, grammar, alphabetical filing, spelling, name comparisons, and meaning of words." Civil service examiners told the newspaper their test was designed to measure skills at a seventh-grade level.

The school district claimed their problems were because city residents voted down a property tax increase. The *Free Press* concluded the district's miserable performance was on account of an inferior "sandbox and custard" curriculum (to use the newspaper's description), counselors who "made no effort to steer students to more demanding programs," and teachers "who resented questions, seemed unprepared for class, and appeared bored with their jobs."

Despite this condemning report, the district and the city government lobbied the public for a tax increase and also a $60 million bond issue to build new schools. Residents ultimately agreed that the school system needed and merited a huge investment in its future and voted in 1959 in favor of both proposals. This gave Detroit schools their most secure financial underpinning since before the Depression.

At the same time, the resulting short-term financial victory set up challenges that would appear later. Higher property taxes would drive more residents to the suburbs, reducing the number of urban tax-payers and actually lowering tax revenues even as tax rates increased. The bonds saddled the district with interest payment obligations that would remain constant regardless of revenue or enrollment figures. Future voter initiatives produced still higher taxes and still more bonds. Another long-term obligation stemmed from a 1954 state law that, in exchange for receiving two-thirds of state sales tax revenues, required school districts to fund the teachers' retirement system enough to keep it "actuarily sound."

A short nationwide postwar recession hit Michigan and Detroit in 1957–58, slowing the market for new cars and raising unemployment. In 1958 Detroit introduced what may have been America's first public entitlement program, giving residents free rent, fuel, medical care, and a weekly cash allowance. On May 1, 1959, amid political infighting and gridlock in the state legislature, Michigan ran out of money. After missing one payday for state employees, the lawmakers worked out a compromise and eventually raised the state sales tax, among other remedies.

Detroit's financial obligations kept expanding even as population and revenues fell. Yet the city focused not on reducing expenses but on raising more money. Once again, long-term consequences were overshadowed by short-term gain. In 1962 a reform-minded lawyer named Jerome P. Cavanaugh took office as the youngest mayor in Detroit history at the age of thirty-three. One of his first major policy moves was to enact a municipal income tax of 1 percent on residents and ½ percent on non-residents who worked in the city. This new revenue stream meant that for the first time since the Depression, Detroit bonds were given a prime rating by underwriters. But it also added another financial burden to everyone who lived or worked in town.

Thus began the increasingly desperate cycle of taxing and spending that would spiral out of control a generation later. The combination of new highways and the dismantling of urban public transportation further accelerated Detroiters' move to the suburbs.

How times had changed. During the Depression, when Detroit and so many other cities struggled to pay their bills, Mayor Frank Murphy acknowledged the "unsatisfactory governmental administration" of years past and took on racketeering and corruption interests fed largely by the Prohibition-era liquor trade. Murphy vowed not to allow deficit spending, but rather to cut the city budget "to the bone" without resorting to "financial acrobatics." In a letter accompanying the city's 1930 annual report the mayor declared, "This is a great, rich city. It has never repudiated on an obligation nor defaulted upon a debt—and it never will."

Through the 1950s and 60s as more property owners decamped for the suburbs, payrolls and property valuations—and thus tax revenue—fell in proportion. Yet while the population and city revenue declined, the municipal budget kept increasing, as did the debt assumed to cover budget shortfalls. Leaders of the 1960s saw their financial obligations in a far different light than Mayor Murphy had.

Middle-class flight to the suburbs increased the percentage of black residents in Detroit, since there were more whites than blacks in that departing demographic group. (The motivation for this migration, which accelerated dramatically as living conditions in the city declined, was economics and lifestyle and not a matter of race, since in 1960 Detroit was still 70 percent white.) Blacks' economic and political strength grew as their numbers increased, putting them in a position to expect and demand faster progress toward equal treatment and equal opportunity. In the wake of the severe housing shortage for black workers during the war, ongoing discrimination and prejudice, and continuing evidence that Detroit's severely dysfunctional school system offered a poorer education to black students than their white classmates, the city took new initiatives to provide equal opportunity for all.

Dr. Remus Robinson was elected to the school board in 1955, becoming the first African American elected official in the city. In 1958 a Citizens Advisory Committee on School Needs included Mrs. James J. McClendon, wife of a former president of the NAACP, and other distinguished black members. After taking office in 1962, Mayor Cavanaugh appointed Alfred Pelham the first black controller in Detroit history. Tentative as these steps were, they put black residents in responsible, high-profile city-wide positions for the first time, paving the way for future progress.

Slow and frustrating though it was, the concept of racial equality was taking root in Detroit. Mayor Cavanaugh and other urban leaders knew public patience was wearing thin. They saw the bitter fruit of racial conflict in August 1965 when a traffic stop in the Watts area of South-Central Los Angeles exploded into destructive riots setting block after block ablaze and costing thirty-four people their lives.

Detroit was moving ahead with the times, its black citizens were prospering, and the city had no reason to believe trouble was brewing in the streets. So when disaster struck, the city was shocked, saddened, and surprised. Did Detroit's leaders ignore warning signs of unrest, or could it be the horrors to follow were carried out through unwitting pawns by outsiders with their own agendas?

Let us look at the history as it has been passed down to us. Then let us look at the facts. ■

Chapter 5

Inferno

"There's no real benefit when you tear up and burn down the place where you live, the places where you shop."
—Pastor Daniel Aldridge,
riot area resident, 1967

■ ■ ■

THE SUMMER of 1967 was pockmarked by racial unrest across America. Not only were there marches and protests in the Deep South where race relations had a long and troubled history, but also in Minneapolis, Kansas City, Wichita, Boston, Newark, and elsewhere. Still fresh in the public memory were the horrors of the riots in Los Angeles two years before, when a black motorist was arrested in the Watts neighborhood after failing a sobriety test. The incident touched off six days of destruction that left thirty-four dead and $40 million in property damage ($340 million in current dollars). Leaders in Detroit confidently declared their city was less likely to have riots than other metropolitan areas. Several reasons gave them hope.

First, they learned important lessons from the Belle Isle riot of 1943. Even if authorities never knew for certain what touched off the fight, they knew it escalated to its destructive and deadly climax because of mistrust and

"Scorners set a city aflame."
—Proverbs 29:8

friction between black and white. Though housing discrimination was still common more than twenty years later, federal and local anti-discrimination laws gave black residents access to more housing than before. The hopeless, legally sanctioned overcrowding of 1943 was gone. Another possible contributor to the '43 disturbance was the historic migration of poor, unskilled workers from the South, both white and black, who poured into the city to fill manufacturing jobs during World War II. Nothing like that was happening in 1967.

Second, compared to the past, and compared with other cities, black residents of Detroit were pacesetters in the long, difficult journey toward racial equality. Detroit in 1967 had two black members in the U.S. House of Representatives, black state legislators, and a black city councilman.

Third, black Detroit families were in a relatively strong financial position, thanks largely to the United Auto Workers Union and the automobile industry. Black workers held important positions in the union and supervisory jobs at the auto plants, where wages averaged $3.40 an hour (about $29 today). At the time, the UAW was negotiating for nearly a billion dollars ($8.5 billion) in additional salary and benefits, which would be its biggest increase ever.

In 1967, the average black Detroit family earned 95 percent of white median income. Black unemployment in the city that summer was 3.4 percent, lower than the national rate for whites. Forty percent of black heads-of-household owned their own homes, the highest percentage of any major city in America. Some of those homes were fine brick houses on tree-lined streets appraised as high as $50,000 ($425,000).

Beginning in 1961, more forward-thinking police commissioners made it a priority to treat black citizens fairly, a conscious break from attitudes of the past when police discrimination was commonplace and African Americans were routinely singled out for harsh treatment. Mayor Jerome Cavanaugh took office in 1962 with 85 percent of the black vote, running on a platform of racial reconciliation and civil rights. Under Cavanaugh's administration, Detroit received more than $40 million ($340 million) in federal funds for local anti-poverty programs. Even before federal programs were in place, Detroit's own public assistance plan offered rent, health care, and fuel relief plus a cash food allowance of $10 per week for adults and $5 for children.

On July 23, 1967, a Gallup poll reported that despite recent riots in Newark and elsewhere, 78 percent of residents of large American cities believed it was unlikely there would be "serious racial trouble" in their communities over the next six months.

That same day, Detroit burst into flames.

Considering Detroit's awareness of its own racial history, its newly progressive leadership, improving conditions for black residents, increased black political representation, historically low black unemployment, and high black home ownership, how could a race riot have exploded on the city streets?

Why would black Detroiters lead the way in destroying their own neighborhoods? The answer to that question still hangs in the air more than half a century later, yet modern-day accounts and the nation's collective memory of those deadly, destructive days insist that is exactly what happened.

The assertion that the Detroit riots of 1967 were sparked by racial unrest among local residents is accepted almost without question. Calling it the "Uprising of 1967," the *Encyclopedia of Detroit*, published by the Detroit Historical Society, describes the riot as an "insurrection" that was "the culmination of decades of institutional racism and entrenched segregation."

The account continues: "Despite the late hour, the avenue was full of people attempting to stay cool amidst a stifling heat wave." Police raided an illegal bar after hours and while they were waiting for paddy wagons to take the revelers to jail, a crowd formed, became violent, and set off burning and looting.

Encyclopedia Britannica online describes the riot as a "series of violent confrontations between residents of predominantly African American neighborhoods of Detroit and the city's police department." The "immediate cause" of the riot was a police raid at an illegal bar.

"The deeper causes of the riot were high levels of frustration, resentment, and anger created among African Americans by unemployment and underemployment, persistent and extreme poverty, racism" and other reasons.

In its entry on the riots, History.com begins by describing the "sweltering summer of 1967," when Detroit's black neighborhood was "a simmering cauldron of racial tension" and the "entire city was in a state of economic and social strife." On the "warm, humid" morning of July 23, 1967, the police raided an illegal club where partiers were celebrating the return of two servicemen from Vietnam. The people inside "were reluctant to leave their air-conditioned club."

Two weeks after the riots, *Time* magazine described them as "the most sensational expression of an ugly mood of nihilism and anarchy that has ever gripped a small but significant segment of America's Negro minority." The article claimed an informant, "a wino and ex-con," was paid fifty cents to warn police the situation at the bar was "getting ready to blow" and tipped them off that trouble was about to start. In its fifty-year retrospective on the riots in 2017, *Time* added, "Beneath that moment lay deep wells of resentment between the city's black population and its majority-white local government and law enforcement."

In its own fiftieth anniversary review of the riots, the *Detroit Free Press* declared the uprising did not begin with a raid on an illegal bar. "No, it began more than a century before, when escaped slaves making their way north to freedom wound up being re-enslaved in Detroit, leading to a race riot in 1833." The police action in the summer of 1967 was "the latest in a long narrative of oppressive racism, discrimination, injustice and rampant police brutality that a growing city continued to ignore."

The version of events almost universally accepted today is that what happened during those deadly days was an inevitable response to Detroit's suppression of black residents, fostering racial conflict that boiled over one hot summer night when people simply could not take it anymore. Yet according to those in a position to know—officials and eyewitnesses on the scene in the middle of the flames and looting—the actual facts tell a far different story.

Local residents, these observers say, did not initiate the violence but were opportunistic participants and unwitting pawns in the process. These sources present an account of the riot of 1967 far removed from what the wire services reported at the time and which challenges the popular historical record.

To begin, one account after another mentions the stifling heat and a teeming crowd on the sidewalk. Yet according to National Weather Service records, the temperature around the time of the arrests that morning was a refreshing 68 degrees; two mornings earlier it was in the 50s. The police report of the incident described "relatively light street crowds, probably not more than a dozen persons" in the immediate area.

Complaints about poverty and unemployment are undercut by the facts that African American unemployment in Detroit was low, wages for blacks were good, anti-poverty programs were some of the most comprehensive in the nation, and home ownership among blacks was some of the highest.

Readers who see the *Encyclopedia of Detroit* article or the *Britannica* entry—or any other mainstream present-day account of the riot—rightly assume they have the facts. And who can blame them? Digging a little deeper into original sources, however, the story is dramatically different.

In a long feature in the *Detroit Free Press* on July 26, 1967, at the height of the rioting, reporter George Walker wrote, "Of the question of why, no one can say. How do you explain something that can't be identified? It is easier to say what the riot is not than to say what it is. . . . Most important of all, it is not a race riot—and from this simple fact may emerge the only ray of hope in an otherwise totally dismal setting.

"It is not a race riot because there has been almost no conflict between whites and Negroes. Negroes and whites loot together, stand side by side to watch buildings burn, go to jail together."

This perspective will be a revelation to many. Walker's voice and other worthy voices are crucial to understanding the history of this moment. Altering the true narrative deprives all who follow of the opportunity to learn from the past. The more we all know about what actually happened in Detroit in the summer of 1967, the better we can understand it and the less likely we are to let it happen again. Here are the facts.

The United Community League for Civic Action was a small-time political organization run by William Scott Jr., out of an office above the Economy Printing Company at 9123 12th Street in Detroit. Between election cycles Scott operated an unlicensed bar in the space. In this he had plenty of company. Known locally as "blind pigs"—from the Prohibition-era offer to show someone a blind pig for a fee then serve them a clandestine drink instead—illegal drinking establishments operated throughout the city, relics of the speakeasies that flourished then because of easy access to alcohol from Canada.

On the night of Saturday, July 22, 1967, Scott hosted a party for two soldiers recently returned from Vietnam. The League office was jammed with more than eighty merrymakers who got merrier as the night went on. Neighbors complained to the police about the racket. It was not the first time locals had gone to Precinct 10 headquarters to file a complaint about Scott and his after-hours revelry. They had tried for months to stop these parties.

Police Sergeant Arthur Howison, who led a previous raid at the location, was familiar with Scott's operation and took the lead on the department's response that Saturday night. According to the police report, in order to document the fact Scott was selling liquor without a license, two undercover policemen knocked at the door around 10:30 p.m. with plans to order drinks, then make arrests after the drinks were served and paid for. The doorman turned them away. Finally, about 3:45 in the morning, Officer Charles Henry slipped in and ordered a beer. Ten minutes later—no word from Henry after that time meant he had made the buy—Sgt. Howison and two other officers, one of them black, entered the room and Howison announced that everyone was under arrest. Another carload of officers on patrol nearby came to assist.

Expecting maybe thirty-five or forty people inside, Howison and his squad found eighty-three, far more than they could transport. The sergeant radioed for three more patrol wagons and started processing his roomful of suspects. In his official report, Howison noted "relatively light crowds, probably not more than a dozen persons at the corner of 12th and Clairmount" when he entered the building. "It was just an average raid," he later recalled. "We arrested the people and made out the papers. There was absolutely no trouble with the people we arrested."

In the meantime, however, as the police waited for the extra paddy wagons, a crowd started gathering despite the late hour. By the time the bar patrons were loaded up and driven away around 4:45 a.m., the mood on the street had shifted. Curiosity hardened into disdain. Rumblings of police brutality swirled through the crowd.

At the time, the reason for the change in atmosphere was a mystery. Officers were there because members of the community requested them; neighbors had gone to the police station asking for help. Officers knew the lawbreakers from past encounters; recently the same police sergeant had responded to complaints about the same rowdy behavior at the same address. There wasn't a big crowd around when the arrests began—not unusual for the pre-dawn hours of a Sunday. The people taken into custody went quietly. Soon afterward, all but about a dozen of them were released without charges. By all accounts the officers on the scene handled the situation fairly and professionally despite the large number of detainees they had to process.

As Sgt. Howison drove off, a bottle shattered against the back window of his patrol car. Within minutes, what had been a routine police deployment was suddenly ground zero for violence. As wire services later reported, "Youths began smashing store windows, looting, and setting buildings afire. They hurled rocks and bottles at policemen, firemen, and newsmen." Taken by surprise and hopelessly outnumbered, the police retreated and called for reinforcements. By dawn all police leaves were cancelled and all available officers ordered to report for duty.

Arsonists and looters took over the streets. Businesses were torched and emptied. Fire alarms came in virtually nonstop. Every piece of firefighting equipment in the city was deployed, as well as brigades from surrounding communities and across the Detroit River bridge in Windsor, Ontario. When word passed through the neighborhoods that the police were not shooting lawbreakers, the mob surged through block after block breaking windows, setting fires, and stealing merchandise by the carload.

Mayor Jerome Cavanaugh and Police Commissioner Ray Girardin believed opening fire on the looters would cause a bloodbath. Hoping the situation would de-escalate on its own, they waited hours before allowing police to shoot in an effort to restore order. Even then, police at first could only fire in self-defense and to protect firemen, who were dangerously exposed as they perched on ladders. Countless police and firemen were hit by bottles, bricks, and rocks.

When firemen in one area started abandoning their equipment under a hail of projectiles and sniper fire, around twenty black members of a neighborhood association armed themselves and surrounded the firefighting equipment to protect the men. "They say they need more protection," one of the club members said, "and we're damn well going to give it to them." Rioters taunted the weary fire crew by dropping off a six-pack of looted beer.

Touring sections of the devastation with Michigan Governor George Romney and a National Guard general, Mayor Cavanaugh was appalled by the "carnival spirit"—the riot was "a great lark" to the vandals, who seemed to be enjoying themselves and their newfound merchandise rather than promoting any particular position or theology. One reporter described "a strange, happy-go-lucky mood." A young boy later told an interviewer, "The riot was very good because my father and I looted four color TVs, two bottles of beer, and a washing machine—just for the fun of it. My nephew got about 32 rugs and a bottle of Johnny Walker."

Governor Romney mobilized the National Guard and requested military assistance from the federal government. Romney and President Lyndon Johnson—considered possible rivals for the 1968 presidential election—traded barbs in the media over Romney's alleged inability to control the violence and Johnson's supposed delay in sending troops in order to make Romney look weak. By Monday night, July 24, army paratroopers from the 101st Airborne were on the ground in Detroit and National Guard tanks rolled through the smoke, flame, and debris.

Speaking live to a nationwide television audience, President Johnson confirmed he was sending in federal troops "with the greatest regret," but "extraordinary circumstances" required him to do so. The president added, "Law, order, pillage, looting, murder and arson have nothing to do with civil rights."

From its first hours, national reporters and commentators labeled the destruction in Detroit a "race riot." As the city burned newspapers declared, "Thousands of rampaging Negroes firebombed and looted huge sections of the nation's fifth largest city . . ." "Negro sniper squads waged guerrilla war early today . . ." "Negro outlaws engage[d] federal paratroopers, National Guardsmen and police . . ." On July 27, the Associated Press described the destruction as "the nation's worst racial explosion in recent history." Certainly there was a history of racial tension in the city. In past years the police had a reputation for being heavy-handed with black suspects and discriminatory in hiring and promoting black officers. Though under Mayor Cavanaugh these conditions were changing, black residents were right to insist the department still had a long way to go.

Nonetheless, there is no evidence the arrests at 12th and Clairmount were racially motivated. Black citizens requested the police action and one of the responding officers was black. There was no basis for any claim of police brutality during the incident. And it was not long before the *Free Press* published its report that far from being a "race riot," this was an instance of blacks and whites looting stores and going to jail together. Damon Keith, chairman of the Michigan Civil

Rights Commission, denounced the riots as the work of "hoodlums with a total disregard for the law."

Middle-class blacks and black community leaders were as appalled and horrified as any white resident by what was happening. James Del Rio, a black state legislator, stood on Grand River Avenue with a Bible in one hand and a chain in the other trying in vain to calm the mob. Congressman John Conyers, an African American member of the U.S. House of Representatives, stood on the roof of a car with a bullhorn imploring looters to stop. The mob answered with catcalls and rocks and surged ahead. Later Conyers's office was torched.

Anyone who disagreed with the wave of destruction was condemned regardless of their race. Reverend Nicholas Hood, the only black member of the Detroit City Council, told reporters he and his family were threatened and were moving out of their house. Another black minister, Daniel Aldridge, described walking through his neighborhood "trying to discourage young people from looting, trying to tell them, 'This is not what it's about . . . I do think there's no real benefit when you tear up and burn down the place where you live, the places where you shop.'"

Black professionals were also targets of the mob. One nervous resident, Dudley Randall, later said, "There was no harm done to me or my family, although there were a few anxious nights when there were rumors that they would get the 'rich black folks.' I never thought it was a crime to have a job." Another resident, a well-dressed psychiatrist walking down the street, recoiled as black looters screamed at him, "We're going to get your rich niggers next!"

Conversely, whites were widely reported among the looters. The first sniper taken out by police was a white man shooting at white officers. Snipers were arguably the most dangerous element of the whole uprising. Hidden on rooftops or between buildings, they took shots at policemen, firemen, and unarmed civilians as well as soldiers. It was risky and difficult to flush them out. Military sharpshooters and police helicopters with searchlights did their best, yet the threat remained. Tuesday morning news summaries reported one sniper shot and killed three civilians.

The situation was most dangerous at night. Police and soldiers began shooting out streetlights to protect themselves, leaving blocks of stores in darkness. One neighborhood police station was besieged by rioters with guns until a National Guard tank came to the rescue. At least three other stations faced sniper attacks.

Almost every news report began with an account of snipers shooting and police and soldiers answering with tanks and machine guns. Twenty-five police officers were shot Tuesday night as hidden assailants advanced through the west side of the city near where the riot began. The death toll stood at thirty-three, including a four-year-old girl. One of three white snipers charged with attempted murder for shooting a National Guardsman in the stomach was the son of a retired police officer.

The east side of town became quieter and safer after army paratroopers were deployed. Looters quickly learned the seasoned soldiers stood their ground and returned fire faster than nervous and inexperienced National Guardsmen in the west. Testifying later before a congressional committee, the military commander in Detroit, Lt. General John L. Throckmorton, explained how he ordered National Guardsmen to unload their weapons because they were "trigger happy" and "nervous." Guardsmen were ordered to put their ammunition in their pockets and load only upon orders of an officer.

"I had no intention of having innocent women and children killed. It was not a red hot situation." The general added, "The situation did not warrant the use of total force."

In the billowing smoke of a thousand fires, neighborhood churches distributed food and clothing as residents struggled to get through the day without grocery stores, gas stations, pharmacies, restaurants, laundromats, theaters, or playgrounds. White and black alike stayed indoors, afraid to risk driving to work and having their cars smashed.

By mid-week, workers were returning to their jobs downtown even as snipers still roamed the west side. Military and police units were waging an "all-out war" against the hidden shooters, who were operating in coordinated squads. There were now 13,000 troops and police in the city. Paratroopers moved into the western streets to help the beleaguered Guardsmen. Army sharpshooters set up a protective perimeter on rooftops around a hospital where the police established a command post.

On Thursday morning the death toll reached thirty-six, surpassing the 1965 Watts riots in Los Angeles as the deadliest civil uprising in American history. The killing and destruction continued, though that day Detroit's exhausted firefighters got a six-hour break from answering emergencies around the clock. By then thirty firemen were hospitalized, most with burns. Four suffered heart attacks. One, a thirty-year-old husband and father, was killed by a sniper. Among the department's small victories was to save the home where Charles Lindbergh was born as the house next door went up in flames. Damage to firefighting equipment from gunfire and vandalism topped $100,000 ($850,000).

As residents, officials, and reporters began processing all that happened, many believed if police had restored order and put an end to burning and looting on the first day, rioting would have been stopped in its tracks. Mayor Jerome Cavanaugh campaigned as a reformer looking to improve the lives and opportunities of the city's minorities. Police Commissioner Ray Girardin was a former reporter for the defunct *Detroit Times* who built his newspaper career as a tireless crusader for the underdog. As commissioner, he was the symbol of a new approach to policing intended to make a clean break from the past. "Now," the wire services reported, "Girardin's compassion is bringing him criticism. There are widespread charges that the riot raged out of control because Girardin's men were under orders, for nearly two days, to hold their fire."

The mayor and police commissioner were so determined to avoid charges of police brutality and discrimination that they failed to act when they could still have stopped the destruction from spreading. They kept thinking the mob would burn itself out until it was too late.

Girardin said he believed the riot was started by "half-drunken young Negroes . . . Once the riot was underway a sort of looting fever seized many Negroes that I bet never stole anything in their lives before. . . . Looting was the thing to do at the moment, and they did it. Now they are ashamed."

Far from approving the police's hands-off response, many black residents condemned the mayor and police commissioner for failing to crack down on looters when the trouble began. Charles Tindal, executive director of the Detroit chapter of the NAACP, and Longworth Quinn, editor of the black-owned *Michigan Chronicle*, joined the chorus of criticism. An eight-column headline in the *Chronicle* blared, "It could have been stopped." The story that followed claimed, "If the police had stopped looting when it centered on one 12th Street block early Sunday, when the mood was allowed to become a Roman holiday, the riot could have been prevented."

According to the newspaper, a witness said when a police car arrived at a store being looted at 4:00 a.m. on Sunday, "'fifty kids piled out of that store.' But later, when Negroes realized that the police weren't going to stop them, the gathering of mobs, looting and burning intensified. William Greene, an official of the United Automobile Workers Union Local 600 at the Ford plant, who lived in the riot area, told a newsman, 'If they had started shooting the first few hours it wouldn't have lasted a day.' Other Negroes also said the crowds joined in the riot, which took on a carnival atmosphere, only after they realized the police weren't cracking down."

Police appeared anxious not to "inflame" black crowds. Twelfth Street was cordoned off but "little attempt was made to break up the crowds in the then-small riot area about six blocks long. Once the outbreak spread to other sections of the city there weren't enough policemen, firemen, or even National Guardsmen, initially, to prevent looting and burning."

In his newspaper feature published by the *Free Press* as the riot unfolded, George Walker returned repeatedly to compelling evidence that whatever else the riot was, it was not a race riot. He observed, "A crowd that burns the office of Rep. John Conyers—one of the city's two Negro congressmen—is not rebelling against the white man."

Reflecting further even as smoke and flame engulfed the city, Walker wrote, "The city's Negroes have good numerical representation in the state Legislature and Congress. For years, Negroes have played an important role in shaping the destiny of the city – running welfare programs, planning housing, planning how to spend millions of dollars in state and federal money that have poured into the city.

"For years, hundreds of thousands of white and Negro workers have worked side by side in factories, so long that most of them have become color blind. The city's anti-poverty program, a model for the nation, is controlled, for the most part, by Negroes. Gov. Romney likes to tell audiences throughout the country that Michigan is the only state with a Civil Rights Commission that is built into its constitution. State, city and federal committees abound, encouraging, threatening employers to hire more Negroes and promote them to jobs equal to their abilities. . . .

"If the riot is not a racial riot and not a lot of other things, what is it?"

More than fifty years later Walker's question remains unanswered. Though histories and commentaries have long since labeled the 1967 Detroit conflict "a racial riot," other accounts support Walker's observation that it was not. For whatever reason, these alternate narratives have been pushed aside.

One alternative in particular merits special consideration. Let us look at the events that unfolded near the corner of 12th Street and Clairmount on a cool (not sultry) summer morning through the eyes of a history-making black reporter who breathed in the dust and smoke of the street, clambered over jagged debris, and worked his inside contacts to capture a version of events that puts this chapter of American history in an entirely new light. ■

Chapter 6

Minority Report

"The riot was instigated by out-of-town forces."
—Sandra West, riot-area resident
and UPI reporter, 1967

■ ■ ■

A LITTLE-KNOWN alternate account paints a vastly different picture of the uprising of 1967 than the historical record. Its chief artist was Louis E. Lomax.

Lomax was a vanguard in the history of journalism. As a reporter for the *Chicago Herald-American*, he was the first black journalist hired by Hearst Newspapers. In Los Angeles during the 1960s, he was the first black personality to have his own major-market television and radio shows. By then he was already well-known on the air. In 1958 he joined WNTA-TV in New York, becoming America's first mainstream black television journalist.

A year later he made journalism history again as writer, co-producer, and co-host of *The Hate That Hate Produced*, a WNTA documentary on the firebrand Malcolm X and his Nation of Islam, collaborating with future broadcast news icon Mike Wallace. Malcolm X refused to be interviewed by a white reporter.

"Buy the truth, and do not sell it."
—Proverbs 23:23

Lomax gained access to the controversial radical and his inner circle in a way no other reporter could.

Lomax was also an author, syndicated columnist, and screenwriter who landed a deal with Hollywood mogul Richard Zanuck and 20th Century Fox for a movie script about Malcolm X. For years he cultivated sources that gave him access to information unavailable to other mainstream media figures. Not only did black leaders, pastors, politicians, and activists trust Lomax, people who had reason to be wary of the law or any "official" authority learned he was a reporter who protected his sources. He was invited to North Vietnam in 1966 to interview Communist leader Ho Chi Minh as secret negotiations with America to end the Vietnam War were being considered. Though the interview was cancelled at the last minute after Lomax had already traveled as far as Cambodia, the invitation was yet another indication of his respected position and his ability to gather information from both sides of a deeply divided issue, inside or outside the law.

Beginning about two weeks after the Detroit riots ended, Lomax syndicated a series of columns through the North American Newspaper Alliance, a syndication service for African American newspapers, about what he saw, heard, and learned. He was on the ground as events unfolded and presented vivid eyewitness accounts of the conflict, including essential background information that was downplayed or lost in the shuffle by the mainstream news services—and by history. This minority report, drawn from notes made at the scene and the reporter's own sources, rewrites the story of the Detroit riots.

Though Detroit had good reason to believe it would be spared the racial conflict that flared in Minneapolis, Newark, and elsewhere in 1967, according to Lomax a civilian task force had taken the extra precaution of drawing up contingency plans to contain a riot, a plan of action to stop the conflict before it could spread. The existence of this task force is reinforced by political commentator Marquis Childs, who as the riots unfolded described a "summer task force on watch to try to anticipate and checkmate tensions" that was on 24-hour call just outside Mayor Jerome Cavanaugh's office.

While long years of legal housing discrimination were coming to an end, most black residents still lived in segregated neighborhoods. Even so, Detroit was largely spared the miserable black ghettos of New York and cities in the Deep South. The closest Detroit came to a black ghetto in this sense was the west-side neighborhood along Clairmount Street. In writing up their simulated riot, the task force picked the location at the corner of Clairmount and 12th as the flashpoint.

Three days later, the real Detroit riots began on that very corner.

The task force plan turned out to be useless, Lomax wrote, "because it overlooked the fact that an organized group, largely from outside the Detroit area," instigated the riots, not local residents protesting local conditions. These outsiders were "highly organized and well trained . . . revolutionaries" dedicated to burning and destruction by starting the conflict then urging "innocent and uninformed" bystanders to pitch in.

Lomax reported that this outside movement, which he labeled "Operation Detroit," began several weeks earlier when a group of young black men canvassed the neighborhood posing as magazine salesmen. Once a member of the group was admitted to someone's home, he said he was a recent high school graduate from the South selling magazines to pay his college tuition. But after completing his magazine spiel, the conversation took a shocking turn.

As Lomax quoted one homeowner, "I thought I was helping a worthy Negro boy get to college. . . . Then he started talking to me about Black Power. He asked me 'why the hell we let whitey, particularly the Jews, run the stores in our neighborhood.' Then he started asking . . . who was who, who had guns, who owed big bills at local stores and might be interested in seeing the building burn down."

When the homeowner declined to answer his questions, the man left. The homeowner learned the "salesman" and his cohorts asked the same questions throughout the neighborhood. Residents worried something was brewing and the neighborhood association began to investigate. In response, "leaders of the group were immediately threatened by young Negro men they had never seen before. Honestly frightened, they remained silent until after the riots."

To start a riot, Operation Detroit needed a spark. Ideally, this would be some minor altercation with the police in a crowded area where a mob could coalesce quickly. Outside instigators could then take advantage of herd mentality by fanning the flames of anger toward police for detaining or arresting someone on the street. Next, the outsiders would break a few windows and set a few fires. They didn't loot or steal. They didn't need to. Once the disturbance reached critical mass, the instigators' job was done and the residents were left to destroy their own community.

The first attempts failed to ignite. In June a black man was shot and killed while allegedly protecting his wife from three white attackers. But there was no crowd around. Nor was there a crowd a couple of weeks later when a black woman alleged to be a prostitute was killed by police who said she threatened them with a knife.

Then early in the morning of Sunday, July 23, police raided an unlicensed bar on the corner of Clairmount and 12th. Aside from the police report, Lomax was one of very few sources to note the police were there because local residents complained about the place for months and asked them to come.

Despite the large number of suspects, the arrests went smoothly. It was only as the police were driving away that someone broke a car window and the atmosphere changed. Lomax reported a woman who was in the bar yelled, "They called us niggers!" A bystander said he heard the same thing. Other rumors swirled: some of those arrested were thrown down the stairs; they were kicked while handcuffed.

More windows shattered and the looting began, though even then the situation was not necessarily beyond hope. A professor at Wayne University who lived in the area (possibly Dr. James Boyce, quoted elsewhere by Lomax) noted, "I was standing on the street when the looting started. It was a normal breaking and looting scene. They happen all the time. Then the people became aware of the fact that the police, following orders, were not interfering with looters."

Early on the police realized they were hopelessly outnumbered. At the time the raid took place, there were only a handful of uniformed officers on the street and they could not possibly control the rampaging crowd. By 5:30 a.m., all police leaves were cancelled and officers were reporting for duty as fast as they could get to their precincts. Later in the morning, reportedly at the request of leading black pastors in the community, police commissioner Ray Girardin agreed not to open fire on the looters, hoping the disturbance would run its course and play out.

"At this point," Lomax reported, "the professionals moved in," one squad of them making its way systematically up 12th Street "with hammers and crowbars, smashing windows."

"Come on, baby, help yourself," they shouted to the crowd in the street. Another squad spread the word a few blocks away: "Hey man, the fuzz is letting people take all they want. Get up to the corner of Clairmount."

The looters, said Lomax, had no idea they were "pawn[s] in the revolutionaries' game." He added, "The professionals wanted hundreds of people running, yelling, and looting near the corner of 12th and Clairmount. Add to that the nonaction by the police and you have a recipe for chaos and riots—perfect food for revolutionaries. Within two hours, 12th Street was a human jungle."

By dawn Sunday, July 23, 1967, the neighborhood was in flames. Looters went up and down the blocks unchallenged except by a few desperate business owners trying to protect their property. Outsiders methodically worked the streets breaking windows and setting fires, then encouraging locals to come in and take what they wanted. White and black alike hauled away stolen merchandise by the carload. Color televisions, still a novelty and more than twice the price of old-fashioned black-and-white sets, were a special prize. One young man loaded a refrigerator across the back of his open-top convertible.

Sandra West, a young UPI reporter who had lived since 1954 with her parents two blocks from where the riots began, reported cars with New York, Illinois, and Ohio license plates filled with stolen goods, price tags still dangling, cruising the neighborhood. "The feeling is growing in my neighborhood," she wrote in a wire service story, "that the riot was instigated by out-of-town forces."

Watching neighbors run from their burning homes with small children and only what they could carry wrapped in a bedsheet, West "saw sights I never dreamed possible. Raging fires burned out of control for blocks and blocks." She and her parents packed a few necessities and prepared to abandon their home if necessary.

Her neighbors were certain the riots were well-planned and professionally carried out. They knew the residents and the cars of the neighborhood and realized the strangers and strange cars they saw flooding the streets and filled with looted merchandise were from somewhere else. "When the looters finished stealing and generally tearing up a shop," one eyewitness told her, "a man who seemed to be the leader would give a whistle, a special 'match-man' would set all the debris on fire, and the looters would move out. And they seemed to know just where to head for next." Shortly after daybreak, the electricity went out. Smoke was so thick that West couldn't see across the street.

Louis Lomax also saw out-of-towners leading the mob. "Methodically breaking store windows," he reported, "the revolutionaries urged the milling Negro people to loot and steal," adding, "at least a dozen" eyewitnesses confirmed the professionals did no looting. "They are not thieves; they are men at war. . . . The streets teemed with whites and Negroes who stole with abandon and glee. People came in cars from miles away and hauled off freezers, sofas, television sets and clothing."

Hampered by orders to hold their fire, police chased looters from one scene only to have another group go to work a few doors away. As soon as officers left to deal with the second incident, looters at the first location resumed their work. Locals who saw this were furious, but the police insisted they were helpless because of orders not to shoot.

Lomax quoted a local resident who owed a big debt to a furniture store. Living on public assistance, she was so far behind in payments that the interest due ballooned to more than the original purchase price. "I burned that damn Jew store down," she declared. "That's one bill I will never have to pay. I made sure the office and all the records went up in flames first!"

The black owner of a nearby drug and liquor store fielded complaints for years about high prices and poor treatment. His was the first black-owned business to be torched. Arsonists systematically continued their work. A man who went to buy groceries looked on in horror as a group of six strangers, working with efficiency and precision, set his local grocery store on fire. He drove to another store and had just finished shopping when the same six arrived and burned down that market as well.

Lomax wrote, "A weary but happy arsonist approached a Negro school teacher on La Salle Street. 'We have Twelfth Street in flames,' he said. 'Linwood is next.' Half an hour later Linwood Boulevard was aflame. A Negro woman . . . bragged that she was getting paid to set fires."

By Sunday afternoon the fires had spread to an integrated neighborhood of tree-lined streets and fine brick homes near Seven-Mile Road. Middle-class blacks watched as their front lawns were marked with crosses by rioters. Middle- and upper-income blacks were afraid their white neighbors would turn against them, but they all stood together in this time of crisis. White bystanders fearing for their lives were allowed into black homes for protection.

Lomax confirmed reports that one of the early, persistent, and most dangerous features of the riots was snipers. From the first day, hidden gunmen took aim at policemen, citizens, and most sinister of all, firemen, who were sitting ducks on their ladders as they struggled against fires in the area that eventually numbered over a thousand. At least some of the snipers had no interest in race relations. They just wanted to shoot at something.

Sandra West heard and saw snipers crossing her lawn. They harassed her as she sheltered inside against the "burning, choking . . . heavy smoke . . . daring me with their stares to order them off my property." Another resident saw her next-door neighbor firing on officers through her hedges. "Why are you doing that?" she yelled.

"It's fun," he answered. "This is the first time I've had a chance to try out my new rifle." He resumed shooting.

Lomax believed the snipers were local but well-prepared. He reported that they, "on the whole, were Detroit's own sons—Black Power advocates who are trained in guerrilla warfare. . . . They knew the terrain, the alleys, the streets, the by-ways, and the roof-tops. They monitored police calls, set off sniper activity and then vanished through the alleys. By midnight Monday, they had set up a telephone squad whose job was to make false reports to the police and thus lure the officers into traps."

According to Lomax, Detroit's "responsible Negroes" suspected six people in their community of working with outside actors to organize the riots: attorney Milton Henry, former Black Muslim, confidant of the late Malcolm X, and former city councilman in Pontiac, Michigan; his brother, Richard Henry; bookstore owner and Black Power advocate Edward Vaughn; Congregational minister and former political candidate Albert Cleage; and John Boggs and his wife, Grace Lee Boggs, both allegedly tied to the Progressive Labor Party, a China-based group calling for open revolution in America.

Vaughn's bookstore was rumored to be a meeting place for the Revolutionary Action Movement, a militant Black Power group with ties to Communist China. The *Detroit Chronicle*, a black community newspaper, sent an undercover reporter to investigate. Lomax wrote, the journalist was "so frightened by what he saw and heard that he refused to write the series."

These black organizers, Lomax said, "communicate with and have relationship with the people who ran amuck in Detroit. The established Negro leadership [pastors, politicians, NAACP, etc.] does not. It is further clear that the dedicated revolutionaries who came into Detroit and worked a brilliant military miracle were packed and gone by Wednesday. Everybody knows they were there; many people know who they were. Reporters talked to some of them but could not prove their organizational ties. Nevertheless, the threat has become reality. The dedicated revolutionaries have left Detroit—bound for other cities."

Lomax had no doubt the Detroit riots were planned and instigated by outsiders. He also believed the uprising was as much about class as race. Middle-class blacks were threatened just as whites were. White looters and snipers were involved from the beginning, often targeting other whites. Black as well as white businesses were destroyed as locals took advantage of the opportunity to settle old scores with merchants they thought mistreated and overcharged them.

"Several factors about the involvement of white people are clear," Lomax wrote in his syndicated column. "They were there and deeply involved. The first sniper taken was white. Many of the looters involved were white. There are those white liberals who felt that the only way to solve the problems of the slum is to burn it down. The dedicated Negro revolutionaries do not have the money to carry out their plans."

White looters, like their black counterparts, "can be disposed of easily," Lomax continued. They "were simply out to steal. . . . But a white sniper, a white man firing on the police, and a white home sheltering three white men firing on police pose yet another question. Who are these white people; what are they up to and why?"

The ashes of Detroit had not yet yielded an answer, Lomax observed, but he concluded, "Black Power advocates who are committed to burning down America's cities have white allies." As a local civil rights leader told Lomax, "I can understand a Negro with a pistol and a switch blade. But when a Negro sniper attacks the police station with a high-powered rifle equipped with a telescopic lens, then we are dealing with something new. White money and white bodies are involved . . ." Lomax concluded there were Americans both white and black who "feel that an urban bonfire is the only thing that will make the white power structure sit up and take notice."

Notes for an unpublished essay about the Detroit riots express the depth of Lomax's belief that Detroit had gone out of its way to encourage and lift its black residents. A look at his introduction raises the tantalizing question of what he would have written had the project gone forward: "Detroit, like every other American city since Watts, poured millions of dollars into Federal, State, and County programs to make sure a riot would not occur there.

"Detroit, more than any other American city, deliberately gerrymandered to give Negroes a quantity of political representation unmatched in the U.S. Detroit is the only American city with two Negro congressmen.

"Detroit has the strongest Mayor's Human Relations Council in America.

"Detroit's Negroes boast one of the highest standards of living in the nation.

"You name it, Detroit tried it. Yet Detroit exploded with the worst racial uprising in modern history."

In the last of his five columns on the Detroit riots, Lomax declared it was "irrefutably evident that a Black Power revolutionary organization . . . took over and directed the riots," and drew a bright line between responsible black citizens and those bent on destruction. The revolutionaries claimed there had been no change in the lot of black Americans since the historic Supreme Court *Brown v. Board of Education* decision of 1954, which ruled the "separate but equal" approach used to justify legal segregation for generations after the Civil War was unconstitutional. A flood of civil rights and welfare legislation in the 1960s gave African Americans new legal rights and recourse, even though in practice there was wide resistance to them.

Lomax argued that since 1954 there had been tremendous improvement in legal protection and individual opportunity for black Americans. But those changes happened "for the Negro with training, brains, and talent," not for ignorant, opportunistic migrants from the South who "have taken over the slums of our major cities and inbred their children with something approaching a congenital inability to live and work into the American mainstream, something those of us who were the original participants of the Negro revolt aspired to do."

The original dream "as articulated by Dr. Martin Luther King" was that white and black would "walk, live, and pray together." However, "the Negroes and whites who made sure Detroit exploded are yet another breed. They are bent upon bringing down both the nation and the system that undergirds it. They have lost faith. They are now convinced that neither the white power structure nor I as a successful Negro really care about what happens to them . . ."

By the time Lomax wrote those words, Detroit Mayor Jerome Cavanaugh had convened a group of black leaders to chart the city's future. But, Lomax noted, "They were the same old crowd, the same old Negro leaders who have not the slightest communication with the Negro masses; the Negroes who could not foresee or stop a racial insurrection if you gave them a detailed blueprint."

Middle-class blacks were more interested in the news that Walter Reuther, head of the United Auto Workers, promised manpower and trucks to clean up the rubble.

Detroit and the nation were slowly moving forward toward racial equality. But it appeared to Lomax that discontented blacks saw only a half-empty glass, justifying continued violence. Commenting on this element, bookstore owner Edward Vaughn said to Lomax, "You told them [in Lomax's book *The Negro Revolt*]. Martin King told them. Everybody who cares, white and black, told them. They did not listen."

Would America listen and respond to the voice of non-violent blacks in the days and years ahead? The alternative, Lomax concluded, was, "God forbid, the only thing they will hear is the crackling of flames, the burp of gunfire and the wail of police sirens across the nation.

"The bad people are now organized. They are subsidized, trained, and ready.

"Are we?"

Lomax never identified his sources for the fact the riots were planned and started by outsiders. His field notes taken during the thick of the conflict are tantalizingly sparse. He jots down a few names and phrases that appear later in his articles but there are no interview records, no phone numbers or addresses of contacts. A few pages are loose sheets of blank newsprint and the rest are torn from a spiral notebook visible in archival photos of Lomax standing in the rubble.

However, he did mention in passing—again without noting his sources—how "one of the agitators" in Detroit participated in the riots in Newark, New Jersey, a week before the Detroit disturbance began. The Newark revolt was touched off when a black taxi driver was allegedly beaten by police. Over five days of fires and destruction twenty-six people were killed. In columns published in the *Newark Star-Ledger* around the same time as his syndicated pieces about Detroit, Lomax described Newark as a "hub for black revolution-aries" and Black Power advocates from Detroit were in Newark before departing "for their hometown to aid in carrying out an ever greater holocaust."

Lomax identified Willie Wright as a "central figure" in instigating the riots. Describing him as a thirty-six-year-old college dropout who worked as an engineer for the Pennsylvania Railroad, Lomax reported White "has carried a vendetta against the white man that traces back to the time the city fathers of Albany, Ga., took 18 city blocks of choice land from his grandfather 20 years before Willie was born."

In another column early the following year, Lomax added, Willie Wright was a key source for information about black nationalism: "When assigned to do a series of articles on Newark it took but one phone call to black nationalist leader Willie Wright to discover that a carefully conceived plan to burn much of Newark's main business section was already in execution when the cab driver incident set off the major conflagration . . ."

Specifically connecting the destruction in Detroit and Newark, Lomax declared, "Newark's revolutionaries were congratulating them-selves for having staged the biggest ghetto revolt to date. Then, as one of the top leaders of the rebellion put it, some of the out-of-town revolutionaries emplaned for Detroit where they helped set off a holo-caust that made Newark's uprising look like a tea party."

In a later interview with media columnist Bob Hull in Los Angeles, Lomax added, the information he gathered in Detroit "unerringly points to one of the nationally known civil rights organizations."

Lomax also believed politicians were duped into shoveling money at poor blacks, but these recipients did not have the skills to formulate programs; they just took the money. Quoting Dr. Nathan Wright, whom Lomax described as a Black Power intellectual leader, Lomax asked, "How in the hell can you build a bridge by taking the money allocated for a bridge and dividing it among people who need a bridge but don't know how to build it?"

Louis Lomax's reporting from Detroit in the summer of 1967 was a historic account of events by a seasoned, professional observer with extensive contacts relevant to the story. His conclusions were supported by others including Sandra West—a vanguard in her own right as a black woman reporting for UPI. Only a few years later in 1970, Lomax's career was cut short when he died in a one-car crash on a deserted highway outside Santa Rosa, New Mexico. He probably fell asleep at the wheel. He was forty-seven years old.

▨ ▨ ▨

Another prominent African American commentator shared Louis Lomax's skepticism about the origin and objective of the Detroit riots. Journalist and author George S. Schuyler looked on the uprising as opportunistic class warfare by Communists, agitators, and migrants with no historical connection to Detroit and no interest in seeing its racial problems solved. Writing for the same North American Newspaper Alliance that syndicated Lomax's columns, Schuyler believed, as the lead-in to his first essay about the riots explained, "that the government, by pandering to the least responsible and least ambitious of the Negro community, is creating a social and moral problem that will become more tortured with each passing year."

Schuyler insisted it was a mistake to let looters run loose and for police not to crack down early and hard. Blame should be on the lawbreakers, not the police or the white community or the legal system.

What good, he asked, could come "in the face of the depressing spectacle of supposedly intelligent and responsible people excusing the crime wave" on the grounds it was justified by discrimination? "What can be expected when some police forces hold off shooting down these arsonists, vandals and guerrilla fighters for fear of further inflaming them? . . .

"Cops who try to suppress insurrection are accused of 'police brutality.' Responsible Negroes, in the vast majority, are terrorized into silence, their homes gutted, their property destroyed, their womenfolk lined up to get refugee rations because grocery stores and meat markets have gone up in smoke."

Schuyler had little patience for city leaders who claimed they were unaware of "black racists" looking for opportunity and "of the subservience cells dug into the framework of their communities and parked on the antipoverty payroll." A running controversy during and after the riots was the claim that numerous instigators were on the public payroll working for federally funded anti-poverty programs.

But rather than hold the rioters accountable, Schuyler wrote, city leaders "impertinently accuse the white victims of their outrages of being actually at fault and demand, as the price of communal peace, that the wastrels be provided with residential Taj Mahals and jobs for which they are untrained."

Part of the problem, he continued, was local political leaders' "trancelike fascination for the theories of guilt-ridden intellectuals who, for lack of anything better to do, would remake the world. . . . This has pathetically raised the expectations of the cretins and incompetents and encouraged the delinquent and criminal element which lurks in the shadows of every city on earth."

Schuyler described how politicians' response to the riots was sending middle-class residents, both black and white, to the suburbs, abandoning the city to waves of newcomers who come only for the entitlements. Organized leaders who direct the violence, Schuyler said, indoctrinate these new arrivals along with resident malcontents "to despise and defy the forces of law and order, to make them sorry for themselves for being 'deprived' and to stir hatreds which are never far from the surface. The more handouts they are given, the louder they clamor for more . . ."

Schuyler noted that although far worse conditions existed for black Americans in the past, it was only now, since the "onset ten years ago of the campaign of agitation and incitement by Negro activists," that riots exploded across the country. This outside influence, not local conditions—which were improving by almost any metric—was the spark touching off the destruction.

Pulling no punches, Schuyler continued, "The vandalizing of our cities today is the product of 50 years of brainwashing. . . . [M]illions of whites have fallen for the line that they are today, in 1967, responsible for the evils of slavery and for the 'century of neglect' that followed it. The fact is that the 'century of neglect' produced the most prosperous, civilized and educated Negro community anywhere on the globe in history.

"So successful was this line that even relatively recent immigrants from Poland, Italy or Ireland have been duped into feeling guilty for what some slave owners in the American South might have done a hundred years before they were born.

"Similarly, Negro intellectuals have been brainwashed into thinking that the only reasons for Negro backwardness in America are those attributable to whites. The successful Negro has been downgraded as a self-seeking opportunist; the jobless, embittered, violence-prone Negro has been idealized as the true voice of his people."

For decades black leaders have "harped interminably on the faults of the American society. . . . Where the Negro needed hopeful plans for the future and an optimistic plan to achieve them, there was a continuous campaign of denigration, denunciation and pessimism. . . . Under these circumstances, it is remarkable that the Negro population acquired so many skills, so much education and such an accumulation of wealth in so short a time, but mostly through individual rather than community effort."

This success and future trends stemming from wide-ranging new anti-discrimination laws "would seem to be reason for optimism and hope, but the prophets of doom shout louder than ever and, unfortunately, they have progressively either brainwashed the Negro upper class or have frightened them into silence. . . . They have almost uniformly taken up the chant of 'Police Brutality' and screamed for civilian review boards to further handicap the police in using necessary force to maintain law and order. They have refused wholeheartedly to condemn hoodlumism and those who led the street packs—for fear of being dubbed 'Uncle Tom.' And one seeks far and wide for a trade school any group of them have set up to teach young Negroes a skill which they can sell in the labor market. A conservative Negro with vision is denounced as an enemy of his people if he speaks up against the criminal trends in his community."

Schuyler continued, "So this has given the agitator-activists full sway and no one has been tearing apart their vicious lies. There is always a holding back for fear of appearing 'anti-Negro.'. . . Every excuse and alibi possible has been made for Negro backwardness, shiftlessness and criminality, instead of facing up to the facts and telling the truth . . . yet how are you going to improve a situation unless you admit it exists? . . .

"The agitators gather crowds by blaming the white man for all of the Negroes' ills while the responsible Negro leadership either defends this falsehood, cravenly remains silent, or whimpers 'we didn't really mean it' after the cities have burnt to ashes."

Louis Lomax, Sandra West, and George Schuyler had plenty of company in their belief that outsiders sparked the Detroit riots for reasons that had nothing to do with local issues. Soldiers and policemen on the ground during the violence believed the snipers were organized by some central authority, though the military commander, General Throckmorton, did not think the gunmen were widely coordinated.

Police Commissioner Ray Girardin said he found no evidence of outside agitators or conspiracy, and the riots were started by young blacks who had too much to drink. On the other hand, Michigan

Governor George Romney believed "there have been certain indications in Detroit of outside agitators and certainly the tinder was prepared for conflagration by outside influences."

House GOP Minority Leader (later President) Gerald Ford of Michigan said, "I can't help but believe that there is in the background some national plan." Other high-profile political figures agreed that Detroit was part of a wider conspiracy. Tennessee Senator Howard Baker highlighted the need to investigate possible "external sources" of the riots, adding, "With violent upheavals in one city after another across this country, I think it is inescapable that we start thinking about whether there is some subversive master plan behind these riots." Illinois Senator Everett Dirksen wanted to know "if there is a Red touch" behind the riots nationally. California Governor (later President) Ronald Reagan believed "there is a plan" behind the Negro rioting, currently carried out by "mad dogs . . . no longer concerned with civil rights . . . I just don't believe these are spontaneous uprisings. It would be pretty naïve to believe it. I believe there is a plan."

On July 31, only days after the violence ended in Detroit, *Barron's* published a lengthy article surveying similar riots across the country and evidence pointing to the conclusion they were all set in motion by outside rabble-rousers. The piece began with a quote from their story two years earlier on August 23, 1965, just after the Watts riots in Los Angeles: "In the name of civil rights, a small band of ruthless men has not hesitated to stir up violence, break the law and undermine duly constituted authority.

"Since then," the article continued, "compelling evidence, including eyewitness testimony and the findings of a Cleveland grand jury, has shown that the riots are less spontaneous outbreaks than carefully planned subversion. . . . Civil unrest is not only organized but subsidized. Thanks to the Office of Economic Opportunity, the U.S. taxpayer now has a chance to finance his own destruction. . . .

"Last year's riots in Cleveland, charged Sen. Frank Church (D-Ohio), were the work of a 'national conspiracy by experts.' After hearing the testimony of detectives who penetrated the conspirators' ranks, [a Cleveland grand jury] found that 'the outbreak of lawlessness and disorder was organized, precipitated and exploited by a relatively small group of trained and disciplined professionals.'"

The story reports William Epton, vice chairman of the Communist China-oriented Progressive Labor Party, was convicted of criminal anarchy for his role in the Harlem riots of July 1964, which broke out following the shooting death of a black teenager by an off-duty policeman. *Barron's* also mentioned a meeting between reporters for *Life* magazine and "members of the sniper organization" active in the Newark, New Jersey, riots that took place only days before the Detroit conflict.

Barron's supported the allegation that government workers had leading roles in stirring up civil unrest. "Last fall the mayor of Perth Amboy, N.J., accused the local anti-poverty leader of seeking 'to foment and incite unrest, agitation and disorder,' . . . which the city manager of Rochester echoed last week. Newark's police chief warned weeks ago that the city faced anarchy because of agitation by federal anti-poverty workers, several of whom were arrested during the riots. In New York City, five marauding young Negroes, collared while looting stores on Fifth Avenue, worked for the anti-poverty program: one wore a sweater emblazoned after the OEO-funded agency, 'Harlem Youth Opportunities Unlimited.'"

By the time Michigan Governor George Romney lifted the state of emergency in Detroit on August 6 and sent the last of the National Guard home, forty-three people had been killed, more than 7,200 arrested, over 1,100 injured including 214 police and 134 firemen, and 412 buildings destroyed.

Of all the lines of inquiry into what led to the riots and what set them off, no official response has ever been accepted as the final word. Certainly African American Detroiters were discriminated against. But the record also shows that black residents were in a better position legally, economically, and practically than ever before.

On Wednesday, July 26, at the height of the destruction, the *Detroit Free Press* had proclaimed, "Most important of all, it is not a race riot . . . because there has been almost no conflict between whites and Negroes. . . . A crowd that burns the office of Rep. John Conyers—one of the city's two Negro congressmen—is not rebelling against the white man."

The day after that story ran, Mayor Cavanaugh and Governor Romney sent telegrams to a list of community leaders requesting their attendance at 4:00 p.m. that afternoon for a meeting "in connection with the city's current and future problems." It turned out to be the organizational gathering of the New Detroit Committee, a group of thirty-nine members chaired by civic leader and department store owner Joseph Hudson Jr. There were nine black members, including the head of the NAACP.

While Hudson said the committee represented all stakeholders in rebuilding Detroit, the *Michigan Chronicle*, the city's black-owned weekly, condemned the group as "people who don't care or are unaware about what happens to the inner city." Congressman John Conyers claimed the "voiceless people in the community . . . anyone poor or black" had no advocate among the committee members.

This was a curious comment from Conyers, a black congressman elected to represent black constituents who had himself implored rioters to disperse and had his office burned down for his trouble.

At this point there was no mention in the press of the city's ballooning deficits, high municipal property and income taxes, heavily pro-suburb transportation system, miserable public schools, ill-conceived urban renewal, or the relocation of manufacturing to outlying areas, all of which had already begun to shrink the city's population and sap its strength.

Even before the smoke cleared, history was taken hostage. ▪

Chapter 7

Shorthand for Hopeless

*"There is no question that Detroit was in much worse
shape when Young left office than when he first entered it."*
—*The Journal of Law, Economics,
& Organization,* 2005

■ ■ ■

IN MAY 1968, the New Detroit Committee released a report titled
"A Crisis of the People," concluding that the city could solve its problems if it and the nation were willing to invest vast amounts of money
to deal with root causes of the riots. The committee also rejected black
nationalism and supported maintaining law and order, though they
suggested the city consider an independent civilian review board to
investigate a history of alleged police brutality and misconduct.

The committee's first recommendation was for "federal involvement in terms of great sums of money and leadership . . . in order to
address the continuing growth of inner city hopelessness and despair."
Housing and jobs, the committee reported, were the two most
important needs. The city, state, and federal government needed to
spend hundreds of millions of dollars on housing, along with endorsing laws to promote racial integration. Major corporations and the
government needed to provide more jobs, especially for the "hard core
unemployed." The report also called for new spending on an array of
social welfare programs.

"A Crisis of the People" was issued two months after the Kerner Commission report and embraced much of its thinking. Named after its chairman, Illinois governor Otto Kerner, the commission was appointed by President Lyndon Johnson to find reasons for and solutions to the racial unrest plaguing American cities during the mid-1960s.

The chief author of the Kerner Commission report was commission member John Lindsay, mayor of New York from 1966 to 1973, whose findings echoed his personal belief that white racism was the cause of civil unrest in America and money was the solution.

Reviewing Lindsay's policies from a historical perspective years later, Fred Siegel, a senior fellow at the Progressive Policy Institute, observed that in 1965, "New York City had a black male unemployment rate of 4 percent. We were in the midst of the greatest economic boom in U.S. history. The city was thriving. Five years later, there were 600,000 more people on welfare. Now, this was a tragedy in many ways, especially for the city's African Americans. They were on the up escalator of jobs and participation in the economy, but they were pulled off the up escalator and shunted off into welfare. The effect on the city was twofold: Fiscal calamity and family breakdown. . . .

"The city actually was advertising for people to come on to welfare. What was the logic? It was the logic of the Kerner Commission Report. It was the sense that African Americans were so damaged that what they needed was not help making it into society, but a respite from society; in effect, they should be pensioned off."

Published commercially after its release, the 426-page report sold more than two million copies. Though history eventually revealed the fallacies of the Kerner Commission and New Detroit Committee findings, they were roundly applauded at the time by many of the public as well as the leaders and politicians of Detroit.

The New Detroit Committee continued to meet over the years and to issue reports and recommendations. While it established an important forum for discussion, there is little evidence it had any significant effect on local policies.

Statistically speaking, the 1967 riots did not drive whites away or damage Detroit's economy to any significant degree. The city's population loss during the 1960s in the aftermath of the riots was about 159,000 residents, less than its loss of about 179,000 during the 1950s when freeways were being built, downtown transportation was withering, neighborhoods were being razed in the name of urban renewal projects, and manufacturers were relocating to cheaper sites in the suburbs.

According to John Mogk, a law professor at Wayne State University in Detroit and an expert in urban planning, the mass exodus of population and resources was not a reaction to urban unrest, but a response to ham-fisted efforts to legislate change in Detroit's public school system and the failure of that system to educate its students.

As Mogk explained, "Everybody thinks it was the riots that caused white families to leave. Some people were leaving at that time but, really, it was after *Milliken* [*v. Bradley*, a landmark 1974 Supreme Court desegregation case that denied Detroit schools the power to force suburban districts into a regional desegregation program,] that you saw mass flight to the suburbs. If the case had gone the other way, it is likely Detroit would not have experienced the steep decline in its tax base that occurred since then." Statistics confirm this statement. During the 1971–72 school year, following the original lawsuit that led ultimately to this landmark Supreme Court decision, more than twice as many students left the system as departed in the year following the 1967 riots.

Though the Detroit public school system has already demonstrated its essential role in the decline of the city's appeal to families with children—the backbone of communities and of the workforce—in the years before the riots, Dr. Mogk's statement about the school system being a greater driver of out-migration than the infamous week of urban violence merits a closer look.

Detroit public school enrollment continued its postwar climb even as the overall population fell, peaking in 1966 at 299,962 students. Then after more than a century of scrambling to keep up with demand, the district started shedding pupils. Between 1966 and 1971, enrollment declined by 15,000.

Educational leaders were poorly equipped to deal with the change. From the Depression through the war years and into the prosperous post-war economy, the school district struggled to build and maintain buildings, hire teachers, and establish a vital curriculum for all its students. After the student population shifted to majority black in 1963, white residents more strongly opposed school financing measures. Some black parents also opposed spending increases, believing the extra money would only go to support a segregated system leaving them with an inferior education and old, tumbledown buildings.

When the black population of Detroit was a small minority, the divisions in school policies had been along class lines. With the student population majority black and the general population about 45 percent black, lines of conflict were re-drawn on the basis of race.

By about the time of the 1967 riots, new more radical voices among black leadership began labeling schools as part of the white racist establishment, condemning integration as a tool for maintaining white supremacy. Their goal was no longer integration but to promote a separate "Black Power" agenda.

White working-class voters, whose children were now a minority in city schools and who were a subset of a shrinking white majority, looked at the educational establishment in Detroit and saw nothing but failure. Why would they want their children there? Why would they vote to raise their own property taxes to support it? When the 1968 campaign to increase taxes was voted down by more than 62 percent of voters, this marked, in historian Jeffrey Mirel's words, "the virtual end of white working-class political support for the public schools of the Motor City."

Meanwhile the quality of education remained low. After the end of the school year, in June 1969, the *Michigan Chronicle* published test scores for fourth-, sixth-, and eighth-graders on the Iowa Test of Basic Skills showing 80 percent of students scored below national norms. Yet as the crisis continued and various groups jockeyed for power and influence, the conversation turned more and more away from education and toward politics.

In 1969 the Detroit school system was reorganized to give residents more local control through a process of "decentralization" to begin in 1971, including plans for a limited bussing program. At a school board meeting on April 7, 1970, nearly two hundred furious parents crowded into the boardroom as hundreds more milled around in the hallways and staircases. Some of them tried to break the glass doors leading into the meeting area.

Representatives of the NAACP, Urban League, and ACLU endorsed the board's proposal. White parents vowed their children would never be transferred to low-achieving black schools. Other African Americans were just as opposed as the whites. A black speaker representing the Inner City Parents Council, the Black Teachers Caucus, and other minority interests said, "these black organizations are unalterably opposed to the plan presented here today. . . . So-called integration is not only destructive to the best interests of black people, in fact, it is a form of genocide from our point of view."

The conflict resulted in an alternative plan from the governor that was then challenged by a lawsuit from the NAACP. The District Court judge hearing the case, Judge Stephen J. Roth, ruled Detroit was legally obligated to integrate its schools but the district did not have enough white students to develop a satisfactory plan. Therefore, fifty-two suburban school districts in three counties surrounding Detroit—780,000 students in all—had to participate in a region-wide desegregation effort.

Suburban school boards and parents were livid. They insisted Detroit schools' problems were the city's own doing, the suburban districts were not responsible, and they should not be forced to help solve the city's racial imbalance. Suburban taxpayers, looking at the long history of mismanagement and corruption in Detroit schools, saw no reason to support such a dysfunctional system when their own system was working vastly better. They also did not want to see their children bussed long distances to unfamiliar neighborhoods, some of which were rife with gang activity.

The defendants appealed Roth's decision to the Sixth Circuit Court, which affirmed the lower court ruling. On September 6, 1973, defendants requested a Supreme Court review of the case, which was granted. On July 25, 1974, in the matter of *Milliken v. Bradley*, the Supreme Court overturned the earlier ruling, holding that outlying school districts which had no part in creating a segregated environment in Detroit could not be forced to help resolve it. The court also ruled while desegregation required elimination of a dual educational system, it did not require racial balance; the lower court had over-reached its authority in presuming to control local schools.

Around this time the school deficit ballooned to a projected $40 million, teachers went on strike for forty-three days at the start of the 1973–74 school year, and columnist Bill Black wrote in the *Michigan Chronicle*, "Detroit schools are filled to overflowing with nonteachers who rely on that 'socially disadvantaged' bull as the alibi for their own failures. . . . When the people of this city wake up and realize how many alibi artists there are working supposedly as teachers in our school system, there is going to be hell to pay."

In the face of poor performance and uncontrolled spending, the *Detroit Free Press* reported in 1974 school board members spent $150,000 on travel and $200,000 on chauffeur-driven cars, which they viewed as "rightful perks of their office."

Black middle-class families, once eager to participate in school reforms, began throwing up their hands. By the end of the 1970s, many of them, including a large number of public employees, abandoned public education entirely and enrolled their children in Catholic schools. Meanwhile, between 1972 and 1979, standardized test scores for ninth- and eleventh-graders on the Sequential Test of Educational Progress declined from the thirty-third to the twenty-fourth percentile in reading and from forty-third to twenty-ninth in math.

Such results support Dr. Mogk's claim that poor schools were a bigger factor in Detroit's decline than racial conflict as its downward slide gained momentum. Though the city had lost more than 300,000 residents since the end of World War II, it was still the fifth-largest city in the nation in the mid-1970s. Detroit was off its peak but still viable, its momentum reduced but not yet spent.

The next two decades set the Motor City on a trajectory to becoming a hollow shell of its former self, making "Detroit" shorthand for hopeless decay. The man at the helm during those historic years was Mayor Coleman Young.

In 2014 the *Detroit Free Press* published its list of the five best mayors in Detroit history. One of the list was the city's first African American mayor, Coleman Young. "Now hear us out on this," the segment began. "There is no doubt that he is often wrongly blamed for single-handedly destroying the city. In fact, if you look at just the facts, he was actually one of the city's best mayors. Seriously."

More than twenty years earlier, when Young was still in office, Israeli-American journalist Zev Chafets observed, "Under Young, Detroit has become not merely an American city that happens to have a black majority, but a black metropolis, the first major Third World city in the United States. The trappings are all there—showcase projects, black-fisted symbols, an external enemy, and the cult of personality."

Young's champions point out that he produced five years of budget surpluses in the 1980s and trimmed the city workforce from more than 25,000 to 15,600. There were those who appreciated his pragmatism and focus on the future. Yet he also eventually lost a $600 million federal transportation grant, revoked after years of turf wars between Young and suburban governments.

Critics accused him of running a political machine that "valued patronage and loyalty over efficiency and progress." City residents and suburbanites alike blamed him for escalating racial tensions. During Young's first three terms in office, the percentage of Detroit's residents on welfare increased from 1.9 percent in 1973 to 20.3 percent in 1986. Over the course of his twenty-year administration, the city lost about one-third of its population, eventually falling below a million residents for the first time since 1920. No other major city in American history has fallen so far so fast.

In *Coleman Young and Detroit Politics: From Social Activist to Power Broker*, Young biographer Wilbur C. Rich writes, "Despite intense competition from the city's suburban neighbors for residents, resources, and industry, Coleman Alexander Young has been an effective leader in the face of political obstacles and a wayward economy. . . . The flamboyant style that gives investors pause is what black constituents love."

Rich also noted Young employed the race card to great effect: "Since blacks have few economic penalties which they can impose on erring reporters or media executives, they use the only weapon they have: criticism is termed *racist*. Indeed, this particular characterization of reporting seems to keep many white reporters in line."

Reviewing Young's autobiography, *Hardstuff*, for the *Washington Post*, award-winning Michigan novelist Loren Estleman offered a contrasting assessment: "This is the Coleman Young of *Hardstuff* . . . defensive, shrill, blaming racism, Republicans, knee-jerk white liberals—everyone but himself for his boarded-over city with its empty blocks littered with rat droppings and used syringes. Hard to take."

As is the truth about the 1967 riots and the truth about why the city began its historic population decline, the truth about Detroit's most controversial mayor is an elusive quarry. What is certain is that from the beginning, he was driven, focused, fearless, and unwavering in the pursuit of his objectives.

Coleman Young was born in Tuscaloosa, Alabama, in 1918 and moved with his family to Detroit five years later. Denied financial assistance—evidently on account of his race—that would have enabled him to attend college, Young went to work for Ford Motor Company, which eventually fired him under suspicion of being involved in Communist-leaning union activities.

During World War II Lieutenant Young was a bombardier and navigator for the renowned Tuskegee Airmen. He was briefly jailed after leading a successful protest against the exclusion of black servicemen from the officer's club. After the war, Young became a union activist for the Congress of Industrial Organizations and in 1951 helped found the National Negro Labor Council.

Though his photo once appeared in the Communist *Daily Worker* newspaper, he refused to say whether or not he was a member of the Communist Party. In 1952, when called to testify before the House Un-American Activities Committee, Young declared, "I consider the activities of this Committee as un-American," adding, "You have mixed me up with a stool pigeon." He later disbanded the National Negro Labor Council rather than turn its membership list over to authorities.

Young was elected to the Michigan state senate in 1964, where he served for ten years. In 1968 he became the first African American member of the Democratic National Committee. Next, he set his sights on becoming the first black mayor of the Motor City.

In 1969, Richard Austin became Detroit's first viable black mayoral candidate. Austin, a member of the Wayne County Board of Auditors, was the first African American certified public accountant in Michigan and ran his own successful accounting practice. He outpolled his chief opponent, white Wayne County Sheriff Roman Gribbs, in the primary yet lost to Gribbs by one percent in the runoff election. Austin received only 18 percent of the white vote but 94 percent of the black vote.

After his unsuccessful run, Austin left city politics to accept an appointment as the state secretary of state for Michigan. Mayor Gribbs chose not to run for reelection in 1973 and became a judge. The two new candidates for mayor that year were police commissioner John F. Nichols and state senator Coleman Young. Once again the precincts voted overwhelmingly along racial lines. Every white precinct and more than 90 percent of white voters favored Nichols, while every black precinct and more than 90 percent of blacks voted for Young. Young won just enough white supporters to win by a margin of about 17,000 votes out of more than 400,000 cast.

One of Mayor Young's first acts upon assuming office in 1974 was to fulfill his campaign promise to disband STRESS (Stop the Robberies Enjoy Safe Streets), a special undercover police unit Mayor Gribbs launched in 1971 to control escalating street crime. Over three years the unit killed twenty-four people including teenagers, all but two of them African Americans. The operation was accused of excessive force, planting evidence, and targeting black men.

Young also redoubled integration efforts to attract more black officers and in 1976 hired Detroit's first African American police chief, William A. Hart. Overall police strength declined, however, because residents moving to the suburbs reduced city revenues and caused a 20 percent reduction of the force in 1976. Young, fiercely protective of Detroit's independence and local control, adopted a confrontational attitude toward neighboring municipal governments and federal authorities. Relations with federal agencies were so bad at times that police officers resisted helping with an FBI or Drug Enforcement Administration case for fear of being demoted.

Detroit seemed to land a huge opportunity in 1976 in the form of a $600 million federal grant to fund a regional transportation system, which would give Detroit residents easy access to the suburbs and also encourage suburbanites to come into the city for its world-class cultural and entertainment attractions. For a cash-strapped city lacking public transportation to and from its thriving outskirts, the opportunity seemed ideal.

A key requirement of the project was to merge regional and city bus services, but Mayor Young envisioned using the grant to build a twenty-mile subway system underneath major downtown thoroughfares. The suburban Southeastern Michigan Transportation Authority (SEMTA) countered that improving the bus network was the best way to use the grant. Young replied that if he did not get his subway, he would block the bus merger. Looking ahead to his reelection campaign in 1977, Young saw the subway project as a way to deliver thousands of jobs to his constituents.

It would be a hard sell. The Detroit bus system already depended on a $32 million annual subsidy. Between 1970 and 1975, crime and vandalism on the line rose by 50 percent and ridership dropped 25 percent. The federal Urban Mass Transit Administration claimed there was not enough demand to build a subway in Detroit, even though SEMTA projected 137,000 subway riders a day by 1985.

The regional merger required by the 1976 grant never took place. Had Detroit been more intentional in collaborating with surrounding towns and county governments in the 1970s, the city might well have avoided the insurmountable problems that brought it down decades later. Each side could help the other in the battle for residents, businesses, and tax dollars. In Detroit's case the relationship between the two sides hardened into a belligerent standoff. Seeing the crime in the city, the waste, the failing schools, the blustering irrationality of public policies, rising taxes, and corruption, outlying communities wanted no part of the city's well-publicized problems unless they had some say in dealing with them.

Whatever Detroit did to deal with its transportation problem, it would do on its own. Near the end of 1980, between the election of Ronald Reagan and his inauguration, outgoing President Jimmy Carter secured for Mayor Young enough money to build a proposed small mid-town monorail, knowing the rest of the ambitious regional project would be cancelled.

A few months after the October 1983 groundbreaking of the monorail system, christened the People Mover, Mayor Young again urged approval of a regional master plan to ensure him a position of control. But as the *Detroit Free Press* noted at the time, the city-suburban standoff was still a stumbling block. "Construction has yet to begin on most of the proposed system because of city-suburban bickering over key elements—particularly sentiment in Oakland and Macomb counties against a Woodward subway." The light rail portion of the proposal also came under fire, "equally opposed by suburban and outstate politicians, who charged their constituents would be forced to subsidize a Detroit boondoggle."

Problems and cost overruns hounded the People Mover from the beginning. Due to poor design and construction, dozens of guideway beams and support pillars failed even before the system was finished. The project ran more than $70 million over budget. Eventually, SEMTA voted to turn control of the People Mover over to the city if Detroit would be primarily responsible for any further cost overruns.

The People Mover was finally finished in 1987. The 2.9-mile system cost $200.3 million dollars, "having survived bungled management, poor design, cracking concrete, cost overruns, political attacks and ridership predictions so low some critics say the system is doomed. Originally designed as the downtown end of a regional system of subway and rail lines, the People Mover stands without those unfinanced projects."

Taking a ride on the People Mover ahead of its official opening, *Detroit Free Press* reporter Jim Fitzgerald found the thirteen stations so "ridiculously" close together "a reporter could easily hold his breath between stations," which were "big and gorgeous," and cost $2 million each. He observed, "The best way to get our money out of it would be to put a mini-casino in each station." The system, moving at a pace "not much faster than walking," was "a dogless tail, filling a need that isn't here yet."

Ten years after it opened, daily ridership on the People Mover, projected to be 55,000, hovered around 7,500. Today a rider still usually has no trouble finding a seat even though rides are free in an effort to boost interest.

In dealing with the problem of public transportation—one of Detroit's most pressing needs—Coleman Young fell short. He had more success in holding onto one of the city's professional sports teams after others followed their fans to the suburbs. Though the process was as fraught and controversial as the People Mover, the saga of the Joe Louis Arena had a happier ending.

As Detroit's downward spiral accelerated in the 1970s, professional sports teams were decamping to the suburbs. In 1975 the

Detroit Lions moved to the Silverdome in nearby Pontiac. The NBA Detroit Pistons followed in 1978. When the owner of the Detroit Red Wings, Bruce Norris, signed an agreement to move to Pontiac as well, Mayor Young was determined to keep them in town by building a new sports arena on the riverbank.

When Norris said he wasn't interested in a new arena, Young insisted on going forward with the project even though the proposed venue had no tenants, no financing, and no architectural plan. The mayor said he had a federal grant for seed money, insisting, "I've got five million Jimmy Carter dollars, and if nothing else we're going to dig the deepest f—— hole in the state of Michigan. Now either get on board or get out of the way."

Young eventually scraped together money, including millions earmarked for the public lighting department, millions more from a hospital fringe benefits fund, and a state grant. The Red Wings agreed to move into the arena after all. But from the beginning, fans noticed a host of glaring problems. There weren't enough aisles for emergency exits. The outside steps were narrow, steep, and fully exposed to ice and snow.

The arena opened without executive suites. Jammed between the Detroit River and a tangle of freeways, it was hard to access. As opening night approached, someone realized there was no press box. The back rows of seats in one area were hastily ripped out and a makeshift pressroom added. Despite the venue's prime waterfront location, there were no windows, producing a gloomy indoor environment. Even when new, the place was damp and smelly. Restrooms were awkward and inadequate. Men who got tired of waiting relieved themselves in the sinks; the line for women's facilities was always long and slow.

Despite its flaws, the team and its fans made the most of the situation. Joe Louis Arena became known for fast ice and a classic hockey experience. Before they left for Little Caesar's Arena in 2017, the Red Wings won four Stanley Cup Championships during their years at "The Joe." The building was demolished in 2020 and the site bought by a developer with plans for a twenty-five-story residential tower plus offices and hotels.

To help manage the municipal budget as population figures and tax revenues declined into the 1980s, Mayor Coleman Young took several bold measures. As the threat of bankruptcy hovered on the horizon in 1981, Young lobbied to raise the local income tax both for residents and for commuters who worked in the city. His argument for the increase, which had to be approved by the voters, was it had to pass or the white people who once ran the city (and who, by the way, were his political opposition) would take it back. As he put it to an audience of pastors, "Are we willing to do what is necessary to see that the city's destiny remains in our hands? Or will we do what thousands of bigots hope we do—vote no and let the state take us over?" The tax proposal passed only after Young convinced more than thirty city labor unions to take a pay cut and issued $135 million in bonds.

The flamboyant Young was associated with several scandals, though the mayor was never charged with a crime. In 1980 he awarded a water department sludge hauling contract to a company formed by his friend Darralyn Bowers without consulting the city council. Federal investigators claimed Bowers's company later paid kickbacks to the head of the water department, Charles Beckham. Bowers and Beckham were eventually convicted of racketeering and mail fraud.

In 1991 Young's brother-in-law Willie Volsan was arrested for taking money to guard cocaine and cash from undercover federal agents posing as dope dealers. He was eventually convicted and sentenced to nineteen years in prison.

The next year Police Chief William Hart, appointed by Young in 1976 as the city's first black chief, went on trial for embezzling $2.3 million. As recapped later by the *Detroit Free Press*, "While the city was scrambling for money and police officers to fight drugs, thousands of dollars and entire top-flight investigative crews were diverted to protect the mayor's niece as she romped with a teenage dope lord."

The trial also revealed, "money from a police fund intended to pay informants and snare drug dealers had been used, in part, to armor-plate the mayor's two Cadillac limousines, pay for a satellite TV system for the mayor's residence, and buy submachine guns for Young's police bodyguards." Chief Hart was convicted and sentenced to ten years in federal prison.

The one point about Coleman Young all parties can agree on is that he was a controversial and divisive figure. Some have called him one of Detroit's best mayors while others have branded him a disaster. A scholarly study by experts with no connection to Detroit may be the most equitable way to consider Coleman's legacy and his ultimate effect on the city.

In 2005, Edward L. Glaeser of Harvard University and Andrei Shleifer of the National Bureau of Economic Research published a paper in *The Journal of Law, Economics, & Organization* titled "The Curley Effect: The Economics of Shaping the Electorate." In this study, the authors compare Mayor Coleman Young's political philosophy and practice to those of James Michael Curley, the fiery Irishman who served as mayor of Boston for four terms in the first half of the twentieth century.

Mayor Curley, they write, "used wasteful redistribution to his poor Irish constituents and incendiary rhetoric to encourage richer citizens to emigrate from Boston, thereby shaping the electorate in his favor. As a consequence, Boston stagnated, but Curley kept winning elections." Boston's poor Irish voters loved him, while wealthy Brahmins in the city disdained his corrupt policies and always voted against him. The more of the former and fewer of the latter there were in the city, the more secure Mayor Curley's power became.

Glaeser and Shleifer call this phenomenon of "increasing the relative size of one's political base through distortionary, wealth-reducing policies" the Curley Effect.

One of their prime examples of other political leaders pursuing the Curley Effect is Coleman Young. As mayor of Detroit, they say, Young "drove white residents and businesses out of the city."

The Curley Effect, the authors say, "turns traditional views about the requirements for good government on their head," making "bad policies more, not less attractive to incumbents. . . . By differently taxing different groups of voters, the incumbent leader can encourage emigration of one of the groups, and maximize the share of voters who support him. While benefitting the incumbent, these taxes may actually impoverish the area and make both groups worse off."

The Curley Effect assumes the incumbent has "an innate appeal to the lower-status group" resulting from "ethnic or class identity." The authors explain their model "follows the work on inefficient distribution through public employment and other means" and "relates to the large body of research on inefficient but politically motivated public policies. . . . Our innovation is the idea that such wasteful redistribution and other public policies shape the electorate by influencing the migration decision."

As Glaeser and Shleifer explain, "A key feature of our model . . . is that leaders derive utility from holding office (they want reelection), but not from governing a richer area. . . . In practice, politicians often care about both the wealth of their community and the probability of reelection—and this concern mitigates the Curley Effect. In this situation, incumbents will try to enrich the community while also shaping the electorate. In the urban context, this might mean that they try to create jobs for nonresidents, who expand the tax base without being able to vote."

In discussing Coleman Young in particular, the authors revisit the fact that in the Detroit mayoral election of 1973, every white precinct and more than 90 percent of white voters favored police commissioner John F. Nichols, while every black precinct and more than 90 percent of blacks voted for Young. The key to Young remaining in office, they say, was to increase the number of black voters.

Between 1970 and 1990, the black population of Detroit grew from 43.7 percent to 75.7 percent. The authors quote Tamar Jacoby, author of *Someone Else's House: America's Unfinished Struggle for*

Integration, saying Young "encouraged the black city to cut itself off." *Detroit News* columnist Pete Waldmeir observed, Young "was trying to drive whites out and he cut their services." Irene McCabe, an early opponent of school bussing whose opposition helped set the stage for *Milliken v. Bradley*, believed Mayor Young "wanted everything black and treated whites as second-class citizens."

While we cannot know Young's intentions, Glaeser and Shleifer observe, "it is hard to ignore the impact of Young's twenty-year rule." Whites moved to just outside the city limits, specifically escaping Young's ". . . regime. Young's policies created an overwhelmingly black city that overwhelmingly supported him."

The authors offer examples of policies Young enacted that they say encouraged wealthier residents to leave the city. "Young's racial favoritism can be seen in his tax policy and his distribution of city services." The 1982 tax referendum, held as the city faced the threat of bankruptcy, raised the city income tax from 2 percent to 3 percent on residents and .5 percent to 1.5 percent on non-resident commuters. This tax, say the authors, had no impact on Young's poor black supporters and encouraged better-off residents to move: "Young eagerly sought to tax his richer constituents to fund redistribution, arguably to drive them out."

Young supported major building projects (Joe Louis Arena, the People Mover) that put his supporters on the payroll. He lobbied for federal public housing when there was a huge stock of available housing selling for less than the cost of new construction. This was to keep his supporters in the city as opposed to whites. At the same time, Mayor Young cut services important to whites including police and fire. Cutting the police force by 20 percent in 1976 led to a spike in crime. Trash collection services declined 50 percent.

Young worked to add jobs and tax revenues without adding residents. For example, the mayor supported Henry Ford II's Renaissance Center office development on the riverbank, which generated tax revenues but kept workers in the suburbs. The authors add, "Young's other construction projects had a similar flavor of Curleyism."

Considering all the evidence, Glaeser and Shleifer conclude, "Did Young hurt Detroit? Did he hurt the black residents of Detroit? There is no question that Detroit was in much worse shape when Young left office than when he first entered it. Its population fell from 1.51 million in 1970 to 1.03 million in 1990, a 32% decline. The unemployment rate as a percentage of the civilian labor force rose from 10.3% in 1969 to 20.6% in 1990. The percentage of households living below the poverty line rose from 18.6% to 29.8%. Nearly all the victims of this unemployment and poverty were Young's black supporters. Over Young's 20 years surely in part due to his policies, Detroit became an overwhelmingly black city mired in poverty and social problems."

Detroit was losing ground, and the crisis would only get worse. After nearly a century as the Motor City, Detroit began watching car makers both foreign and domestic leave the area to re-establish their industry in more business-friendly and partnership-oriented communities. And despite all the commentary about the "collapse" of the automobile industry, the automobile industry never collapsed; it just left town. ▪

Chapter 8

Stalled

*"The ultimate irony of Detroit's demise is that it has been defeated
by companies that do the job that Detroit once did."*
—Micheline Maynard,
auto industry historian, 2003

■ ■ ■

THE STORY of Detroit's downfall is also the story of the auto industry's migration from its birthplace to more business- and family-
friendly communities as, over time, Detroit offered its residents and
employers less and less while demanding more and more. And just as
Detroit lost its way in a tangle of missed opportunities and misguided
choices, the American auto companies similarly fell from their position as world leaders in the industry, some of them reduced to tattered
remnants of their former glory, going hat in hand to the government
for money to save them from bankruptcy.

While automotive manufacturing in Detroit has shrunk to a
shadow of itself in the 2020s, the American-based automotive industry is thriving. Today's factories, however, are not concentrated in
the Motor City but widespread in Alabama, Tennessee, South Carolina, Kentucky, and other states and communities with a welcoming environment, allowing companies to operate with a high degree
of flexibility, low taxes, and low regulatory burdens. Toyota, Nissan,
Mercedes-Benz, BMW, Hyundai, and other foreign makers bypassed

Detroit as a prospective manufacturing center despite its decades of tradition, a seasoned workforce, and a ready list of suppliers and sub-contractors nearby.

From the time foreign cars became a force in the U.S. market beginning in the 1970s, domestic manufacturers bemoaned the competitive disadvantage of the American factories' costly United Auto Workers agreements. But as Micheline Maynard wrote in *The End of Detroit: How the Big Three Lost Their Grip on the American Market,* "To blame the union alone for what's happened to the Detroit companies is just plain wrong. Detroit's problems haven't been caused only by the fact that its workers are unionized and those at the transplants are not. There are two signatures on every contract—one from the UAW, the other from the auto companies. The work rules, wages and benefits at the Detroit companies weren't imposed on them—they were agreed to."

The United Auto Workers made demands that rendered union automakers uncompetitive with nonunion rivals. Yet instead of negotiating an agreement allowing them to build more economical cars, automakers acquiesced to terms that set their manufacturing costs too high to be competitive in the retail showroom. Detroit's part in this was to side firmly with the unions, supporting the state regulation allowing unions to require employees to be union members as a condition of employment. These closed shops protected workers, but by the 1970s produced an unproductive workforce and, like the city of Detroit, massive unfunded retirement and health care liabilities.

These legacy costs diverted corporate income away from product development and competitive pricing at the very moment when American car makers encountered their first real challenges from foreign imports. But, in parallel with the leadership of Detroit, the car companies kept kicking the can down the road, buying labor peace in the short run with wages and unsustainable benefits in the long run. Then on top of everything else, the oil embargo of 1973 suddenly brought fuel economy front and center. Middle Eastern oil producers halted shipments to the U.S. over its support for Israel in a war against

Egypt and Syria, causing gasoline prices to skyrocket. Still, Detroit industry leaders looked at the small and strange-looking offerings from Japanese car makers and others and decided they had nothing to worry about.

The skepticism about foreign competition was well-ingrained in the minds of Detroit's top auto executives. In March, 1948, Henry Ford II was in Germany meeting with British army officers. The army brass offered Ford a partly bombed Volkswagen plant for nothing. Ford vice president Ernest Breech commented, "Mr. Ford, I don't think what we are being offered here is worth a damn." Ford declined the offer. Sixty years later, Volkswagen would be worth more than General Motors, Ford, and Chrysler combined.

In the 1970s, as gas mileage requirements and federal safety standards threw a host of new challenges in American auto makers' path, car companies agreed to ever more generous and wide-ranging benefits that siphoned off money needed for developing and marketing new technology. In 1970 after a sixty-five-day strike against General Motors, the UAW won a 30 percent wage increase over three years. After only a two-day strike in 1973, the union won from Chrysler the right to retire at any age after thirty years' employment at full pension with no health care co-payments. These union members might well live longer in retirement than the thirty years they worked.

Management's resistance to union wage increases was often half-hearted because of a corporate policy keeping an "appropriate" spread between blue- and white-collar compensation. An increase in UAW pay thus produced an increase in company salaries.

American companies complained about foreign makers having an unfair advantage because they did not have to deal with the UAW. When Japanese and other foreign corporations starting building cars in the U.S., however, domestic manufacturers were in for an unpleasant surprise.

One of Japan's advantages over Detroit was that the Asians declared union or not, they would not produce a unprofitable car because of the wage scale. Toyota's first manufacturing effort in the U.S. was a joint venture with GM at a recently closed plant in Fremont, California. As part of the agreement, the UAW insisted the joint venture hire workers from the closed plant. These workers were notorious for drug abuse, absenteeism, and poor performance.

The manager of the new enterprise, former Ford executive Gary Convis, held a five-hour meeting with Bruce Lee, the UAW official in charge, explaining how the previous behaviors would destroy the project. Convis took Fremont workers to Japan to spend three weeks working alongside Toyota factory workers there. When the Fremont factory opened in 1985, it quickly became one of the most productive plants in the industry. Union-built cars could be competitive in the American market after all with the right planning, training, and leadership. Toyota did not sell an American-made Corolla for two years, until the quality of those cars matched the imported models.

In the early 1980s, Honda opened its first American auto factory in Ohio, and Volkswagen operated a plant in Pennsylvania. The Honda plant was a non-union workplace while Volkswagen workers were represented by the UAW. Detroit executives expected Japanese companies to employ UAW workers in order to "level the playing field." However, workers in Ohio were satisfied without union representation. The UAW petitioned Honda for an organization vote in 1986, but learning they would lose the count, withdrew their voter petition. The VW plant in Pennsylvania closed in 1988. By 1990 Honda was selling over 800,000 cars a year in America, more than half of them made in the USA.

Honda focused on giving its American workers a job that paid well and showed respect. When the company announced it was hiring 2,000 workers for a new plant in Lincoln, Alabama, it received 16,000 applications. The company invited 5,000 to enroll in their training program; 3,000 completed it. Looking at the local culture, the company modified its rules and practices to accommodate its workers. Since many of them smoked, Honda made an exception to its no-smoking rule and allowed smoking at tables outside. The factory cafeteria served large portions of local favorites. There were no after-hours meetings scheduled on Wednesdays because many employees traditionally went to church functions on Wednesdays.

Meanwhile, UAW assembly line workers earned ever more lavish wages and benefits while job performance sank ever lower. Many Detroit-area factories had to close on the first day of deer season because there were so many unexcused absences they could not run the line. When a machine broke down, only skilled tradesmen were allowed by union rules to repair it, even if the line worker could do it. Often the skilled repairman took his time so the shift would go into overtime and everyone would receive extra pay for the shift.

As car makers considered modular manufacturing systems to improve efficiency and lower production costs, the UAW balked at the prospect because it would reduce the number of factory jobs. Modular production gave vendors responsibility for pre-assembling whole components of a car, such as the instrument panel, rather than having assembly line workers build them from scratch at the plant. As a Nissan executive in the United States observed of the modular process, "The ones who do it, love it. The ones who can't envy those who do."

Of all the missteps made by the great American auto companies in Detroit, arguably the worst was the creation of the Jobs Bank, negotiated with the UAW in 1984 to ease the union's fears about automation. Workers displaced by automation joined the Jobs Bank, where they would sit around all day earning 95 percent of their wages until the company found them a new job. By 1990 the Jobs Bank agreement was changed so workers furloughed for any reason could join the Jobs Bank indefinitely without having to look for another job.

Like the Motor City, the domestic auto companies were swamped in legacy costs even as their business shrank and the number of workers fell. Between 1985 and 2007, the GM hourly workforce declined from 450,000 to 74,000. Legacy costs added more than $1,600 to the cost of every General Motors vehicle, compared with less than $200 per vehicle for Toyota. Foreign nameplates far outstripped American producers in efficiency on their own turf, in more than two dozen U.S. factories.

As foreigners built the more efficient cars many American drivers wanted. American auto makers had to rely on high-margin gas-guzzling SUVs, pickups, and minivans because, as automotive historian Paul Ingrassia observed, "their cost structures were bloated by soaring health care costs, gold-plated pensions, union work rules, and lavish white-collar perks. At Chrysler, for example, every retired executive got free use of two new cars, every year, for life."

Four thousand furloughed workers at GM's Delphi division earned an average of nearly $100,000 a year in wages and benefits— about twice the compensation of other car component employees— without working a single day at a cost to GM of about $400 million per year. By 2009 General Motors had ten retirees for every active employee and $172 billion in liabilities.

Meanwhile, foreign car makers were investing in new automotive technology to improve driving performance and fuel economy while American companies spent millions on unrelated projects, reallocating money they could have used instead to remain competitive. Detroit's Big Three spent $20 billion on non-automotive acquisitions in electronics, aviation, finance, and other businesses, while Mercedes-Benz, for example, focusing on its core operation, built a $300 million factory in Alabama.

Foreign car companies thrived building their cars in America. The Toyota Camry, perennially the best-selling car in the United States, is built in Kentucky. Every one sold in the United States is made just outside the famous bluegrass fields of Lexington. By the early 2000s, the Nissan plant near Nashville was ranked by a Michigan consulting firm as the most efficient factory in the United States.

Just as Detroit was unable to see its own faults and acknowledge its own history, the UAW, American automakers, and Detroit boosters failed to see the demise of the Detroit auto juggernaut was their doing. As industry historian Micheline Maynard wrote in 2003, "The ultimate irony of Detroit's demise is that it has been defeated by companies that do the job that Detroit once did with unquestioned expertise: turn out vehicles that consumers want to buy and vehicles that capture their imaginations." The previous year, Toyota's operating profit was nearly $12 billion, more than the combined profits of Detroit automakers over the previous five years, and the company had $34 billion in cash.

Yet—and here is a clear example of Detroit's convoluted sense of self-awareness—in June 2003, *Detroit News* columnist Daniel Howes argued that because of its growing clout, Toyota had a responsibility to fund charities, schools, and cultural institutions in Detroit the way the Big Three did in the past. If it was to be considered the industry's leading company in America, Toyota had to assume a leadership role in "the epicenter of the American automotive universe." Somehow Toyota owed Detroit. The truth was Toyota succeeded in spite of Detroit by avoiding the mistakes that made American car makers stumble.

The Detroit mindset reached a fever pitch after General Motors and Chrysler asked Congress for a financial bailout to avoid bankruptcy in 2008. A local business magazine ran a cover story calling a bailout a "moral imperative" for the nation. "Hear Us Out," shouted a front-page headline in the *Detroit Free Press*, "We're in Crisis."

During congressional hearings on the prospect of a bailout, Tennessee Senator Bob Corker was dumbfounded at an explanation of the Jobs Bank. "I find it very difficult [to] believe," he told one executive, "you're asking for $25 billion when you have an agreement in place to pay 95 percent to workers who are not working."

In the course of researching the industry, Steve Rattner, head of the federal auto industry task force, former *New York Times* reporter and billionaire investment banker, concluded General Motors might be "the worst-managed company" he had ever seen.

On June 1, 2009, General Motors, once the biggest employer in the nation, filed for bankruptcy in the U.S. Bankruptcy Court in lower Manhattan.

■　■　■

As American automakers fought to stay alive, Detroit continued its own struggle for survival. After the tension and drama of the Coleman Young years, Young's successor as mayor took a different approach to leadership. Dennis Archer was a former Michigan Supreme Court justice who came across as "cerebral, scholarly and gentlemanly." He took an accommodating attitude toward racial politics as opposed to Young's sharp confrontations and fiery rhetoric. During his term several important developments signaled a slowing of the pace of decline in Detroit's finances and future prospects.

In 1996, following years of opposition from Coleman Young and others, casino gambling was approved in Michigan and three casinos were authorized in the city of Detroit. The first casino opened in 1999. Taxes from casino operations became the most reliable source of city revenue. (In 2022 Detroit casinos earned $1.276 billion, paid $155.6 million in taxes to the city, and contributed nearly $102 million to the state School Aid Fund.) In 2000 Comerica Park, new home of the Detroit Tigers, opened downtown. Two years later, Ford Field, a domed football stadium for the Detroit Lions, opened nearby, marking the Lions' return downtown after decades at the suburban Pontiac Silverdome.

Unfortunately, Dennis Archer was followed in the mayor's office by Kwame Kilpatrick, rated by the *Detroit Free Press* as the worst mayor in city history. Youthful, charismatic, and campaigning under the slogan, "Our Future: Right Here, Right Now," Kilpatrick captured the attention of an electorate desperate for good news and a vision for rebuilding the city. But while cutting public expenses, he was padding his own pocket.

Kilpatrick cut the police force by more than a thousand officers, making dangerously long police response times even longer. He cut trash pickup, which increased illegal dumping. Broken streetlights went unrepaired. Meanwhile, he charged more than $200,000 in public funds for personal trips, massages, French Champagne, and a Lincoln Navigator for his wife.

In a Hail Mary effort to delay the city's complete financial melt-down, Mayor Kilpatrick engineered a complex, risky, and almost certainly illegal transaction that yielded $1.4 billion in loan proceeds. When a $400 million balloon payment came due, he pledged the city's casino gambling income and engaged in more fancy financial footwork. Eventually, the city found itself $2.8 billion in debt.

During this time, Kilpatrick was having an affair with his chief of staff. When he thought policemen on his security detail might expose the liaison, he allegedly sabotaged their careers. The guards sued and won a $6.5 million judgment settled with city funds.

In 2010 Kilpatrick was indicted by the federal government on a host of corruption charges including extortion, bribery, fraud, and money laundering. Three years later he was convicted on twenty-four counts and sentenced to twenty-eight years in prison with no possibility of parole. Kilpatrick was released in 2021 when his sentence was commuted to time served by President Donald Trump.

After City Council President Ken Cockrell Jr. served out the balance of Kilpatrick's term following his 2008 resignation, the next mayor gave the city another glimmer of hope. Dave Bing was a seven-time NBA All-Star who played nine seasons with the Detroit Pistons. Following his sports career, Bing founded a steel company in Detroit to serve the auto industry and bring jobs to Detroiters. He was elected mayor in 2009 and set out to do what he could for his adopted home-town as an encouragement and example of cooperation, goal-setting, and personal responsibility.

He described his philosophy years later in his biographical memoir, *Attacking the Rim*. Bing especially encouraged "those in the Black community struggling with the highs and lows" of life. The ex-sports star's recipe for success was hard work, respect for others, and telling the truth.

Bing explained that this list of life lessons "lets Black folks know that, number one, we can't use our Blackness as an excuse for failure. We need to prepare ourselves from an academic standpoint so that we can go to the highest level that we can achieve. . . . It's hard, but it can be done."

After Bing left office at the end of 2013, he set up the Bing Youth Institute and BINGO mentoring program for "young Black boys in Detroit." Standards are high. "We are strict," Bing admitted, "that you've got to go to school, you've got to be on time, you've got to get your grades, because if you don't, you can't stay in the program." After working with four graduating classes of boys, the program had a 100 percent high school graduation rate. Eighty-five percent of those graduates went on to college.

Dave Bing was a man of accomplishment and vision who knew how to get things done. Yet he was new to the rough-and-tumble world of Detroit politics, and he came on the political scene too late to save Detroit from financial ruin. He clashed with other city and community leaders at every turn. He tried his best, battling with the bureaucracy over budgets and layoffs, but he was hopelessly outnumbered and outmaneuvered. And Detroit was out of time. ■

Chapter 9

Hope to the People

*"The only way you could restructure the city was
to have an honest conversation. . . . If you don't tell
people the real story, you can't get anything done."*
—Detroit bankruptcy attorney, 2013

■ ■ ■

WHEN DETROIT declared bankruptcy in federal court on July 18, 2013, it began a voyage into uncharted territory. The sheer size of its debt dwarfed any previous similar case. Up to that time, the largest municipal bankruptcy in American history was Jefferson County, Alabama, in 2011, with $4 billion in liabilities. The largest city by population to seek protection from its creditors had been Stockton, California, in 2012, with 290,000 residents. Detroit came to court underwater to the tune of approximately $18 billion with a population of about 700,000. Its municipal debt of $25,700 per resident roughly equaled the city's average annual per capita income.

Congress instituted Chapter 9 bankruptcy in 1937 to give insolvent municipalities a way to clear their balance sheets and make a new start. When a business goes bankrupt, its assets are liquidated to pay creditors as much as those assets will bring. But a city cannot realistically or practically be liquidated. Bankrupt or not,

*"Through
presumption
comes nothing
but strife."*
—Proverbs 3:10

it has to maintain fire and police protection, utilities, roads, schools, and other basic services. Chapter 9 is a means for reducing debt to the point where the city can continue to function.

Detroit's path to insolvency was long and winding, with many opportunities over the years to change course and prevent the historic financial meltdown that waited at the end of the road. Endless books and analyses have offered reasons why the city failed so completely. Most of them put racial tension and the decline of the auto industry at the top of the list. Other cities, however, have lived through racial strife and a decline in traditional heavy industries without ending up in Detroit's desperate shape.

Sifting through decades of information and interpretation, the reasons for Detroit's unique situation gradually emerge from the shadows of history. They are not because of racism, the auto industry, federal policies, greedy capitalism, or other often-quoted causes. Detroit went broke because of a spectacular failure on the part of its leadership to live within its means, and because that leadership refused to face the truth about its own shortcomings and poor decisions, obscuring the facts and attempting to rewrite history to deflect attention elsewhere.

For decades the city agreed to unsustainable pension and health care obligations, so-called legacy costs. As the city's population and tax base withered, legacy costs soared to 40 percent of the city's budget by 2013, sapping funds for police and firefighter salaries, school maintenance, police cars, busses, garbage trucks, park maintenance, and everything else the municipal government was responsible for. Left unchecked, pension payments, retiree health care costs, and debt service were on track to gobble up 70 percent of the budget by 2020.

The warning signs were there as early as the 1950s when the city's tax base first started to shrink. In the '80s, Mayor Coleman Young waved the possibility of bankruptcy as a cudgel to enact his fiscal agenda even as his intransigence and refusal to share power with suburban leaders cost the city a $600 million federal grant. In the 2000s, Mayor Kwame Kilpatrick used the fear of bankruptcy to push through a complicated and legally suspect lending scheme to take on more debt than the city could assume under state law. In the fall of 2011, Mayor Dave Bing announced that without some major changes, the city would go broke in 2012. Though he and other elected officials insisted they could clean up Detroit's financial mess without outside assistance or oversight, they could never reach a consensus and failed to launch a successful plan.

"Detroit needs to be run by Detroiters," the mayor declared at a press conference to the cheers of his audience. Bing vowed to take care of the problem even though it only got worse under his administration. At the same time, however, he also endorsed an effort to get 162,000 signatures on a petition to repeal a Michigan state law allowing the governor to appoint an emergency manager to run a city when its government was hopelessly in debt and unable to find a solution. So at the same time the mayor was scrambling for an answer to Detroit's chronic financial problems, he was also trying to make sure no one else could step in and take control.

In April 2012, the Detroit City Council signed a consent agreement allowing them to avoid an emergency manager if they could control their financial obligations by consolidating departments and streamlining their bureaucracy. They also agreed to repair streetlights, improve public transit, and take other initiatives to restore the city's ability to serve its residents.

Unfortunately, Bing and the council failed to deliver. According to Michigan state treasurer Andy Dillion, "It could have worked. The problem was that Bing and the Council didn't get along. They couldn't govern themselves." Personalities and power politics were ultimately insurmountable barriers to saving the city.

Neither financial crises nor corruption are new to Detroit or any other city. The difference is that in the past, the city was willing to change its ways and clean up both its balance sheet and city hall. The Motor City could have learned a valuable lesson from its own history. For example, as America emerged from the dark days of the '30s and the world prepared for war, Detroit citizens took the lead in uncovering the biggest corruption scheme in the city up to that time.

In August 1939, a resident named Janet McDonald killed herself and her daughter, leaving behind a letter alleging her ex-lover was involved in gambling activities and payoffs to police. When county prosecutor Duncan McCrea said he was too short-staffed to pursue the case, a citizens' group went to court to demand action. The court appointed Judge Homer Ferguson to investigate.

After two years of work, Judge Ferguson indicted the county prosecutor, county sheriff Thomas Wilcox, and former mayor Richard "Little Dick" Reading on charges of accepting a total of $400,000 in bribes from underworld figures. All three were convicted, with Reading sentenced to 4½ to 5 years in prison. Unrepentant to the last, Reading responded to the verdict exclaiming, "This is the greatest injustice since the crucifixion of Christ!" City council members were also indicted for accepting $25,000 in bribes to award contracts in an $8 million public housing project.

During the 1950s, when the population of Detroit fell for the first time ever, the mayor and city council would have been justified in trimming their budget to match the smaller population that now needed city services and paid taxes to support them. Mayors Hazen Pingree and Frank Murphy used that strategy when the economy collapsed generations earlier. This time around, city leaders focused not on reducing expenses but raising revenues. Detroit introduced its municipal income tax in 1962 (currently 2.4 percent for residents and 1.2 percent for non-residents who work in the city; this is on top of a state income tax of 4.05 percent). Nine years later the city imposed a tax on utility bills (currently 5 percent on electricity and gas). Between 1962 and 2012, revenue in constant dollars fell 40 percent as the population declined. Although the assessed value of property sank 77 percent in constant dollars, the city shed only 28 percent of its workforce. While revenue dropped 20 percent between 2000 and 2012, healthcare obligations shot up 46 percent.

Going beyond even contractual obligations they could not afford, the city paid out extra bonuses to city workers and retirees to the tune of about $1 billion over more than twenty years. From 1985 to 2008, instead of investing returns back into the retirement fund, the city paid out money in the form of a so-called thirteenth check, an extra bonus payment to each participant every year. Had this money been reinvested instead, it would have been worth an estimated $1.9 billion by the time the city went bankrupt. Twice the city tried to halt the practice, once through a change to the city charter and once through a ballot initiative. Both times, furious union and retiree groups sued to block the changes and won.

It was between 2000 and 2012 when the wheels finally came off the Detroit budgetary wagon. During that period the deficit doubled to $8 billion. When Mayor Kwame Kilpatrick refinanced Detroit's debt with his doomed restructuring deal, bankruptcy became inevitable.

Time and again, mayors let the opportunity to trim expenses slip by. Mayor Coleman Young insisted the city had to raise more money by increasing taxes, though he also made the hard choice to freeze city wages, reduce services, and lay off 6,000 city workers including 2,000 police department workers and 500 in the fire department. One reason Young cut employees was that the city tried to reduce compensation to union workers but an arbitrator ruled against the city. Faced with spending more per worker, Young had no choice but to reduce the number of people on the payroll.

Though services suffered under his administration even as taxes went up, Young stabilized the city's budget and earned an investment-grade rating from Wall Street. The fact that this lowered Detroit's borrowing costs was a mixed blessing. From 1987 to 1994, Detroit's debt increased 72 percent in constant dollars.

Young's successor as mayor, Dennis Archer, had his own opportunity to rein in spending and reset the local government on a new, more modest, more sustainable financial path. In the 1990s, the rate of Detroit's economic decline slowed and the city could have taken the moment to catch its breath. Instead, Archer added workers to the public payroll Young previously trimmed, even though the population kept dropping. He justified it, Archer told the press, because the budget was balanced and the city could afford it. Moreover, in a prosperous national economy, cutting workers would have been a political liability.

Not only did the new hires add their salaries to the budget, they piled on more of the legacy costs already threatening the city's financial future. By the end of the 2001 fiscal year, there were more than 18,000 employees on the payroll, about one worker for every fifty-one residents. Indianapolis, another midwestern city of similar size, had one worker for every 115 citizens.

Even after the city realized legacy costs were a ticking time bomb, they ran into vigorous opposition from unions in cutting expenses. Court rulings and arbitration decisions strongly favored workers. The mayor and city council thought they had no choice but to keep paying. From 2007 to 2011, unfunded healthcare liabilities rose 19 percent even as the city reduced its active payroll by thousands. Over ten years the city cut 8,000 employees while retiree healthcare benefits rose from $99 million to $145 million per year.

During this time, many employers found relief from overwhelming healthcare costs by switching from defined benefit programs, which guaranteed certain benefits regardless the cost, to defined contribution plans, which provide a set amount of money for benefits and no more. Under union pressure Detroit stayed with the old system, even after the state government switched to a 401(k) defined contribution plan in 1997.

Forty-five years of overspending were the backdrop for Mayor Kwame Kilpatrick's Wall Street magic trick that brought in enough cash to fund the city's pension deficits nearly 100 percent. Kilpatrick heralded the agreement as a way to free Detroit from its financial constraints and bring the city solid financial footing and valuable flexibility. Several council members questioned the deal because, they said, the stock market was too volatile and the structure of the deal too murky.

If the council blocked the deal, Kilpatrick warned, he would have to lay off 2,000 city employees, whose job losses would be their fault. The *Detroit Free Press* editorialized in favor of the plan, calling skeptical council members "heads-in-the-sand" obstructionists who "have become a threat to the stability of the community." Unions lobbied relentlessly for the deal to go through. After months of delay, the Detroit city council approved the Wall Street infusion of cash by unanimous vote.

Wary council members were right after all. Three years later the stock market went into freefall and the United States entered its worst recession since the Great Depression. As interest rates tanked, the city was obliged to pay 6 percent on its millions. This was when the city pledged its casino gambling tax revenue to make a $400 million balloon payment.

When at long last Detroit's leadership realized they were out of maneuvering room, they looked to their biggest creditors, the unions and pension managers, for relief. No one wanted to give an inch. They insisted their members worked for these benefits and the city owed them. Since the city's poor financial management was not the workers' fault, they should not have to suffer because of it.

The financial crisis was at the breaking point. As the Citizens Research Council of Michigan reported in December 2011, Detroit municipal income tax and property tax revenues continued their decline. The council concluded, "With local tax revenue reductions exacerbated by reductions in state revenue sharing payments [due to the city's decline in population], the city's strategy of financing current operations with future revenues is not sustainable."

Even when demands for wage increases were justified, the city had no money to fund them without taking it from other budget items or borrowing. Between 1967 and 1992, Detroit teachers went on strike six times. The 1992 strike lasted four weeks as teachers defied a court order to return to work. Over the next year 15,000 students—more than 9 percent —left the district for other educational options. In 2013 Detroit Public Schools enrollment dropped below 50,000.

Fine arts organizations ran into financial trouble like every other part of the city's economy. Yet when faced with the reality of a twenty-first-century financial crisis, the musician's union representing the

Detroit Symphony Orchestra dug in its heels. Unlike the Detroit Institute of Arts and the Detroit Public Library, whose worth was concentrated in their world-class collections, the symphony's value was in its acclaimed players. Without them, the symphony had nothing to offer. And players were accustomed to being well-paid.

During its heyday, the Detroit Symphony Orchestra was a nationally renowned performer. Founded by a group of visionary women in 1914, the orchestra hired internationally renowned conductor Ossip Gabrilowitsch and built the magnificent Beaux Arts Orchestra Hall. In 1922 the Detroit Symphony became the first orchestra ever to broadcast on the radio. In the 1950s and '60s, they made dozens of popular recordings.

But as the local economy shrank, symphony expenses continued as they had when the organization was a cultural jewel in a prosperous, cosmopolitan city. By 2009 the orchestra was $3.9 million in debt. In 2010 Detroit Symphony musicians earned a base salary of $104,650 plus nine weeks of paid vacation. By comparison, the 2010 salary for a Detroit public school teacher with a master's degree and ten years of experience was a little over $65,000, a 10 percent reduction from the year before.

The symphony board proposed a pay cut to $70,000, about a 33 percent reduction, with three weeks of paid vacation, plus pension and benefit cuts. Representatives for the players offered a 22 percent reduction, insisting that deeper cuts would affect the quality of the orchestra and make it harder to recruit new players. The board held firm, determined to avoid commitments they knew they could never keep. The players went on strike for six months, eventually settling for a 25 percent salary cut to $79,000.

The symphony's conductor at the time, Los Angeles native Leonard Slatkin, donated four weeks of his salary back to the board and took a 34 percent pay cut. Had everyone else involved done the same, a strike would likely have been avoided and the symphony debt would not have climbed to almost $9 million by the next season.

Downtown Detroit in its 1920s heyday: Woodward Avenue streetcars, the Opera House, Hudson's Department Store, and streets bustling with cars and trucks.

Graf Zeppelin over Detroit, October 26, 1933, as part of a nationwide celebration of the Chicago World's Fair. The pilot circled the city in only one direction to hide the swastikas on the other side of the tail fins.

UAW representatives Walter Reuther and Richard Frankensteen beaten and bloodied for handing out pro-union literature at the "Battle of the Overpass," May 26, 1937.

When these 1940 Plymouth Roadkings came off the line, the company's Lynch Road plant was the largest auto assembly building in the world.

Assembling tracks on a Sherman M4 at the Chrysler tank arsenal c. 1942. During WW II the Motor City was transformed into the Arsenal of Democracy.

Huge new highway projects in the 1950s condemned more than 20,000 homes, many in thriving ethnic neighborhoods, and accelerated a population shift to the suburbs.

Not right through our bedroom! Concerned Detroiters anxiously look to see if their homes are in the path of destruction for a new right-of-way.

National Guardsmen advance with fixed bayonets as riots intensify, July 24, 1967. Later they were reinforced by more experienced army paratroopers.

Soldiers protected utility workers and firemen from deadly sniper fire. Some eyewitnesses reported snipers were directed by out-of-town coordinators.

Determined to avoid a bloodbath, city leaders ordered police not to shoot looters. Within hours, the neighborhood was in flames.

A collection of newly-acquired bicycles on display in front of a burned-out grocery store, Hamilton Avenue, July 25, 1967.

With neighborhood stores looted and burned, local residents line up for food donations on John R Street near Adelaide, July 25, 1967.

Vanguard African American journalist Louis Lomax saw the Detroit riots first-hand and had sources on both sides of the law. He reported the cause was out-of-town instigators.

Louis Lomax and author James Baldwin join host Hugh Downs on the live network TV program *Today*, February 1, 1963.

eset by poor construction and $70 million over budget, the 2.9-mile People Mover is the "dogless tail" of an otherwise unbuilt regional transportation plan.

Joe Louis Arena gave fans fast ice, a classic hockey experience, and four Stanley Cup championships despite treacherous steps, smelly concourses, and a lack of windows.

A wonder of the steam age when it opened in 1913, Michigan Central Station symbolized Detroit's place as a national transportation hub.

A fter it closed in 1988, Michigan Central was stripped by vandals and defaced with graffiti, becoming one of the most popular stops on the city's "urban blight" tours.

F ord bought the decayed site and in 2024 reopened it as the hub of their $950 million Michigan Central Project to build innovative transportation solutions for the future.

At this critical moment, had the various parties involved put aside their differences, their political posturing, and their self-serving perspectives to pull together for the sake of their city, they could have honored their promise to the state to right their own ship. What could have been done then—reducing obligations, attracting new investment, holding officials accountable—is exactly what happened under different leadership in the wake of Chapter 9 bankruptcy. Because the city lacked the courage and resolve to take the right steps, outsiders eventually had to take over when all other options were exhausted.

In 2012 Governor Rick Snyder began looking for an emergency manager to guide the city in negotiating with its creditors if possible or, as a last resort, steering it through a massive and unprecedented bankruptcy. Jones Day was one of several law firms applying to advise the city in restructuring. One of their attorneys was Kevyn Orr, who earned his law degree from the University of Michigan in 1983 and worked in the firm's office in Washington, D.C., where he lived with his wife, a doctor at Johns Hopkins, and their two children.

During Jones Day's first meeting with the governor's advisors, one lawyer asked whether Detroit even needed an emergency manager. Orr was astonished at the question. Spontaneously he exclaimed, "You've got to be kidding me!" It was painfully clear all other efforts had failed miserably. "Elected officials won't get this done. You've been coming this way for sixty years. You just had six and a half years of kleptocracy. Debt ratios to your income are out of whack. This is a dumb question. You're so far beyond needing an emergency manager, it's not funny."

His impromptu outburst convinced the rest of the players that Kevyn Orr should be Governor Snyder's emergency manager. He was experienced in bankruptcy law, grasped the situation quickly, had no political baggage to deal with or political reputation to protect, was known to be steady under fire, and he was black.

For forty years mayors and other leaders of Detroit labeled criticism and calls for reform as racist. Incapable of fixing the problems themselves, they invariably accused their critics of discrimination and trying to "take back" majority-black Detroit from its elected black leaders. It was their failed policies and poor outcomes being challenged, not their skin color. Yet accusations of racism effectively muffled legitimate, productive conversation and left people in charge who would never otherwise have stayed in office on the strength of their performance.

Before Governor Snyder even chose his emergency manager, civil rights activist Reverend Malik Shabazz, born Paris Lewis and one-time chairman of the New Black Panther Party, denounced the pending appointment as "white supremacy," telling residents they should "burn down the city of Detroit before letting the state take over."

After Orr's appointment was officially announced on March 14, 2013, activist Reverend Jesse Jackson condemned the move as a white Republican governor replacing the democratically elected city council and mayor, which he described as a "plantocracy—a plantation-ocracy—replacing a democracy." Though Snyder wisely chose a black appointee, Orr's education and position as a partner in a major law firm prompted unions and liberal leaders to condemn him as what one journalist called "an elitist outsider."

One of Orr's first orders of business was to meet quietly and out of the media spotlight with leaders of the city's black churches, who as a group were key influencers in the community. As the son of an African Methodist Episcopal Church minister, Orr knew how valuable these church leaders could be. He believed if he could engage them in conversation off the record, he could convince them he was on their side.

The plan worked. As word spread about Orr's appointment, a parade of black activists came to town to rail against the "racist" governor who was "stealing" Detroit from its black leaders and citizens. Louis Farrakhan, Al Sharpton, and Jesse Jackson were three of the best-known figures who came to the city to air their grievances. Thanks to Orr's preemptive move to embrace the black pastors, the out-of-town militants failed to get any traction.

Orr got down to work, first to assess the situation as it stood, then to see what he could do to avoid the biggest bankruptcy in American history.

Orr soon confirmed that Detroit reduced its active police force by thousands of officers because so much of its budget went toward retiree benefits it could not fund more positions. In 2012 the city had 389 murders reported, more than Cleveland, Pittsburgh, and St. Louis combined. The average time for Detroit police to answer a 911 call was half an hour. Forty percent of streetlights were out, the darkness encouraging more crime. Only about 53 percent of property taxes due—a major source of operating revenue—were being collected, either because residents could not afford them or they withheld payment in protest of the city's incredibly poor levels of service.

The violent crime rate was five times the national average. The police force was 40 percent smaller than ten years before. In addition to nearly half of the streetlights being out, more than 84,000 empty or ruined buildings sat decaying across the city, which would take $850 million to remove. Bus service was some of the most unreliable in the nation, owing to a broken-down bus fleet and an average daily absenteeism rate in the Department of Transportation of 35 percent from drivers' fear of unruly riders.

As he gathered facts about the disastrous state of the city, Orr made a historic decision. Rather than liquidating all possible assets and dividing the spoil between retirees and debtholders, he resolved to put the residents of Detroit first. The initial step was to make the situation clear to all the stakeholders. For decades people refused to acknowledge and discuss the cold, hard facts. As one attorney on the team observed, "Things were . . . probably bleaker than people thought. . . . The only way you could restructure the city was to have an honest conversation with people: 'Here are the facts. We're confident you won't like them.' But if you don't tell people the real story, you can't get anything done."

In a meeting on June 14, 2013, Orr explained to the city's biggest creditors that about 42.5 percent of the annual budget currently went to retiree healthcare benefits, pension payments, and debt service. By 2017 the figure would be 64.4 percent. Pension shortfall and unfunded retiree healthcare liabilities were $9.2 billion, roughly nine times the city's annual budget. Orr's decision to put the health and safety of Detroiters ahead of creditor claims meant setting aside about $1.25 billion over ten years for "blight removal, public safety investments, and information technology upgrades," with the rest going to creditors. Unsecured creditors were furious at Orr's initial offer of ten cents on the dollar. Pension representatives were livid because they insisted the state constitution protected them from any cuts whatever.

Pensions and benefits were also the biggest political hot potato for Governor Snyder, since most retirees still lived in Michigan and voted for governor. Furthermore, Article IX Section 24 of the state constitution declared public pensions were a "contractual obligation" that could not "be diminished or impaired."

After the city filed for bankruptcy on July 18, creditors' attorneys argued the state constitution gave ironclad protection to pensions. Thomas Morris, attorney for pension managers, told the court, "If the City of Detroit were to cease to exist, if there were to be some horrendous natural catastrophe that . . . wiped the city off the map, then we believe the city would still owe that obligation." Orr and his team countered that the guarantee in the state constitution was a contractual guarantee and subject to cancellation just as any other during bankruptcy. He added that federal bankruptcy law trumped state law. To the charge that Orr and Governor Snyder had usurped the power of elected officials, Snyder reminded the court he had been elected governor by all the residents of the state and was discharging his duties as such.

To charges that Orr failed to negotiate in good faith with his creditors, the emergency manager pointed out how the pension and benefits lawyers said they would not accept any cuts because of their constitutional protection, making any further negotiation a waste of time. Also, it was practically impossible for the city to negotiate in good faith with a list of creditors thirty-five hundred pages in length, about 170,000 of them in all.

On December 3, 2013, bankruptcy judge Steven Rhodes ruled the city was eligible to file for bankruptcy and could cut pensions. "We in bankruptcy impair contracts all day, every day," he said. "That's what we do." Creditors would fight to get all they could, especially the revenue stream from casino gambling taxes pledged as collateral. But soon creditors set their sights on a far richer prize which, if they could claim it, would dramatically reduce their enormous losses with a single stroke.

In 1885 a group of citizens founded the Detroit Museum of Art. Years later when the organization ran into financial trouble, the city donated money to keep it financially afloat. After the Michigan Supreme Court ruled the city had to stop subsidizing the museum because it was not a municipal agency, museum trustees offered its collection to the city as a gift. The city accepted it in 1919, noting as a result, art "shall become in its broadest sense democratic, with the museum and its valuable collections actually belonging to the people." In 1927 the city opened a magnificent new Beaux Arts museum building for what had been renamed the Detroit Institute of Arts.

This bit of history meant that, unlike a typical art museum where the collection is owned by a nonprofit corporation or trust, the Detroit Institute of Arts was city property and as such could be liquidated as part of the city's bankruptcy settlement.

Advisors working with Kevyn Orr contacted the museum and explained that the institution had only a limited time to raise hundreds of millions of dollars to transfer the art to a trust and keep it from being auctioned off. Selling art paid for with taxpayer dollars might be inevitable. The museum replied they would not sell a single piece of the collection under any circumstances. Selling except to buy other art was against professional standards and could endanger their accreditation.

Ken Buckfire, an investment banker advising Orr, said, "If it came down to selling a Van Gogh so that the city's retirees can live on tuna fish and not cat food, it's not even a close call," adding the museum's "position was not well thought out."

Of the more than 2,700 museum works purchased with taxpayer money, eleven works comprised 75 percent of the total value, including Bruegel's *The Wedding Dance*, Van Gogh's *Self-Portrait with Straw Hat*, and Rembrandt's *The Visitation*. Though difficult to estimate because of the unique quality of the art, estimated value for the whole lot ranged up to more than $800 million, with a value of $200 million for the Bruegel alone, which was the most valuable single work.

The bankruptcy team made it clear that the museum's professional standards and accreditation meant nothing to them. If the Detroit Institute of Arts tried to stop them, Orr had the power to fire the museum's executives and sell whatever needed selling. Once this somber news sank in, the museum leadership realized it had to act or die.

A key first step in saving the museum was to convince nonprofit foundations with a stake in Detroit to join forces for the good of the cause. Mariam Noland, president of the Community Foundation for Southeast Michigan, canvassed her contacts to see who was willing to help. On November 5, 2013, she hosted a meeting with representatives of top nonprofits including the Ford Foundation, Kresge Foundation, Knight Foundation, and Mott Foundation among others.

Darren Walker, president of the Ford Foundation, spoke for many when he observed, "What you're asking us to do is to help correct the bad decisions of leadership in the past." Foundations, he added, invest in the future; they don't dwell on previous decisions. Largest by far of Detroit-related nonprofits with an endowment exceeding $10 billion, the Ford Foundation was founded by Edsel Ford in 1936 and headquartered in New York. It would set the bar for everyone else. If Ford declined to participate, the rescue plan was likely dead in the water. Kresge was the second largest at $3.5 billion, followed by Knight and Mott foundations at $2 billion each, with many smaller foundations whose help would also be essential. A handful of big players alone would not generate either the money or the community support the proposal required.

Speaking later at a meeting of the Knight Foundation board, trustee Beverly Knight Olson said, "I think this is wonderful. . . . I think this is exactly what my father and my uncle set up the foundation for. But I don't think $20 million [the original amount proposed as a contribution] is enough. I think we should do thirty . . . because Jack Knight loved Detroit, and the *Free Press* was his paper."

The spirit of Olson's offer evidently spurred other foundations to go big. The Ford Foundation pledged $125 million. Kresge offered an "astonishing" $100 million, the Kellogg Foundation gave $40 million, and other nonprofits stepped up in similar fashion. Reporters John Gallagher and Mark Stryker of the *Detroit Free Press* dubbed the plan the Grand Bargain.

Once the foundations got behind the Grand Bargain, Kevyn Orr thought the museum should make its own financial commitment. He suggested they contribute $100 million. After all, they were the recipients of all this largesse. Museum leadership refused. Museum chief operating officer Annmarie Erickson said it was "completely unfeasible" to raise that amount "and continue to raise what we do to cover expenses and what we've committed to raise in endowment dollars." She and her colleagues seemed at first not to realize that without a commitment on their part, there would be no expenses nor endowment because there would be no museum.

But the museum did begin raising money to make a contribution to the Grand Bargain and donors eagerly pledged their support. General Motors, Ford Motor Company, and Penske Corporation each pledged $10 million; Chrysler offered $6 million; Dan Gilbert, Detroit's biggest champion and founder of Quicken Loans, offered a corporate donation of $5 million.

In the end, the Institute pledged $100 million over twenty years, the goal Orr set for them. Total pledges for the Grand Bargain were $816 million over twenty years, which would allow the museum to set up a nonprofit entity to own its artwork and make money available to honor city pension and benefit obligations. This saved an art collection valued at $4 billion or more (when donated works were included), though liquidating everything at once in a "fire sale" could have reduced the value by half.

The generous, visionary benefactors who funded the Grand Bargain had already donated millions in cash and art to the museum over generations to establish its world-class collection in the first place. Despite decades of incompetence that now endangered those gifts, the same people demonstrated a level of grace and sense of civic responsibility in rescuing the institution that no other group could have matched. They eventually saved the Detroit Institute of Arts and also paved the way for tens of thousands of city pensioners to keep their benefits.

Meanwhile, negotiations with the creditors continued. No one wanted to give any ground and no one seemed to understand this was a new day with new rules. Pensioners and retirees who were set on liquidating the Detroit Institute of Arts began to change their position as the Grand Bargain took shape against long odds. Here was a chance to bring hundreds of millions of dollars of free money into the equation. But the Grand Bargain commitments were contingent on these creditors agreeing to big cuts. Without a compromise, the $800 million-plus donation pledges would disappear. The alternative was a years-long battle over whether liquidating the DIA was legal or not.

As negotiators worked their way through the seemingly endless layers of claims and counterclaims, contending parties gradually agreed on a way forward. Police and fire pensions would not be cut, though cost of living increases would be limited to one percent. Other city workers agreed to a 4.5 percent pension cut and no cost of living allowance going forward. The city paid $450 million to two new independent trusts to administer reduced healthcare benefits with no further financial obligation from the city. Bondholders agreed to major cuts as well, leaving bond insurers as the only holdouts. In the end they settled for pennies on the dollar and the final piece of the agreement was in place.

In trying to scrape together as much money as possible, Governor Snyder offered to make Belle Island a state park. This once-popular recreation area on a thousand-acre island in the Detroit River was hopelessly rundown, yet the city spent $6 million per year maintaining what was an uninhabitable, derelict mess. The city council refused Snyder's offer, considering it an insult that the state would propose to take over such a historic landmark. Orr also saw both the potential of the location and its pointless drain on the city's non-existent resources. He also saw it as a valuable asset the city's creditors could latch onto. When the city balked at a sale, Orr leased the island to the state instead.

Poor municipal water service was a long-time headache and health threat. After decades of leadership failures and financial mismanagement, the city's outdated system was failing fast. Most of the three thousand miles of pipes were 70–90 years old, leading to more than 5,000 water main breaks in the past three years. In March 2014, nearly half the city's water accounts were delinquent, totaling $118 million in unpaid water bills. To strengthen its finances, the water company started shutting off overdue accounts at the rate of 3,000 per week. The city also persuaded municipal bondholders to exchange old bonds for new ones with better terms for the city, saving the water company more than $100 million over time.

Another part of solving the water problem, long resisted by city leaders, was to establish a regional water management utility. In September 2014, the Great Lakes Water Authority began leasing the city's water assets for $50 million a year. This payment would go to overhaul the water system and set aside $4.5 million per year to limit rate increases and help low-income residents pay their bills.

As part of the bankruptcy agreement, the state legislature set up a financial oversight board to make sure Detroit did not slip back into its old fiscal habits. After Orr returned control to the city council, the oversight board "would retain the authority to veto budgets, reject debt, and approve major contracts, including union deals—possibly for more than a decade." The board would be disbanded after three straight years of balanced budgets and debt payments.

In the end, the bankruptcy of Detroit slashed more than $7 billion in liabilities accrued over the years like barnacles on a ship and "scrubbed its balance sheet of 75% of the legacy costs that had prevented it from investing in core city services." The city projected having more than $1.7 billion over ten years in new money to spend on city services.

In his meticulous and definitive history of the Detroit bankruptcy, *Detroit Resurrected: To Bankruptcy and Back*, reporter and historian Nathan Bomey sums up the saga as follows: "What emerged from the city's bankruptcy was not an ideological trampling of democracy or union rights . . . [but] a plan that, for the first time in decades, offered hope to the people of Detroit. . . . Opponents accused Snyder and Orr of shattering promises that were made to retirees who relied on pensions and health care benefits and promises that were made to bondholders who relied on the city's financial wherewithal. But the city had broken those promises years ago—perhaps decades ago—by failing to reach labor deals it could afford and by borrowing to pay the bills instead of correcting course to avoid a fiscal iceberg."

To citizens of Detroit who were angry about the final result, bankruptcy judge Rhodes said, "I urge you now not to forget your anger. Your enduring and collective memory of what happened here, and your memory of your anger about it, will be exactly what will prevent this from ever happening again. And so I ask you, for the good of the city's fresh start, to move past your anger. Move past it and join in the work that is necessary to fix this city."

Every step Kevyn Orr took to rescue Detroit could have been taken over the years by the mayor and city council: curbing entitlement costs, rebuilding infrastructure, shoring up police and fire protection, extracting value from Belle Isle and other assets, reducing waste and corruption, clear and honest communication, accepting responsibility and accountability. Yet the city failed to do so. As a result, under a withering barrage of criticism, Governor Snyder and Orr grabbed the reins as the stagecoach careened to the edge of the cliff.

They saved the stagecoach. Now, catching their collective breath and stepping carefully away from the abyss, what would the passengers do next? ■

Chapter 10

Hard Lessons

*"There's a real roadmap to drive Detroit into a ditch.
It's been clearly articulated. . . . So there's got to be
a different roadmap to make Detroit great."*
—Darren Walker, Ford Foundation CEO, 2013

■ ▓ ■

IN THE aftermath of bankruptcy, the rate of Detroit's population decline has slowed even though residents are still leaving at a rapid pace. While the regional Metro Detroit population has remained remarkably constant over the years—its population in 2022 was 3.5 million, the same as in 1960—the city has continued to lose its people. Between the 2010 census and 2020, the city population fell 10.5 percent from 713,000 to 639,000, one of the steepest declines of any major city and one of only a handful to lose rather than gain residents. More black Detroiters than white departed the city during that ten-year span. Sixteen percent of the black population moved, reducing their numbers from 83 percent to 77 percent of the total.

Tracing the history of Detroit's bankruptcy in his book *Detroit Resurrected*, Nathan Bomey made a number of observations as the city stood on the threshold of a new era in its history.

Education was still a topline issue. "The appalling state of public education in Detroit remains a barrier to the city's resurgence," he wrote. In 2013 the National Center for Education Studies reported

54 percent of Detroit's eighth-graders scored below basic achievement levels in reading, far exceeding the average of 32 percent below standard for large U.S. cities and 23 percent for all schools.

Enrollment in Detroit public schools fell about 102,000 between 2003–04 and 2013–14. As Bomey noted, "The governor's attempts at rehabilitating public education in Detroit by appointing a series of emergency managers for the school district and assigning the worst schools to a new entity called the Education Achievement Authority have failed to erase deficits or markedly improve test scores."

At the same time, Bomey underscored promising signs of improvement including the governor's Community Ventures program, "a feasible route into the workforce for the chronically unemployed in Detroit, providing practical help such as funds for daycare, a ride to work, or help building a resume."

Detroit Resurrected ends on a generally hopeful tone, highlighting billionaire Dan Gilbert's ownership or control of more than seventy buildings in the city at the time, including the headquarters of his Quicken Loans, now the largest home mortgage lender in the nation. Gilbert's investments "have included substantial renovation projects and a private security apparatus that has improved public safety but also drawn scrutiny from concerned citizens. On the whole, Gilbert has breathed new life into streets that were mostly abandoned a decade ago." There is also fellow billionaire Mike Ilitch and his family, who built a new downtown arena for the Detroit Red Wings, though critics opposed the decision to commit future city and state taxpayer dollars to the project.

Ford Foundation CEO Darren Walker described Detroit's post-bankruptcy options by pointing out "there's a real roadmap to drive Detroit into a ditch. It's been clearly articulated. All we need to do is look back over the past two or three decades. So there's got to be a different roadmap to make Detroit great. . . . That's what the leadership in Detroit has to do. That's what we in philanthropy have to do."

Despite their hard-learned lesson, at least some city employees retained a deeply ingrained sense of entitlement. In April 2013, four of the men running the city's pension fund were charged with spending $22,000 on a conference trip to Hawaii. They claimed it was for work but Bill Nowling, a spokesman for Kevyn Orr, said the trip didn't look good when there were city employees taking pay cuts. "Middle-class, blue-collar workers, their dream vacation when they retire may be a two-week trip to Hawaii—they don't associate Hawaii with a place you go to work."

Problems evolving over decades would take time to resolve. Only a third of the city's ambulances were in service in the first quarter of 2013. Forty percent of streetlights were still out and the backlog of complaints was more than 3,300. Average response time for an emergency call grew to fifty-eight minutes, compared with a national average of eleven minutes. City law enforcement solved 8.7 percent of crimes in town compared to an average 30.5 percent rate in Michigan.

In analyzing Detroit's downward trajectory over the past seventy-five years, observers consider why Detroit fared so much more poorly than other cities facing similar challenges. Writing in *Forbes* in 2018, Scott Beyer wondered why Detroit never recovered from the loss of its core automotive industry jobs to Alabama, Tennessee, South Carolina, and other southern states and the resultant outmigration of residents. "Why has Detroit continued to decline (and at a faster rate) in the nearly four decades since?" Was the city destined to keep declining in the face of those previous events, or "are new causes to blame?"

Kansas City, Chicago, Milwaukee, Cincinnati, and Philadelphia were all growing, Beyer noted. Even cities continuing to decline such as Pittsburgh, St. Louis, and Cleveland had not declined to the extent Detroit had, "nor do they generally have Detroit's level of poverty, unemployment, service failure, and visible decrepitude."

Beyer continued, "Detroit's decline also makes it an outlier within its own metro. . . . less than an hour west of Detroit is Ann Arbor, a bustling city with an eds-and-meds economy." The Detroit metropolitan area at the time was one of the nation's twenty largest, with 2.1 percent GDP growth in 2016. Six of the ten largest cities in Greater Detroit added population since 2010. "There is significant wealth throughout the metro, and much of it butts up right outside the city border."

Nearby Oakland County, for example, is the wealthiest county in the state. L. Brooks Patterson served as county prosecutor for sixteen years before beginning his twenty-eight years as County Executive in 1992. Patterson's tough-on-crime approach coupled with a commitment to low taxes, good services, and "aggressive courtship of business investment and housing sprawl" yielded twenty straight years of AAA bond ratings.

Patterson's financial team developed a three-year rolling budget to keep the books balanced. In the 1990s he moved county employee retirement funding to a 401(k) plan saving millions of dollars and issued bonds to pay off retiree healthcare liabilities. County sheriff Michael Bouchard praised Patterson, saying, "He got the county out of that financial guillotine that is just crippling other local governments. . . . He provided a great level of service at a very competitive price point."

Though some urban politicians accused Patterson of racism, his successor as county executive, Gerald Poisson, explained, "He got tagged with that because he wouldn't genuflect to Coleman Young." Patterson in fact blamed Young for Detroit's downfall, calling him "the captain of the Titanic."

People who talk about Detroit's decline, Beyer continued, not only "invoke the events from long ago, but their language is often fatalistic, as if some outside force just swooped in and yanked everything out from under Detroit. Often, this is a reference to 'capitalism,' or close cousins like neoliberalism or globalization."

But if other Midwestern cities have been recovering and the rest of southeast Michigan has been diversifying its economy, "then 'capitalism' can't be blamed. Detroit has become an outlier, suggesting that its problems are unique and internal."

Some "experts" claim Detroit's demographics and infrastructure are the problem. Government engineering produced urban renewal, subsidized highways, and discriminatory loan policies that "drove white people to the suburbs, and kept black people inside the core." Leftover houses and factories are expensive to repair or demolish. Others note old housing stock and "non-cohesive neighborhoods." Detroit native and *Forbes* columnist Pete Saunders wrote, "Once the auto industry became established in Detroit, political and business leaders abdicated their responsibility on sound urban planning and design."

Michael LaFaive of the Mackinac Center for Public Policy counters that infrastructure and demographics should not matter. "What's more important is a city's ability to attract capital. And for that, Detroit has failed miserably, with corporations often locating right outside the city border, so they can enjoy the central proximity, without actually having to deal in Detroit.

"My explanation involve[s] the basic idea that capital, be it financial or human, goes where it's welcome, and leaves if it's not. And Detroit politicians for decades have repeatedly made capital unwelcome."

Beyer went on to explain that Detroit has turned capital away in four ways.

First, high taxes. Detroit has high income taxes and the highest property tax of any major city.

Second, poor municipal services in ways "deeply rooted and terminal"—police who don't arrive, schools growing mold, blighted properties going decades without being demolished, waste dumped and never cleaned up, and on and on. High taxes and poor services, writes Beyer, "conjoin around that fact that the city spends much of its revenue on non-services."

The third factor affecting the availability of capital is regulation. According to Florida Gulf Coast University, the city of Detroit ranks 345 out of 384 metro areas in "economic freedom." This is "hard to quantify, instead surfacing through anecdotal tales of corruption and clandestine impediments against business."

The fourth factor is corruption.

"Collectively, these four factors—taxes, regulations, poor services, and plain corruption— . . . are precisely . . . what would discourage—and in some cases directly prohibit—capital from entering Detroit." Thus the arguments that infrastructure and demographics are major sources of Detroit's ongoing troubles are unsupportable.

Beyer says the claim that Detroit's outdated infrastructure is part of the problem is "a complete red herring." Most of America, he explains, has been laid out similarly to Detroit, "but almost none of it performs this poorly. There are countless cities—think New York, San Francisco and Savannah—that have many old buildings, yet have revived them to greater values than before. Again, though, this historic restoration process requires inbound capital."

He considers the demographic argument "flimsy" as well, pointing out how many American cities, including Houston, Dallas, Philadelphia, Chicago, and New York City, have more poor people than Detroit. These cities are all "far more economically successful because they've also managed to attract rich people, who create jobs and fund the services needed for those cities to continue growing. This proves the existence of low-income demographics do not, unto themselves, bring cities down.

"Detroit's struggles are about its inability to attract capital, business, and economic growth. . . . all those things stop abruptly at the city border, on all sides, before immediately resurfacing in the suburbs. And this is because such growth is largely discouraged by Detroit's public administration. That fact is more relevant to the city's ongoing struggles than anything that happened fifty years ago."

After the bankruptcy, Detroit schools remained as dysfunctional as ever. By early 2016, a balloon payment due in February nearly equaled the entire annual payroll and benefits. The school district borrowed $121 million to operate during the school year on top of $139.8 million already owed.

District payroll and healthcare benefits for the year would be $26.8 million per month and monthly debt payments would be $26 million, meaning debt payments would be 97 percent of operating expenses. Debt payments exceeding 10 percent of payroll were "a major warning flag" according to municipal bond analyst Matt Fabian. "That's no longer, really, a normal school district. The school district has turned into a debt-servicing entity. It's making its own mission impossible."

In 2016 the district ranked last nationally among urban districts on the National Assessment of Educational Progress for the fourth year in a row. Meanwhile, in April of that year, twelve school principals were accused of taking bribes for supplies never delivered. Each one, working separately, issued contracts for school supplies to a vendor, who then kicked back some profits to them. The principals raked in a total of $2.5 million.

There were plenty of other problems. Barbara Byrd-Bennett, a top district official under a previous emergency manager, ordered a book series titled *StoryTown* from publisher Houghton Mifflin Harcourt. It was a massive $40 million investment, the single largest purchase in Detroit schools' history, for a series of materials that completely altered the curriculum. Rife with problems, it was replaced after one year.

At the beginning of the 2016–17 school year, a federal civil rights lawsuit was filed on behalf of DPS students. Legislators saw the problems as proof the school board was not ready to resume control from the emergency manager directing it at the time. The complaint gives a devastating snapshot of conditions in the district, including these "horrifying allegations:"

At Cody Medicine and Community Health Academy, a ninth grade language arts class "spent a large part of the year going paragraph by paragraph through a single novel, which had a third-grade reading level."

At Marion Law Academy, teachers searched Google for lesson plans the night before or bought them from teacherspayteachers.com. The teaching resources at Law were "woefully deficient" because at the beginning of the 2012–13 school year, textbooks, library books, and other curricular materials were thrown into a dumpster when the school opened as an Educational Achievement Authority campus under a statewide system for failing schools. "But the new digital information platform was ineffective, lacked existing instructional materials, and was abandoned in the 2015–16 school year. Administrators told teachers at Law that they were expected to buy their own supplies."

At Hamilton Academy, a charter school authorized by DPS, many students had a vocabulary of only a couple hundred words. Some students could not even sound out letters. A math teacher teaching seventh and eighth grade quit a few weeks into the school year. The first replacement was a paraprofessional, who was then replaced by a special ed teacher, who was in turn replaced by the best student in the class, who taught his fellow classmates for a month until a teacher could be assigned.

The atmosphere at Hamilton was as miserable as the learning environment. Meals were sometimes served with moldy bread and expired milk. Students avoided the water fountains, "which are frequently infested with cockroaches and maggots." Even though teachers arrived early every morning to pick up the playground, students at recess still found "bullets, used condoms, sex toys, and dead vermin."

At least in the short term, Detroit did not do so well in learning from its mistakes. Yet as the city moves through the decade of the 2020s, there are more signs of life and resurgence than there have been for generations. Architectural ruins of a once-great city that had long been symbols of Detroit's decline are finally being repurposed or demolished. Thousands of abandoned houses have been razed, depriving prostitutes and drug addicts of long-accustomed hiding places. Adventurous urban pioneers are re-establishing a foothold in formerly empty and lifeless neighborhoods.

The massive void—physical and psychological—of the vacant mid-town block where the iconic Hudson's Department Store once stood is finally being filled by a dramatic new high-rise. With entrepreneur and investor Dan Gilbert in the lead, civic-minded businessmen have poured new resources into the city, building, renovating, and investing in a community they are convinced is worth saving.

The pace of Detroit's decline is slower than before, its outlook brighter than before, its champions more determined. These are the fruits of hard lessons learned from a long history of missteps and poor choices.

If Detroit is learning from its mistakes, what have other cities learned from Detroit?

As Darren Walker of the Ford Foundation so aptly pointed out, the Motor City has given the world a roadmap of how not to run a city. Now Detroit is in the process of drawing a new map. While Detroit is unique among American cities in the size of its decline since 1950, other cities have followed their own paths up and down the economic and population scale over the years. Some have stagnated while others have surged. Some have prospered while others have struggled. Every city has its own set of circumstances, yet some have turned those circumstances into successes as others have surrendered to failure in light of similar conditions.

Even a cursory survey of American cities highlights how cities that make the decisions Detroit has made over the years produce the same poor result. They are headed down the same dismal path Detroit's discredited road map led Detroit. This is the Detroiting of America.

Other cities have managed to hold their own over the years in spite of the historic challenges they encountered. Still other cities have been a reverse image of Detroit, rising as shining examples of success, growing exponentially over the years as families and businesses come to take advantage of an environment promising a safe and prosperous life.

Which cities, then, have prospered most, and what do they have in common? Which cities have held onto the status quo? And which cities today are withering, unwilling to acknowledge and accept the free lessons in charting their future course bought by Detroit at so tremendous a cost?

Numerous cities today are walking boldly and blindly in Detroit's historic path. All of them are sharing, to a greater or lesser extent, a taste of Detroit's self-inflicted misery.

Chapter 11

History Repeats

"Cities only work when people behave according to common standards—and the de-prosecution movement has proven that absent an external deterrent, enough people will behave hellishly to make life hell for everyone else."
—Nicole Gelinas, *New York Post*, 2022

■ ■ ■

IN THE decade of the 2020s, several cities are vying for the top spot as poster child for the Detroiting of America. Today's headlines are proof that Detroit's hard-won lessons are lost on many city leaders and the voters who elected them. One of the prime examples is Chicago, the industrial powerhouse of the Midwest once described by poet Carl Sandburg as the "city of big shoulders." Chicago has been one of the biggest cities in America for more than a hundred years. It held the number two spot behind New York at the turn of the twentieth century and kept its position until Los Angeles pulled ahead in 1990.

Between 1930 and 1970, Chicago's population fluctuated between about 3.4 million and 3.6 million, then started a downward trend. By 2020 the city was home to around 2.7 million residents, the same as in 1920. Over that hundred years its net growth rate was 0 percent. Houston, by comparison, grew

"He who digs a pit will fall into it."
—Proverbs 26:27

1,675 percent during the same period, advancing from forty-fifth in population to fourth. With Chicago losing about 7 percent of its people over twenty years ending in 2020 while Houston gained 17 percent, Houston is poised to overtake Chicago for the third spot in 2030. (You heard it here first.)

Why is Chicago failing? For the same reasons Detroit failed. In recent years Chicago's crime rate has risen dramatically. This rise correlates to lower arrest rates due to criticism of police and policies limiting police response to crime, district attorneys who decline to prosecute, and courts releasing accused and convicted criminals back onto the streets. A spike in 2016 saw an alarming increase in homicides. According to a report by the Institute for Policy Research at Northwestern University, the "most disturbing feature" of the rise was that the police were not solving crimes. The report noted, "the ability of Chicago police to solve gun violence has plummeted to single digits. Because crimes have gone unsolved, the standard model of policing—in which the police receive a call, investigate, and arrest someone—has collapsed."

In early 2017, researchers at the University of Chicago Crime Lab reported homicides in January 2016 were 67 percent above January the year before. By the end of 2016, the city recorded 58 percent more killings than 2015. Though teenage gangs were presumed to be behind the carnage, the average age of homicide suspects arrested was twenty-six, about two-thirds of whom were affiliated with a gang. During that time, as a result of an agreement with the city following a lawsuit by the ACLU, a Justice Department investigation, and public reaction to the fatal shooting of high school student Laquan McDonald by a Chicago policeman (who fired sixteen shots into his back), street stops by police in 2016 fell 82 percent. As police presence declined, crime went up.

Another spike in 2021 produced 797 homicides, the most of any city in America that year. There were 3,561 shooting incidents in Chicago during the same period, more than 300 ahead of 2020 and more than 1,400 over the 2019 figure. Yet again, as the murder rate rose, police response declined. Between June 2020 and February 2021, arrests fell 53 percent as murders increased 65 percent.

Along with a drop in street stops and arrests by law enforcement, Chicago has seen a transformation in charging and prosecuting suspects. Cook County State's Attorney Kim Foxx was criticized for charging decisions that released many suspects back into the community, including a new higher threshold for felony charges in retail theft that some blame for an increase in shoplifting. Foxx also supported increased reliance on electronic monitoring and elimination of cash bail, though the policy change on bail was challenged in the courts. In the summer of 2023, the Illinois supreme court found the law constitutional, making Illinois the first state in the nation to eliminate cash bail. Six months after implementation the law was reportedly "working as intended," though its effect on recidivism and compliance with court appearances was unclear. Meanwhile, Foxx's position prompted an unprecedented rise in the number of resignations from the State's Attorney's office: 136 members of the office resigned in 2022, compared with eleven resignations in 2012.

Running for re-election in 2023, Chicago Mayor Lori Lightfoot was criticized for a 40 percent increase in crime during her four-year term. The mayor vigorously defended her public safety record against concerns of police department attrition and budget issues. Like Detroit mayor Coleman Young, Lightfoot charged her critics with racial discrimination—"I'm a Black woman and, let's not forget, some folks frankly don't support us in leadership roles"—and suggested that if people didn't plan to vote for her, "then stay home . . . don't vote."

Unlike Young, Lightfoot failed even to make the runoffs. Her perceived inability to deal with crime cost her a second term.

Many residents, fearful for their safety, would argue that the criminal justice system in Chicago has switched from serving the citizens and taxpayers to defending and excusing lawbreakers: more about the criminal and less about justice. That fear was reinforced in April 2023 after hundreds of teenagers went on a rampage downtown, smashing car windows, attacking passersby, interrupting traffic, and threatening tourists. Instead of arresting troublemakers wholesale, the authorities defended them. Fifteen people were taken into custody.

State senator Robert Peters of Chicago claimed the assault and destruction was simply "a mass protest against poverty and segregation." Mayor-elect Brandon Johnson called the destruction "unacceptable" but also insisted it was "not constructive to demonize youth who have otherwise been starved of opportunities in their own communities."

Others charged the city with condoning violence, making excuses for unlawful behavior, and ignoring its responsibility to protect the innocent. Even so, Chicago elected Johnson as mayor over challenger Paul Vallas, who promised more support for law enforcement and was endorsed by the police union. *Newsweek* called Johnson's win "the police's worse nightmare." Johnson argues against more money for policing and in favor of more investment in healthcare and other social services. He supports replacing police officers with social workers and EMTs on some 911 calls.

This is in spite of a massive increase in Chicago crime in 2023 over the previous year, with total crimes reported between January 1 and April 9 up 45 percent, including a 135 percent rise in car theft.

The police union predicted a thousand officers would leave the force after Johnson's win because they "will not work for a bigger anti-police mayor than [former mayor Lori Lightfoot]." The result will be even "more crime, violence and blood on the streets."

In assessing Mayor Johnson's first hundred days in office, the Illinois Policy Institute saw "no movement on Chicago's crime, education, or financial problems." The Institute reported overall crime up 39 percent in 2023, including a 50 percent increase in juvenile homicides and a 50 percent drop in arrests since 2019. Debt service and pensions were projected to be 42 percent of the city budget. The report also noted Chicago Public Schools' 2023–24 budget was the biggest ever despite a drop in enrollment of 39,000 since 2018.

In response, Mayor Johnson accused his critics of holding him to a "different standard" as a black man and "perpetuating a particular view of Blackness," opposing "a Black man on the left who leads with love." To anyone who "has a problem" with him as mayor, Johnson said, "come see me in four years."

Together with rampant crime, Chicago shares with Detroit a long history of failed schools. As parents sought better options, Chicago public school enrollment fell by 116,000 between 2002 and 2022, a drop of 27 percent. Then-mayor Rahm Emanuel responded by closing forty-nine elementary schools in 2013, according to *Crain's Chicago Business*. The resulting community outrage produced a moratorium on school closings until 2025, even though enrollment continues to decline. As families transfer their children to new charter schools in their neighborhoods, traditional public school facilities sit underutilized, costs escalate, and student performance remains some of the lowest in the nation.

In 2013 Chicago schools had a $5.3 billion budget and $6.4 billion in debt. Ten years later the budget was $9.4 billion with $8.6 billion in debt and unfunded pension liability of $13.2 billion. The district noted, "For many years, pensions have been the dominant driver of CPS's structural deficit."

With further school closings suspended, the district operates facilities at only a fraction of capacity. According to CPS figures, the twenty emptiest schools during the 2022–2023 academic year were used to an average capacity of under 15 percent, producing an average student-teacher ratio of 3.6. The average cost per student was over $27,400 with one school posting a per-student tally of $62,155.

It would seem that so low a student-teacher ratio would be an educator's dream and produce outstanding results. The facts tell a different story. In these twenty nearly-empty schools, students' average proficiency in reading was 8 percent, meaning eight out of a hundred students could read at grade level. The year before, in twenty-two Chicago schools not a single student could read at grade level according to data from the state board of education, and in thirty-three schools not one child reached grade-level proficiency in math. Graduation rates have risen in recent years, but if only 11 percent of black students and 17 percent of Hispanics can read at grade level, a diploma means little.

Like Detroit, Chicago schools have had their share of corruption. One high-profile case in recent years was the conviction of Chicago school superintendent Barbara Byrd-Bennett (formerly of Detroit Public Schools) for steering contracts to friends. Byrd-Bennett was sentenced to four and a half years in prison for awarding a $20 million training contract to her former employer. After her trial, the school district inspector general uncovered another $10 million in contracts she fraudulently awarded. She solicited jobs for friends, accepted kickbacks, and fed insider bidding information to her preferred bidders.

Chicago continues its long history of corruption on a wide scale. Based on Department of Justice statistics, Chicago has repeatedly been identified as the most corrupt city in the United States. In 2019, for example, there were twenty-six federal corruption convictions. During the year extortion, racketeering, and bribery charges were filed against city finance committee chairman Ed Burke. The chairman of the powerful city zoning committee, Danny Solis, allegedly received massage parlor treatments and male enhancement drugs in exchange for supporting certain business deals. Alderman Proco Moreno was arrested on felony insurance fraud charges. Former Alderman Willie Cochran was sentenced to a year in prison for fraud. Chicago state senate representative Martin Sandoval pled guilty to accepting bribes.

According to Department of Justice records, Chicago led the nation in public corruption convictions for the period 1976–2019 with 1,770 convictions, an average of forty-one per year. By comparison Los Angeles, with a million more people, had 1,558 cases while New York City, with more than triple Chicago's population, logged 1,361. In 1984 an FBI sting called Operation Greylord indicted ninety-two Chicago and Cook County officials including seventeen judges, forty-eight lawyers, eight policemen, ten deputy sheriffs, and eight court officials for federal crimes.

One theory holds that Chicago corruption is so ingrained because of its history of handing out political favors in exchange for support going back more than a century. Political bosses played various ethnic communities against each other, rewarding loyalty with control of parts of city government. An Irishman could count on a job in the police department, for example, while Italians were always welcome at the transit authority.

Other big cities of the day operated the same way. But over time reform-minded leaders often came along who swept those systems away at least for a while. Detroit had Hazen Pingree and Frank Murphy. New York had Fiorello LaGuardia and his friend Franklin D. Roosevelt. Chicago never had such a figure and moved instead more toward a one-party system. The last Republican mayor, William H. Thompson, left office in 1931.

After crime, schools, and corruption, the fourth and final key ingredient for Detroiting is high taxes. According to the Tax Foundation, Chicago is tied with Glendale and Long Beach, California, for the highest combined state and local sales tax rates in the country with a rate of 10.25 percent. Compared to other large American cities, Chicago taxes are also the highest in the country for 911 service, wireless service (more than 36 percent), amusements, soft drinks, cigarettes, parking (28 percent), and more.

Over the ten years ending in 2023, Chicago's property tax levy doubled from $860 million to over $1.7 billion. The city suffers a critical loss of police and firefighters, yet much of any increase to those departments will go to pension funding. Chicago's current pension debt is $48 billion, more than forty-four U.S. states. As happened in Detroit, instead of reducing expenses to live within their means, Chicago leaders keep squeezing their residents for more revenue to pay unsustainable pension costs. Recently some small businesses in the city have seen property tax bills more than double in a single year. This, and a proposal to impose a progressive income tax, will have business owners and their workers packing their bags. Though Chicago posted a net loss (departures over arrivals) of only 155,000 residents between 2000 and 2020, the city saw an out-migration of more than 260,000 black residents disproportionally affected by high crime, high living costs, and underperforming schools.

In addition to Chicago's textbook example, other cities in the 2020s seem determined to follow Detroit's destructive path with policies driving the cost of living and doing business to impossible levels along with a view of criminal justice that excuses criminal behavior and endangers innocent residents.

A generation ago, New York City was a dirty, dangerous place. Under Mayor John Lindsay, law enforcement faded and criminal activity increased. When residents stopped carrying cash for fear of being robbed, street criminals were incensed. The city's response was not to increase policing but rather to advise citizens to carry five dollars for muggers and so avoid a beating. The city budget careened out of hand. Strikes paralyzed the city. Transit fares rose from fifteen cents to fifty cents. Welfare rolls increased 117 percent. Police and other departments were mired in corruption.

The crime rate in New York City rose through the 1960s and '70s and beyond. In 1967, two years after Lindsay took office, there were 746 homicides in the city. In 1990 there were 2,245. To turn this deadly trend around, the city and its police commissioner initiated their "broken windows" policy. Instead of looking the other way at petty crime, law enforcement concentrated on it in the belief that preventing small crimes would make criminals rethink committing more serious offenses. In 2016 the city saw 335 murders—a historic turnaround.

The broken windows concept of law enforcement was first described in 1982 by criminologist George Kelling and social scientist James Q. Wilson after Kelling accompanied beat cops on the streets of Newark, New Jersey. Kelling noticed the police enforced low-level misbehavior that upset "local norms of order," whether stopping panhandlers or telling loiterers to move along. Kelling and Wilson believed communities where public disorder is allowed to continue tended to go into a "spiral of decline." If the public perceives an area is unsafe, they avoid it, abandoning it to petty criminals. As begging and vandalism increase, lawbreakers realize they can operate in that area without consequences. The neighborhood declines, businesses and residences who can, move away, and the neighborhood is lost.

The first test of broken windows policing was in 1984 on the New York subway system, which had been taken over by graffiti vandals. Within five years, the problem was solved and subway ridership blossomed. The theory went citywide in 1994 under Mayor Rudolph Giuliani and Police Commissioner William Bratton, beginning with a focus on rampant turnstile jumping. Giuliani believed ignoring fare beaters led them to believe obeying the law was unimportant. Commissioner Bratton had these petty thieves arrested rather than waiting for them to commit more serious crimes.

Seeing offenders arrested made it clear that citizens would be protected and criminals held accountable. As an added bonus, many fare thieves turned out to possess illegal handguns or be wanted for serious crimes including rape and murder. Now they were off the streets.

The broken windows effect spread to cleaning trash and graffiti off the streets, closing sex shops and strip joints, and revitalizing business improvement districts. Felony arrests went down because criminals were behind bars on misdemeanor charges. The prison population decreased because there were fewer crimes. Between 1993 and 1997, murders declined 60 percent, dropping to the lowest level in thirty years.

In spite of its success, broken windows policing had its critics who claimed it was racist. Giuliani and his successor as mayor, Michael Bloomberg, countered that the policy saved thousands of lives, most of them young black and Latino males. Far more than residents of well-to-do neighborhoods, people in the Bronx and Harlem have been the strongest proponents and beneficiaries of diligent police work. If many of the suspects were black and Hispanic, so were the neighbors who reported the crimes and reaped the benefits of quick police action. According to Heather MacDonald, who has written widely on policing policies, the biggest threat facing minorities in New York City is not "overpolicing" but "de-policing."

The election of Bill de Blasio as mayor in 2014 brought a sea change in the city's approach to law enforcement. He discouraged prosecution of petty crimes, decriminalizing turnstile jumping (ironically), public urination, and other "quality-of-life" crimes. District attorneys increasingly refused to pursue misdemeanor cases, especially drug offenses. Bail reform made it hard for judges to keep even repeat offenders locked up. Between January 1 and August 9, 2021, homicides were up 29 percent from the year earlier. Writing in the *New York Post*, Michael Goodwin observed, "We have twice proven that broken-windows policing works, first by using it and then by abandoning it."

Professor Eugene O'Donnell of the John Jay College of Criminal Justice noted that over de Blasio's term his "impact on public safety and the NYPD has been catastrophic. There's no other word for it."

Along the way de Blasio also had his share of scandals and missteps, including a school reform plan abandoned after two years and $773 million, and a much-derided $1.5 billion mental health program headed by his wife, an English major.

De Blasio's successor, former police captain Eric Adams, promised during his campaign to make New York City safer and better. Yet crime has skyrocketed since Mayor Adams took office. In 2022 reported felonies were up more than 20 percent over the year before, while major crimes—murder, robbery, grand larceny, car theft, and rape—were up more than 22 percent. Shoplifting was up 45 percent over 2021, even though merchants increasingly do not even bother to report it. Misdemeanor offenses hit an eight-year high. These figures are driven by legislative reforms eliminating bail or jail time for many criminals which makes prosecution more difficult and less likely to win a conviction. In poll after poll, crime ranks as New York residents' number one concern.

There were improvements in 2022, including a near 20 percent drop in transit crime following state aid that paid for more police overtime and a 20 percent drop in shooting incidents following a $1.5 million investment in gun violence prevention. Still, overall budget cuts along with legislative changes produced a 46 percent rise in crime over the two years ending in April 2023, including a 45 percent increase in robbery, 54 percent rise in grand larceny, and a 91 percent jump in auto theft.

The trend toward cities advancing criminals' rights to the detriment of public safety has been going on for years. As happened in Detroit, cities whose law enforcement policies make its people feel unsafe have seen an exodus of residents who obey the law, pay taxes, create jobs, volunteer for Little League, and attract similar citizens as new neighbors. Their places are taken by unemployed and often unemployable homeless criminals who do not pay taxes, do not build businesses or anything else, and transform an area into a dangerous, filthy urban camp.

Everyone in a society deserves equal treatment and equal opportunity. The challenge comes when local governments redirect their focus and resources away from protecting the people whose industry, commitment, and sense of responsibility make civil society possible. This trend accelerated dramatically after the death of George Floyd allegedly at the hands of Minneapolis police on May 25, 2020. Floyd reportedly bought cigarettes at a convenience store with a counterfeit bill. In arresting him, an officer subdued him by putting his knee on Floyd's neck for more than nine minutes as the suspect begged for air, went unconscious, and died, a grisly scene posted on the Internet. Medical examiner Andrew Baker said Floyd died of "severe underlying heart disease," which impaired him to the point he could not withstand police restraint.

Though Floyd's official autopsy "revealed no physical findings that support a diagnosis of traumatic asphyxia or strangulation," and although Floyd reportedly had fentanyl, methamphetamine, and cannabinoids in his system and showed symptoms of coronavirus, hypertension, and arteriosclerosis as well as heart disease, the medical examiner ruled the death a homicide, specifically noting the finding was "not a legal determination of culpability or intent."

Floyd, who was black, died in the custody of a white police officer. In the short term, news of Floyd's death set off riots in cities across America. Over the long term, it prompted wide-ranging accusations of police brutality and racism that accelerated and intensified the movement in some cities to defund the police, reduce or eliminate cash bail, raise prosecution thresholds, lower conviction rates, and limit what the police could do to fight crime on the street.

After Floyd's death, numerous cities recast their criminal justice systems in the name of racial equality. Three representative examples of this trend, Portland, Seattle, and San Francisco, have seen crime rates soar, workers and businesses despair, and residents move away to safer places, leaving the cities to be picked over by criminals, vagrants, and now massive numbers of illegal aliens.

Three months after Floyd died, Greg Goodman, co-president of the Downtown Development Group in Portland, Oregon, wrote to the mayor and city council that companies were leaving the city because of "the lawlessness you are endorsing" by allowing anti-police protests and riots to go on seemingly unchecked.

Goodman wrote that companies including Daimler Trucks, Airbnb, Banana Republic, Microsoft, and Google were leaving or planning to leave the area. "You aren't sweeping the streets," he told the mayor and council, "needles are all over the place, garbage cans are broken and left open, glass from car windows," and accused them of neglecting their duties "as elected city officials to keep our city safe and clean."

Portland storeowner Marcy Landolfo made headlines when she permanently closed her Rains PDX clothing store after fifteen break-ins over a year and a half and ruinous losses due to shoplifting. "Our city is in peril," she wrote. "Small businesses (and large) cannot sustain doing business in our city's current state. We have no protection, or recourse, against the criminal behavior that goes unpunished." Landolfo said she was closing her store due to "unrelenting criminal behavior coupled with escalating safety issues for our employees."

Homicides in Portland rose 58 percent in 2020 over the previous year and were up 54 percent in 2021 over 2020.

In response to Rains PDX closure, the mayor's office said they "worked to increase funding" for grants to repair damaged businesses, "strategized" about retail theft, and were working to "streamline the permitting process" for adding more lighting to storefronts. No mention of any change to the city's law enforcement policies.

In December 2022, Walmart CEO Doug McMillon warned that the company's stores in Portland could be closed "if authorities don't crack down on prosecuting shoplifting crimes." As theft ran rampant, all Walmart stores in the city were closed in March 2023 with the loss of 850 jobs. Also in March, Cracker Barrel announced it was closing all its Portland area restaurants. That month, postal service records showed over the previous two years, more than 2,600 businesses filed change of address notices to leave downtown zip codes.

Outdoor retailer REI announced in April 2023 they would close their downtown Portland store as soon as their lease was up. A spokesperson explained, in 2022 "REI Portland had its highest number of break-ins and thefts" since the store opened twenty years before, despite recently spending more than $800,000 on security, surveillance, and safety glass. One week there were three break-ins. Though the company spoke with a representative of the mayor's office about the problem, lawlessness increased to the point where it was "overwhelming systems in place."

In Seattle, officials literally turned part of the city over to a violent mob in the aftermath of the Floyd death. The Capitol Hill Occupied Protest (CHOP) movement occupied the police building in the area, set up barricades, and posted armed guards in the summer of 2020. As police abandoned the area to rioters—businesses were destroyed and burned and the protesters committed murder including the death of a sixteen-year-old boy—Mayor Jenny Durkan proclaimed CHOP part of "a summer of love." Homicides that year were up 61 percent over the year before. The mayor and police chief later deleted tens of thousands of text messages in an attempt to conceal the city's actions. In 2023 the city settled a lawsuit filed by business owners charging that city policies "effectively authorized the actions of the

CHOP participants." Plaintiffs were awarded $3.65 million including $600,000 in penalties for deleting the messages, calling it compensation "for the City's mishandling of CHOP that resulted in a significant increase in crime and even loss of life."

Seattle public schools have been losing students at twice the state average. Though general enrollment is down because there are fewer children in the state, public school enrollment dropped more than 6 percent between 2019 and 2022, while Catholic school enrollment increased 6 percent during the same period. According to the Center for Reinventing Public Education at Arizona State University, private school enrollment in Seattle was up 10 percent per year by comparison, homeschool enrollment was up 27 percent per year, and charter school enrollment up 28 percent per year.

In 2023 the school district started laying off employees, announcing their deficit had grown to $131 million. Budgets have increased and student enrollment has declined every year since 2013. High living costs and the aftermath of the pandemic have sent local families looking for other solutions. The reasons for public schools' decline in particular include overworked teachers, insufficient infrastructure, poor test scores (30 percent of children in 2021 performed at grade level in math), and parents who are "frustrated with the district's overemphasis on social justice issues at the expense of core curriculum lessons."

San Francisco is another famous and beautiful city transformed by a change in policing tactics. In March 2023, resident Jenny Chan described how the historic and picturesque farmer's market was overrun with homeless drug addicts, driving farmers and their customers away. "People are leaving," she observed. "Businesses are closing down." Absent efforts by police to keep vendors and shoppers safe, farmers were afraid to sell at the market because it was too dangerous. Some of the few vendors remaining were selling stolen merchandise.

Two months later, Nordstrom announced it would close its two San Francisco stores as soon as their leases were up because of "the dynamics of the downtown San Francisco market." The store's landlord noted the closure "underscores the deteriorating situation in downtown San Francisco. A growing number of retailers and businesses are leaving the area due to the unsafe conditions for customers, retailers, and employees, coupled with the fact that these significant issues are preventing economic recovery in the area." The company tried for years to convince the city to do more to protect their property, but faced unremitting "lack of enforcement" of laws by police.

In June 2022, District Attorney Chesa Boudin was recalled by voters for policies including elimination of cash bail and "a soft-handed approach toward drug crimes" that many blamed for the crime wave. About 60 percent of voters supported his ouster for a string of reform-minded policies including ending prosecution of minors as adults, commitment to lowering the jail populations, and becoming the first San Francisco DA ever to file homicide charges against a police officer. Defending his position during a press conference, Boudin declared, "We can't arrest and prosecute our way out of problems." When the city's mayor, London Breed, implored Boudin to prosecute open-air drug dealers, the DA attacked her as "knee-jerk."

Commenting on the recall, Nicole Gelinas wrote in the *New York Post*, "Cities only work when people behave according to common standards—and the de-prosecution movement has proven that absent an external deterrent, enough people will behave hellishly to make life hell for everyone else. . . . People don't want to thread their way through open-air drug marts. They don't want their cars broken into multiple times. They don't want sidewalks, homes and storefronts blocked by aggressive panhandlers. They don't want stores to close because of mass-scale shoplifting." When residents have had enough, they move, abandoning the turf to the law of the jungle.

What San Francisco's law enforcement apparatus did have time to do was fine a pair of senior citizens for setting up a box with free books and a bench for their neighbors. In 2023 the couple, a retired psychologist and attorney, installed the items in order to "share books and knowledge with neighbors," according to *The Wall Street Journal*.

They got the idea after seeing other similar boxes in the city. At first, their only problem was addicts using the bench to shoot up.

After an anonymous complaint, the city Board of Supervisors told the couple they had thirty days to apply for a "Minor Sidewalk Encroachment Permit" to accommodate their book box and bench, at a cost of $1,402. Otherwise the encroachments had to go.

Of all the cities following in Detroit's footsteps, none is more faithful than Jackson, Mississippi. Detroit native Chokwe Antar Lumumba promised to make Mississippi's capital city "the most radical city on the planet" when he was elected mayor in 2017 with 93 percent of the vote. He proposed universal basic income, criminal justice reform, and a resolution of the city's long-running water supply problem that had residents boiling water off and on for more than a decade. The city was losing population and businesses for years by then. Since Lumumba took office, crime is up, population is down, and the city's hopelessly dysfunctional water system still needs $2 billion in repairs. In 2020 Jackson had the second-highest homicide rate per capita in America. In 2021 the city moved into the number one spot, with about one citizen in a thousand killed. Though the number of fatalities declined in 2022 and 2023, Jackson remained the most deadly major city in the nation.

Between 2010 and 2020, Jackson was the only sizeable city in America to lose more people on a percentage basis than Detroit, dropping 11.4 percent to about 154,000. Another 10,000 left between 2020 and 2023 as middle-class families both white and black decamped to the suburbs. Residents have been relocating to surrounding areas like the town of Byram, a dynamic and growing suburb to the south that Jackson has tried unsuccessfully to annex.

In the spring of 2023, with the water problem still unresolved, city trash pickup was interrupted when the mayor and city council could not agree on a service provider. The low-bid company had evaluations that were not up to par according to some council members.

With the council deadlocked in a tie vote, trash collection halted. Residents and businesses had to deal with the problem as best they could.

Local restaurant owner Tim Norris called the situation "absolutely ridiculous. We have all of the problems with crime, potholes, dilapidated buildings, and we are putting our effort and energy into garbage. At the end of the day, it's poor leadership."

Reminiscent of Detroit being taken over by Emergency Manager Kevyn Orr, the Mississippi state legislature passed two laws allowing the state to step in and take over some governmental responsibilities from the troubled city. Governor Tate Reeves and the state lawmakers were convinced Jackson was foundering, the situation was going from bad to worse, and they had to step in and take over from incompetent local leadership. Mayor Lumumba and city leaders countered that this was a racist move to take control of a majority (81 percent) black city by white outsiders.

One legislative act expanded the state-controlled Capitol Police jurisdiction from the immediate vicinity of the state capitol in Jackson to a wider area. The second established a new court district including the capitol area downtown, Jackson State University, and nearby neighborhoods, with the district judge being appointed by the state chief justice. The law also authorized temporary special circuit judges and added staff to public defender and district attorneys' officers to work through a backlog of cases.

Elected leaders in Jackson condemned the move as "a slap in the face of our city." Police Captain Christian Vance flatly declared, "We don't have a crime problem," calling crime statistics a matter of people "not valuing each other and not valuing themselves," adding, "You cannot arrest the problem away." Mayor Lumumba insisted a state takeover "says we don't value your voice." Rather, the mayor continued, "I think it says, 'You're a population that is meant to be controlled, as opposed to being supported.' I think this is a message that says that we don't believe that Black leadership is capable of moving forward for itself."

In response to the governor's move, the NAACP filed a federal lawsuit against the state and the governor, claiming the black citizens of Jackson "need real investment in their infrastructure and complete control over the future of their city."

Black residents reportedly feared state-controlled Capitol Police would not be held accountable for mistreating citizens. Black activists called the plan "ruthlessly racist." At the same time, State Representative Earle Banks, an African American Democrat, believed the state was trying to help its capital city deal with its crime wave. "The people I hear from—constituents, lawyers, doctors, other people—are saying they want more police presence and protection in the city of Jackson," he said.

A federal judge later ruled state officials could expand the patrol territory for Capitol Police and set up a capitol district court. However, the state supreme court struck down approval of special circuit court judges. A federal judge also brought in seasoned utility manager Ted Henifin to head the water department. Henifin set up a private corporation to run the water system and handle billing, repaired broken pipes and valves, and improved bill collection rates, telling residents they should no longer expect city-wide boil water notices. His appointment was opposed by the People's Advocacy Institute, which complained that local citizens should have more input into water system reforms. The Institute is headed by the wife of former water department executive Tariq Abdul-Tawwab, who was fired by Henifin.

Cities failing to protect their people, welcome investment, educate children, and keep their political houses in order are destined for decline. Detroit led the way, and other cities are following them down the path to ruin by adapting the same policies. However, it is not only cities that are subject to Detroiting. States do it too. Some of the most stark and illuminating examples of success and failure in governing today are found not by comparing city to city, but by comparing state to state, where Detroiting rears its head on a far wider level. ■

Chapter 12

Altered States

"Talking about crime, talking about ideas on how to fight crime was racist. It was easier to just be quiet and move away."
—Karol Markowicz, journalist
and former New Yorker, 2023

▨ ▨ ▨

STATE GOVERNMENTS have the same choices to make about crime, schools, taxation, and public trust as those in city hall. And like city leaders, state legislatures may choose Detroit's path or another one.

As briefly mentioned earlier, a comparison between New York and Florida puts these different approaches in high relief.

The Empire State and the Sunshine State have roughly the same population, with New York hosting an estimated 19.5 million and Florida with 22 million in round numbers. New York's top state and local combined income tax rate is more than 14 percent, with the wealthiest 1 percent of residents paying almost half the total of all income taxes paid. Florida has no state income tax. The 2023 state budget for New York was $229 billion. The annual budget for Florida that year was $117 billion including a $350 million reserve

> *"He who walks with wise men will be wise, but the companies of fools will suffer harm."*
> —Proverbs 13:20

for public schools, $1.4 billion in tax breaks, a 5 percent raise for government workers, and a projected surplus of $13.5 billion.

While New York endures a dangerous and expensive increase in crime, Florida has cracked down on illegal immigration, made it easier for qualified residents to own guns, and instituted the death penalty for child rape. In April 2023, Miami Mayor Francis Suarez lauded the fact that in an environment where crime was skyrocketing in many cities, Miami had its lowest per capita homicide rate since 1964. The reason, he explained, was Miami's elected officials' belief "that the rule of law and public safety are the foundations of a free and prosperous society; versus another type of cities where elected officials fail to uphold the law, refuse to enforce the law, and blame those who follow the law, from police to small businesses, as the causes of crime."

That year Miami had its largest police force ever, producing a historic low in crime as the city "worked with community partners and law enforcement to ensure that every crime is prosecuted, every victim is protected, and every case commands the best technology to convict criminals."

Mayor Suarez continued, "The defunding of police by elected officials across the country has made us less safe and less free. It excuses violent crime and the destruction of property. When laws are not enforced or not enforced robustly, it creates space for a relatively small, concentrated group of criminals to unleash a great deal of violent crime."

According to the legislative budget, Florida spent $8,648 per student on education in 2023. The state also makes every student eligible for private school vouchers regardless of income. *Public School Review* reports New York's 2022 spending at $26,190 per pupil. Alternatives to public schools have faced opposition in the state from unions, politicians, activists, and other critics over the years. Though New York outspent Florida three-to-one, a 2022 ranking of top high schools in America by *U. S. News & World Report* show 41 percent of Florida high schools ranked in the top quarter of schools nationally, while the figure for New York schools was 32 percent.

New York is a state with high crime rates, problematic public schools, some of the highest taxes and rents in the nation, and a tendency to make decisions for its residents the state feels residents cannot make on their own (such as a recent proposed ban on natural gas in new buildings). Florida has none of those inclinations.

In 2019 New York lost $9 billion in adjusted gross income over the year before. In 2020, as the pandemic surged, the year-over-year loss rose to $19.5 billion. The figure for 2021 was $24.5 billion, ten billion of which went straight to Florida as part of their $39.2 billion gain in resident income in 2021. The exodus from New York has been underway for years—in 2020 the state lost a seat in the House because of its population decline while Florida gained one.

The governor of New York should not be surprised. Reminiscent of Coleman Young's adversarial attitude toward Detroit's white voters in the 1970s and Lori Lightfoot in 2020 telling constituents if they were not going to vote for her they ought to stay home, Governor Kathy Hochul told the state's 5.4 million Republicans they should "jump on a bus and head down to Florida where you belong, OK? You are not New Yorkers." In 2022 New York had the greatest population decline of any state in the country. The average annual income of departing New Yorkers was over $100,000. Two thousand millionaires moved out of Manhattan during the pandemic, along with the money they spent and the jobs they provided. As happened in Detroit, taxes go up, high earners leave, and the lower-income remainder are left to struggle with declining services and still higher taxes.

In her inaugural address on New Year's Day 2023 following re-election, Governor Hochul said the state must "reverse the trend of people leaving our state." Yet her legislative agenda has been focused not on changing the policies driving productive residents away, but on legislation requiring people convicted of hate crimes to undergo sensitivity training and enhancing opportunities to teach about diversity, equity, and inclusion. Though polling has shown high taxes are historically the main reason New Yorkers leave the state, lower taxes do not appear to be under discussion. The top income tax rate in the state went from 12.7 percent to 14.8 percent in 2021.

Karol Markowicz has written for *Time, USA Today,* the *New York Post, The Observer,* and other major publications. She emigrated to New York City from the Soviet Union in 1978. She married, had three children, and built her dream home in Brooklyn. The George Floyd riots shook her, she said, but not nearly as much as the response from health officials who otherwise shut the city down during Covid "saying that the protests were OK or the politicians covering for the destruction of cities across the country with woke platitudes."

Open-ended mask mandates and school restrictions prompted her family to rent a house in Florida and enroll their children in local public school. "For nearly five months, we lived a life New Yorkers like us could not imagine. The kids went to school every day. We went out to dinner. We never wore masks outdoors. It was normal and normal was glorious."

During her Florida stay she interviewed Governor Ron DeSantis. "He said words my New York leaders would not say," she reported. He talked about putting children first and how important it was to him that schools open. He was ready to "fight for these kids."

"Meanwhile," Markowicz noted, "in New York, the politicians were also fighting . . . to give Teachers Unions whatever they wanted at the expense of kids."

After school was out, the family returned home to Brooklyn. When New York schools began in the fall of 2021, masks still were required, even outside. Markowicz's children were chided for wearing masks improperly in class, and one of them struggled to develop verbal skills because he could not make himself understood or understand his teacher.

Crime was getting worse. Her neighbors still had "Defund the Police" signs in their windows. "Police were bad and crime, well, did it even exist? Talking about crime was racist, talking about ideas on how to fight crime was racist. . . . It was easier to just be quiet and move away."

The Markowicz family is one who took Governor Hochul's advice and headed south. In the wake of the governor's change of heart in asking people to stay even as those 2,000 millionaires voted with their feet, the writer concluded, "These millionaires didn't leave 'in search of lower costs and opportunities elsewhere,' they left because of her leadership."

California and Texas, the nation's most populous states, are growing in different directions. Between July 2021 and July 2022, Texas gained about 470,000 people while California lost around 113,000. The trend has been ongoing for years: after the 2020 census reapportionment California lost a seat in the House of Representatives for the first time ever while Texas gained two seats. Residents are leaving California for the Lone Star State and elsewhere because California has embraced Detroiting for years, doubling down in the wake of George Floyd's death and the pandemic to accelerate their turn toward high crime and high taxes.

Discussion of crime in California quickly turns to Proposition 47, a law passed by voters in 2014 that downgraded some theft and drug crimes from felonies to misdemeanors in the name of criminal justice reform. At the time the ACLU claimed the law would reduce "barriers that many people with low-level, non-violent felony conviction face to becoming stable and productive citizens, such as lack of employment, housing and access to assistance programs and professional trades."

California state assemblyman Kevin Kiley is one Californian who now believes results of the law prove it was a terrible mistake. "Voters were egregiously misled about what this would do," he said. Crime in California has increased dramatically since then. In a 2021 survey, the National Retail Federation reported Los Angeles and the San Francisco Bay were the nation's top two areas for organized retail theft.

The threshold for felony theft was raised by Proposition 47 from $400 to $950. As a result, Kiley says thieves now go into stores with calculators. "They'll add up the value of what they're stealing because they know as long as it's under $950, they might as well wave to the security camera on the way out. They know there's going to be no consequences for that."

Higher crime rates embolden other criminals, creating a cause-and-effect cycle with major retailers such as Nike, Nordstrom, Whole Foods, and Walgreens either abandoning high-crime areas or instituting new security measures including putting merchandise behind locked cases and hiring extra guards.

In March 2023, CNN reporter Kyung Lah and a news crew went to San Francisco to report on crime in the city. While they were recording an interview, smash-and-grab robbers broke into their rental car and stole their bags, despite having professional security on the scene.

San Francisco district supervisor Joel Engardio, recently elected to replace his more progressive predecessor, declared, "San Francisco, the most liberal place in America, is saying 'enough.' We want safe streets. We want good schools. That should tell anyone—pay attention."

Attitudes toward homelessness have had a major impact on crime. Proposition 47 and other legislation have made it difficult or practically impossible for police to remove homeless encampments. Between 2019 and 2022, homelessness in Sacramento increased 67 percent. More and more violent crimes and theft have been due to mentally unstable felons allowed to roam the streets and campsites instead of being locked up. Over the same period, homicides in Sacramento were up 31 percent and robberies up 42 percent. In the first quarter of 2022, rapes were up 92 percent over the previous year.

By 2022 California, with 12 percent of the nation's population, had 48 percent of America's homeless thanks in part to authorities' hands-off policies allowing homeless encampments and refusal to arrest or prosecute many theft and drug offenses. San Diego Court Attorney Summer Stephan identified a solid link between homelessness and crime, reporting 98 percent of homeless suspects cited for crimes had two or more new cases filed against them. Homeless people were more than 500 times as likely to commit felony-level offenses as the average population. The cause, Stephan said, was untreated mental health and addiction disorders and "laws preventing law enforcement from deterring petty crime and steering homeless individuals into treatment before lawless behavior accelerates."

Stephan continued, "We have to address mental and substance abuse with a tough-love approach which means supporting and empowering our law enforcement agencies to actually enforce the law." She joins the growing chorus of Californians demanding their elected officials "make crime illegal again."

Changes in law and policing also preceded a massive increase in prostitution in California. A new law went into effect January 1, 2023, repealing a previous law that banned loitering with the intent to engage in prostitution. The law's sponsor, State Senator Scott Wiener, argued it would protect transgender prostitutes who he said were targeted by police based not on what they did but on how they looked. Advocates said it would reduce the criminalization of sex trafficking and protect suspects from the stigma of arrest, difficulty in securing employment, threat of deportation, and other consequences.

As a result, women wearing thongs—or less—stand on street corners in broad daylight, pimps follow mothers taking their children to school, and businesses and shoppers fear for their safety. San Francisco Supervisor Hillary Ronen told the *San Francisco Chronicle*, "It's absolutely out of control and dangerous." State assembly leader James Gallagher said in a statement, "California Democrats' policy of legalizing crime is creating more victims by the hour. . . . Families and businesses are moving out, while human traffickers are moving in."

Los Angeles police said the law handcuffed them from cracking down on the sex trade. Under the new statute, officers can make an arrest only if a suspect admits to prostitution. Emboldened by the new limits on police action, prostitution rings infiltrated neighborhoods, bringing robberies, shootings, aggravated assaults, and other crimes.

Oakland police said the new law "now hinders officers' enforcement across the state." In response, Oakland City Council President Nikki Fortunato Bas countered that her response has been "a comprehensive approach" that included law enforcement and is focused on "the exploiters." The city, she said, would deploy more "violence interrupters" on the streets and add crime prevention initiatives such as better lighting and speed bumps.

Compared with California, Texas has taken a simpler and more pragmatic approach to crime prevention: they arrest criminals. State law bans homeless encampments on public property, punishable by a fine of up to $500.

In the state capital of Austin, the city council had rolled back penalties for homeless encampments but in May 2021, after two years, Austin residents voted to reinstate bans on public camping as well as limitations on panhandling and other activities. A month later the statewide ban was signed into law. The statute requires officers to make "reasonable efforts" to direct the homeless to medical or mental health services and shelters before citing them.

To address prostitution, Texas became the first state in the nation to make buying sex a felony. The 2021 law was designed to shift punitive blame away from prostitutes, many of whom are themselves victims. The law also expanded felony charges against recruiting minors and offered pretrial diversions allowing suspected prostitutes to avoid jail time. The author of the legislation, state representative Senfronia Thompson, said, "We know the demand is the driving force behind human trafficking. If we can curb or stamp out the demand end of it, then we can save the lives of numerous persons." The Criminal Justice Institute at the University of Houston Law School observed the law was "a rethinking of the traditional supply side in prosecutions that tend to target the women . . . and not the buyers."

A key factor in the incidence of homelessness in California, and a chief reason why the state is losing population, is California has some of the highest costs of living in the nation. Developers struggle to build affordable housing because of the heavy cost burdens of environmental regulations, affordable housing mandates, labor laws, permitting hurdles, high taxes, and high land costs.

The same cost structure makes it difficult for middle- and lower-income earners to stay and encourages highly taxed, high-income residents to leave. The California income tax is a graduated scale, with 1 percent on the first dollar of individual income up to $10,099. A salary of $75,000 per year is taxed at 9.3 percent. Over about $677,000 the rate is 12.3 percent with another percent added to incomes over $1 million. The top half-percent of filers pay 40 percent of all state income tax revenue collected. The top 1 percent pay about half the total.

Texas has no state income tax.

The average price of a house in California is $790,000. In Texas it is $335,000.

The fuel tax per gallon in California is 63 cents for gasoline and 88 cents for diesel. The tax in Texas is 20 cents for both.

In July 2023, Texas celebrated a trifecta of success: *Business Facilities* magazine rated its business climate the best in the nation; it added more new jobs than any other state for the twelfth consecutive month; and according to a survey of leading CEOs in *Chief Executive* magazine, it was the best state in America for business—based on business climate, workforce, and quality of life—for the nineteenth year in a row.

Because of its fiscal conservatism, coupled with unanticipated revenues from new residents moving into the state, Texas reported a surplus of $32.7 billion for 2023 and approved a biennial budget of $321.3 billion (Texas budgets cover two years). This surplus is larger than the total budgets of twenty-four states and about the size of the budget of South Carolina. The state constitution requires the Texas legislature to pass a balanced budget. Thanks to the historic growth in tax collection, the Lone Star State took in more than a thousand dollars extra for every resident.

While California projected a nearly $100 billion surplus for 2023, sharp declines in tax revenues turned that figure into a $22.5 billion deficit. Budget analysts warned that the shortfall could be even greater. Revenues were coming off a peak built on Covid payments from the federal government and high capital gains taxes. At $297 billion, the California budget is the largest in the nation.

Between April 2020 and July 2022, California lost more than half a million residents. Setting aside births and deaths and counting only people moving in or out, the net loss was more than 870,000. Eighty thousand of them, a hundred a day, moved to Texas. The decline was part of the reason why California's January tax revenue in 2023 was $14 billion below the same month in 2022.

In February 2023, a *Los Angeles Times* opinion piece claimed that although California had lost residents there was no population crisis. The writers believed "there are more opportunities in California's relative youth and the state's ability to attract immigrants than there are alarm bells." They laid blame for the decline on Covid, "Trump-era policies," and the cost of living, which prompted low and middle-income Californians to leave, replaced by newcomers who "tend to have higher incomes and more education."

Three months later the *Times* reported higher-income Californians were moving to lower-tax states. "For years, we denied that," veteran columnist George Skelton acknowledged. "Maybe it wasn't even happening. But it definitely is now." The story referenced a Public Policy Institute of California report that higher-income residents were leaving and that the wealthier they were, the more likely they were to move to one of eight states with no income tax [Alaska, Florida, Nevada, New Hampshire, South Dakota, Tennessee, Texas, Wyoming].

When asked about the high cost of living, California Governor Gavin Newson responded, "California is not a high-tax state. . . . There's a lazy punditry that California is a high-tax state." Rather it is "the ninth-most tax-friendly state for the middle class." This though the state's 9.3 percent rate for a single filer making $66,000 per year and for a married couple earning $133,000 is the highest rate in the nation for those incomes.

In the same way Jackson is a reflection in miniature of the path Detroit has taken over the past generation, Mississippi mirrors the action of California, New York, Illinois, and other declining states. Reporting in early 2020, just before the pandemic hit, the Mississippi Center for Public Policy noted although the South generally was increasing in population, Mississippi and Louisiana were declining.

The reason, the article concluded, was because Mississippi did not welcome people and businesses the way other Southern states did. People move from one place to another "because of opportunity. And there are policies . . . that would put Mississippi ahead of the curve," in making it more nationally competitive if they were implemented.

Over-regulation was one problem. "Mississippi has more than 117,000 regulations that cut across every sector of the economy," especially high-value businesses such as healthcare and technology. Mississippi should not require professionals licensed in their state to re-certify in order to work in Mississippi. "Today 19 percent of Mississippians need a license to work. It was 5 percent in the 1950s. . . . This serves to lower competition and increase costs for consumers, while not providing those consumers with a better product. . . . we could create a much bigger economic pie if we encouraged more creative disruption, competition, and risk-taking.

"Not that long ago, Charlotte and Meridian were exactly the same size. Economies are dynamic and once they get momentum, amazing things can happen." ("Not that long ago" is slightly wide of the mark but the comparison makes a powerful point. According to U.S. Census figures, in 1890 Charlotte had about 11,500 residents to around 10,600 for Meridian. In 2023 Charlotte was home to an estimated 885,663 people, making it the fifteenth largest city in America; the population of Meridian was 33,222, good for 1,382nd place.)

The Mississippi Center for Public Policy also recognized the state's economically unhealthy dependence on public money, and how the government does not generate income but only redistributes it. "We have the third highest level of economic dependence on federal grants-in-aid in the nation (43%) and the fourth highest level of our economy driven by the public sector in the country (55%). Politicians, state agency directors, and government bureaucrats cannot create the economic growth we need."

What the politicians and policymakers could do, however, is "create an environment that allows and encourages private economic activities."

While Detroiting has produced steep declines in population and business revenue over the years in some places, others have thrived. Turning the focus back to the municipal level, it is clear some cities got it right. These success stories demonstrate how responsible, enlightened leadership has guided some cities to new heights of prosperity in spite of lost industry, missed opportunities, or past mistakes. They rebounded from economic setbacks by scrambling for new business, presenting a business-friendly environment, and investing themselves in their city's future. Many of them, at some point, faced the truth about corruption and other barriers to success, replacing finger-pointing with rooting out the trouble and moving ahead. They are informed by the past but not bound by it.

They set out to become places where residents felt safe, welcome, and free to pursue their dreams. And they succeeded. Noteworthy examples include a mill town that survived the loss of American textile jobs to become a world-class financial center; an isolated desert community that turned a World War II government program into a powerhouse international technology hub; and an inland cotton shipping port that survived a series of setbacks to take Detroit's place as the fourth largest city in the nation.

Chapter 13

Success Cities

"A permissive society is not a civilized society; it's a decaying one."
—Francis Suarez, Mayor of Miami, 2023

■ ■ ■

WHILE NEWS of America's urban decline claims the headlines, many cities are nevertheless growing and optimistic, looking to the future with anticipation and hope. Some cities with long, troubled pasts in the mold of Detroit have recovered their footing and today offer great opportunities for families and businesses.

Akron, Ohio, once the Rubber Capital of the World, saw its core industry disappear yet limited its population loss to 35 percent and has re-cast the city as an international center for polymer research. Though Pittsburgh, Pennsylvania, eventually lost half its residents after the collapse of its legendary steel industry, the city has evolved as a center for healthcare, technology, and education; it has seen property values rise in recent years and limited its population decline between 2000 and 2010 to less than 1 percent. Philadelphia, Pennsylvania, the largest city in America in 1776, has adapted to change over more than two and a half centuries to remain a strong sixth in population according to the 2020 census.

"Go to the ant, o sluggard, observe her ways and be wise."
—Proverbs 6:6

Smaller, newer cities have made decisions that attract residents, even within regions surrounded by decline. In a state mired in a crisis of homelessness, the city of Coronado, California, has no homeless people. Zero. As Mayor Richard Bailey explained, statewide policies tolerating "destructive" behavior were "enabling this situation to increase." When police failed to stop theft, panhandling, public drunkenness, and other disruptive behavior, the behavior became worse.

Mayor Bailey said his city works with police and a homeless service provider to give people the help they need. City funds are available to help them "get back on their feet," but Coronado has a no-tolerance policy for violating the law.

Law enforcement and other officials "make it very clear that we don't tolerate encampments along our sidewalks, and we don't tolerate other code violations such as being drunk in public or urinating in public. . . . An individual either chooses to get help or they end up leaving."

The mayor continued, "Although there are a myriad of reasons that people end up homeless, they eventually only fall into two camps—those that want help and those that do not. . . . Those that are refusing to get help . . . shouldn't be granted additionally the ability to break laws."

Another island of relative calm in America's troubled urban landscape is the city of Miami, Florida. As cited previously, in April 2023 Miami Mayor Francis Suarez published an essay saying the current surge in urban crime reflects a modern tale of two cities, "between cities that invested in their police versus cities that defunded their police." In Miami, Suarez continued, "We increased funding for our police," and saw crime drop "to one of its lowest levels in Miami's history . . . [W]e've also invested in our online presence to address misinformation and forms of violence. . . .

"A permissive society is not a civilized society; it's a decaying one."

Mayor Suarez added, "The successive waves of crime and rioting across American cities are unacceptable and inexcusable. The solution is simple: invest in your police, invest in better policing, and hold everyone accountable. . . . This wave of crime must not be the wave of the future. In Miami, we have a template that works."

A more detailed look at three cities gives a clearer view of successful cities run well. Charlotte, North Carolina, grew from a pin dot on the map in 1890 to a major financial center with a population today approaching a million. Phoenix, Arizona, equally obscure at the turn of the twentieth century, is today the fifth largest city in the country and also one of the fastest-growing. Houston, Texas, the forty-fifth largest American city in 1920 with under 140,000 residents, is now the fourth largest city in the nation with a population of 2.3 million.

Charlotte

Between 2004 and 2014, Charlotte, North Carolina, was the fastest growing city in the United States. With a population of nearly 850,000 in 2020, it is the nation's fifteenth largest city and after New York City, the second biggest banking hub in the nation. In 2021 it was ranked the third best place in America to start a business based on tax climate, business survival rate, education level of residents, housing costs as a percentage of income (19.9 percent), unemployment (4.4 percent), and other factors.

Charlotte's first business boom was in mining. It was the largest gold-producing region in the nation until the 1849 California gold rush destroyed the local mining trade. Charlotte re-focused its efforts and became a regional cotton processing and railroad hub. After the Civil War, local businessmen realized there was money to be made by spinning and weaving fabric themselves rather than shipping their cotton out of town. The first textile factories opened in 1881. Owners then discovered there was even greater profit in lending money to "aspiring industrialists" rather than running their own textile companies. By 1910 Charlotte was the biggest city in the state.

At the turn of the twentieth century, two banks led the way in building a base for the financial services industry, Commercial

National Bank (later Bank of America) and Union National Bank (later Wachovia/Wells Fargo). Charlotte's civic leaders saw the huge potential for banking and related industries. They nurtured these and other institutions into enormous international giants by "thoughtful and light" state regulations. As the UNC Charlotte Urban Institute reported, "The regulatory strategy was partially a result of the state's historic poverty—North Carolina was simply too poor to place the same limits on bank expansion as were found in other states following the Great Depression. . . . Banking not only provided capital to local industry, but it also served as our first example of local knowledge industries successfully competing in national markets." International banks including Toronto-Dominion Bank and the Bank of London now have major operations in the city.

Another need bankers had beyond business-friendly regulation was easy access. Bankers traveled a lot by air and wanted frequent service to a wide range of destinations. Charlotte Douglas International Airport today has direct flights to nearly 200 destinations, far more than a typical airport serving a city the size of Charlotte.

World-class financial services and air connections in turn have attracted international companies including Honeywell, Dole Foods, Lowe's, and Credit Karma.

Journalist Jeremy Markovich wrote in 2014 about moving from Ohio, where his father, grandfather, and great-grandfather worked in the same steel mill, to Charlotte. "Charlotte was the first place I'd lived where droves of people weren't actively trying to leave," he said. He noted that the remnants of the textile industry were being transformed into apartments and businesses instead of abandoned to decay "like the old steel mills up north."

Markovich observed, "When the mills closed here . . . more banks opened. The interstate banking laws that made Bank of America possible also made Charlotte's incredible growth possible. Steel and cloth are commodities. But money to loan is the secret to success. . . .

"Charlotte seems to quickly find other things to do when its main industry goes bad. Textiles died. Banking arrived. When banks took a hit during the recession, Charlotte decided to call itself an 'energy hub,' and to my amazement, that prophecy is starting to become self-fulfilling. Charlotte is an industry town, but it's nimble enough to change industries when it needs to."

When the industries Charlotte built its economy around— mining, textiles, banking—faltered, the city always found a new source of growth rather than bemoaning the losses of the past. Instead of being left to ruin, historical remnants are repurposed to build for the future as seen today by abandoned mills converted into breweries and other businesses providing local employment, attracting tourists, generating tax revenue, and enhancing the city's value to corporate relocation managers. Its 2023 estimated population of over 900,000 (40 percent white, 36 percent black, 16 percent Hispanic, 7 percent Asian) is poised for further success in the years ahead.

Phoenix

In 1920 Phoenix had a population of 29,000. By 1950 its 105,000 residents earned it 99th place among U.S. cities. Between the 2010 and 2020 census tallies, Phoenix was the fastest-growing large city in the nation, surging more than 11 percent to 1.6 million, passing Philadelphia in 2017 to become America's fifth-largest city. Its phenomenal growth continues, driven by a tradition of searching out every opportunity for the future, always eager to move ahead.

The trait of following up opportunities started early. When Jack Swilling stopped to rest his horses in the Salt River Valley in 1867, he noticed the rich soil turned up by the horses' hooves. This was prime farmland if only it could get enough water. Swilling formed a company to dig an irrigation canal and the next year organized the town of Phoenix, Arizona. In 1886 the town built one of the first municipal electricity-generating plants in America, a steam plant fired by mesquite. The arrival of the railroad in 1887 and the opening in 1911 of the Theodore Roosevelt Dam, dedicated by Roosevelt and the largest masonry dam in the world, gave Phoenix the water to grow cotton, citrus, and other crops and the freight cars to transport them. New Deal programs helped preserve and expand the agricultural infrastructure during the Depression.

In the runup to World War II, the federal government was looking for training and manufacturing sites. In January 1941, the city of Phoenix, eager to attract wartime installations and dollars, bought 1,440 acres nearby and leased it to the War Department for dollar a year to build a pilot training facility. Luke Field, where more than 13,500 pilots trained during the war, became the largest advanced flight training school in the world.

Other military installations went up in the area, bringing more than 12,000 defense jobs to town. Factories ran around the clock and so did Phoenix, with restaurants, theaters, and even swimming pools open twenty-four hours a day to serve workers during their free time. To build housing for this huge inflow of residents, the government partnered with developers including Del Webb, a California native who came to Phoenix as a young man to recover from typhoid fever. During and after the war he built military installations, veterans' hospitals, air bases, and missile silos. His revolutionary Sun City retirement development—30,000 homesites around a lake in the middle of the desert—would later help drive Phoenix's growth as a retirement destination.

City leaders scored a major win by bringing Luke Field to the area, as well as the other war-related expansion that followed, with virtually free land and a persuasive sales pitch that it would be hard for the enemy to bomb anything in the Arizona desert. They soon responded to another demand from military brass: clean up your town.

In the early 1940s, Phoenix was an openly corrupt city. Officials looked the other way at gambling and prostitution because "fines" from these ventures brought money into the city's coffers and into its leaders' pockets. The military commanders had their hands full keeping trainees away from venereal disease and/or jail until they were ready for combat.

The crisis boiled over on November 26, 1942, when a black soldier was shot while resisting arrest after a fight. When other black soldiers challenged the authorities, military police began rounding them up. About 150 soldiers panicked and ran, pursued by military police in armored personnel carriers. Over 180 soldiers were arrested and three men died. Four days later the military declared Phoenix off-limits. Venereal disease at the base had tripled in four months. "The city will stay out-of-bounds until it has become untenable for prostitutes," declared a military statement, demanding "an immediate drive on all loose women . . . no matter who it hurts."

This directive was a disaster for Phoenix businesses. Under intense pressure from the business community, the mayor and city commissioners fired the city manager, clerk, magistrate, and chief of police. Payoffs were no longer acceptable. Three days later, the military lifted its ban.

After the war, Phoenix leaders and businessmen were determined to keep the city's momentum going. Wartime contracts showed they could work with the federal government to build local businesses, and Phoenix wanted to attract more federal projects. They knew from experience that city government had to be transparent and efficient. Industrial and military contractors frowned on local policies that seemed sluggish or inefficient, or that had any tinge of old-fashioned cronyism. In 1947 a group of local businessmen led a successful drive to revise the city charter, allowing a professional city manager to run the government.

To win against other cities for new government business, Phoenix offered low taxes and eliminated many business taxes completely. The city's fortunes got a boost when the state legislature passed a constitutional amendment that guaranteed open shops in Arizona (1946), and repealed state sales tax on products made to sell to the federal government (1955). Only the copper industry, long a key part of the state's economy, remained solidly union, making Arizona wages 10–25 percent lower overall than America's major industrial centers.

The 1950s was the decade when Phoenix took off like a rocket. Many ex-military recruits who trained in the area came back with their families for the sunny weather and cheap housing. Motorola chose Phoenix to build its Military Electronics Division. New hires loved the place. As one Motorola manager explained, "We can run an ad in the trade magazines mentioning three places to work—Phoenix, Chicago and Riverside, in California. We'll draw 25-fold replies for Phoenix compared with other cities. . . . We don't have to pay a premium to get engineers and other skilled employees to live here, either. The premium is free—sunshine."

The only real drawback to life in Phoenix was the blistering hot summers, with average daytime highs above 105 degrees and a scant eight inches of rain a year. Air conditioning conquered that challenge in the 1950s, prompting a Motorola executive to note, "refrigeration cooling has transformed Phoenix into a year-round city of delightful living."

Other companies large and small kept Phoenix's technology wave growing, including General Electric and Kaiser Aircraft & Electronics. When representatives from Sperry Rand hesitated about building in the area, a group of Phoenix businessmen raised $650,000 in seventy-two hours to buy a plant site and improve the regional Deer Valley airport. The company made the move. In competition with Tucson and other alternatives, Phoenix took advantage of every opportunity to give prospective employers what they wanted. By the 1960s, nearly 700 new businesses had settled in Phoenix, representing 70 percent of new manufacturing in Arizona. From 1950 to 1960, the city's population rose 311 percent from 106,818 to 439,170. Certainly, air conditioning contributed to the surge. However, all that cool air fell equally upon Tucson, Albuquerque, and dozens of other cities in the desert Southwest. Without the city's other advantages, air conditioning alone would not have made Phoenix the economic powerhouse it became.

Today Phoenix still works tirelessly to determine what prospective employers and residents want and then give it to them. To compete for new business in the twenty-first century, cities have to be technologically savvy and provide the latest in communication innovation and connectivity. In 2019 the Greater Phoenix Economic Council (GPEC), the Arizona Institute for Digital Progress, Arizona State University, and the Maricopa Association of Governments launched The Connective, a collaborative project to develop and promote connectivity, mobility, equity, and sustainability in order to attract businesses.

Its work paid off. Nike sited a new facility in the area after a multistate search, bringing 500 jobs and a $185 million investment. Microsoft opened three new data centers. GPEC president Chris Camacho says Phoenix gives these and other businesses the strong labor supply, strong infrastructure, and "cool tech vibe" they want. Cybersecurity companies, software development, and electric vehicle businesses are some of the sectors behind the latest and biggest wave of growth in the city.

"From a legacy standpoint, we are known largely for aerospace and defense, electronics," Camacho notes. "We began shifting to financial services and call centers in the 1990s. Technology-enabled firms are the new wave." Deloitte and Microsoft are two other industry giants basing new security projects in Phoenix.

Phoenix has a strong and growing international presence. In the wake of the United States-Mexico-Canada Agreement of 2020, Phoenix does $16 billion in trade per year with Mexico and $5 billion with Canada. The city has representatives on the ground in the United Kingdom developing new business partnerships. They recently opened an office in Tel Aviv and see strong potential there. The city partners with Arizona State to host international firms and help them get established.

New American and international firms bring billions of dollars and thousands of residents to town. Another large contributor to prosperity is the growing number of businesses relocating to Phoenix from the West Coast. Phoenix Mayor Kate Gallego noted, "The quality of life here is exceptional and combines with smart policies and a welcoming business operating environment." Businesses in California face an uphill burden of high taxes and regulation and political unpredictability. According to the GPEC, there is a 30 percent cost advantage for business moving from California to Phoenix. California income tax is roughly three times what it is in Phoenix. Californians move to Phoenix, the Council reports, "for our great amenity base, affordability and quality of life. And on the police front, our decisions have helped."

One of the few clouds on Phoenix's horizon has been finding enough water to support future growth. With the population expanding and the threat of a cut in Arizona's share of Colorado River water, Phoenix tackled the challenge by building a $280 million pipeline to import water from the Salt and Verde Rivers. Planning began in 2015, so by the time water flow from the Colorado River was reduced by 18 percent in 2022, the pipeline was finished and ready for business. Whatever the next impediment or opportunity, Phoenix stands poised for action.

Houston

Houston is the nation's fourth largest city, the spot where Detroit peaked a hundred years ago. This connection makes Houston's story especially relevant and merits a closer look at its history from a frontier settlement in the newly independent Republic of Texas to the economic powerhouse it is today.

When brothers John K. and Augustus C. Allen founded Houston on the banks of Buffalo Bayou in 1836, they described it as "handsome and beautifully elevated, salubrious and well-watered." A congressman who visited shortly thereafter called it "the most miserable place in the world," while another visitor remembered it as "the greatest sink of dissipation and vice that modern times have known." It was hot, swampy, and isolated. Briefly designated the capital of the Republic of Texas, the settlement was home to Texas President Sam Houston, whose official residence was a two-room log cabin. During Texas's nine years as a sovereign nation—complete with its own currency, navy, legislature, and foreign ambassadors—the small community became a local trading center for cotton and other commodities. Riverboats traveled the bayou between Houston and the bustling port of Galveston on the Gulf of Mexico.

In 1852 the first railroad line in Texas was built from Harrisburg, a few miles from Houston, to Richmond, a distance of thirty-two miles. When Houston businessmen realized the track would bypass them, they levied a civic tax to build a road connecting Houston to the rail line. They would not be denied the enormous opportunity the railroad represented. From the beginning, Houston was a community of visionaries and doers.

In 1882 Houston and New York became the first American cities to build electric power plants. By then Houston was an important regional rail and water transportation center, moving products to Galveston for shipment to the rest of America and the world. Galveston became the biggest cotton shipping port in the nation.

Three events in the first decades of the twentieth century helped position Houston for its tremendous growth and success in the following years. First was a hurricane on September 8, 1900, that destroyed Galveston. Warnings by observers on the ground went unreported by the National Weather Service. Thus, a massive hurricane with winds estimated at 145 miles per hour and a fifteen-foot storm surge flattened the city. At least six thousand people lost their lives, making it the most deadly natural disaster in American history to the present day. Galveston eventually recovered, but its setback gave Houston businessmen an opening to build a seaport of their own.

Before becoming a seaport, however, Houston found a new identity as a center of the oil industry. Discovery of vast fields of easily extracted oil was symbolized by the famous 1901 gusher at Spindletop Hill above a salt dome outside nearby Beaumont. Just as America was becoming a nation of automobiles, Houston became a new focus of the oil and gas business.

The third and most wide-ranging event in Houston history during those years was completing the Houston Ship Channel. Congress first proposed making Houston a seaport by dredging Buffalo Bayou in 1870. For decades the project remained only a concept. Then in 1910, the Houston Chamber of Commerce offered to split the cost with the federal government. Four years later a fifty-two-mile channel carried oceangoing vessels to Houston. By 1930, thanks to its ocean access and massive growth of the oil industry, Houston passed San Antonio to become the state's largest city with a population of almost 300,000.

World War II brought an explosion of job opportunities in oil and chemical production as well as shipbuilding and other manufacturing. Houston grew 55 percent during the 1940s, reaching a population of more than half a million by 1950. In 1948 the city annexed a vast area around its borders, growing from just under seventy-five square miles to 216. By 1955 the metropolitan area had more than a million residents. (Today's city limits enclose 655 square miles, about two-thirds the size of Luxembourg.)

As other states and municipalities began adding income taxes and further cost burdens after the war, Houston attracted even more attention from real estate investors and businesses. There were no state or city income taxes and, unique among the nation's metropolitan areas, no zoning restrictions. The city planning commission recommended zoning in 1929 but found "scant support." Voters rejected a zoning ordinance in 1948, again in 1962, and again in 1993 even after the city council mandated zoning regulations for the first time. Developers were free to build almost anything they wanted without municipal restrictions.

Houston also avoided the racial upheavals that divided and destroyed other communities during the 1960s. One reason was there were no overcrowded concentrations of black citizens like there were in Detroit's Paradise Valley and Black Bottom neighborhoods. Another reason was blacks were a relatively small percentage of the population. Third and most important was the attitude among Houstonians that though they did not believe in integration early on, they did believe in obeying the law.

As historian T. R. Fehrenbach observed of the 1960s attitude, "Texans disapproved of the so-called civil rights movement; few were badly disturbed or frightened by it. . . . The power structure that had grown up in modern Texas had no belief in integration, but even less belief in civil disorder. . . . Law, not popular sentiments, prevailed." Both white and black communities understood this. At the time, Houston was home to more African American millionaires than any other city in the United States. One wealthy black family descended from a slave who made shoes for ten cents a pair before the Civil War.

Fehrenbach added, "Southern social ethos . . . prevented the flight of middle-class blacks from their own people, and prevented much of the destructive ghetto atmosphere of the North."

As with Detroit, there were times when blacks from outside came to Texas to stir up trouble. Unlike in Detroit, the outsiders were unsuccessful. There were "some . . . instances in which Negroes from outside Texas tried to rouse interest in demonstrations or public protests in the 1960s. In virtually every case, the local black power structure was hostile to these and prevented any such action. . . Few Texas leaders on any level were likely to be gripped by the paralysis that agonized and immobilized Northern political structures in the face of riots. . . . Texans by and large obeyed the desegregation and antidiscrimination laws because these were the law."

In 1971, Shell Oil moved its headquarters to Houston, joining the more than 200 major firms that moved headquarters or major divisions to the area during that decade. By then the NASA Manned Spacecraft Center was long-established south of downtown; in 1969 "Houston" was the first word ever spoken from the moon. The city got another economic shot in the arm in the wake of the 1973 Arab oil embargo. The price of petroleum quadrupled in ninety days, fueling a boom leading to further growth and prosperity.

In 1978 *U.S. News & World Report* declared of Houston, "This is not a city, it's a phenomenon—an explosive churning, roaring juggernaut that's shattering traditions as it expands onward and upward with an energy that stuns even its residents."

In 1982 a deep energy recession crushed the local economy, somewhat comparable to the auto industry exiting Detroit. Between 1982 and 1987, nearly one out of six jobs in the Houston area disappeared. Houston's response was to diversify into computers, electronics, healthcare, and other industries not connected to the oil patch. The crown jewel of the health services industry in town today is the Texas Medical Center, the world's largest medical complex with over 50 million square feet and 10 million patient visits a year.

Even during the recession developers kept developing, refusing to give in to an economy that seemed to be in freefall. In 1983, 155 new office buildings were completed. In 1987 the Brown Convention Center opened with over a million square feet of exhibit space (later expanded to 1.8 million). The same year, the Wortham Center was opened for opera and ballet productions, its $66 million cost financed entirely with private donations in defiance of the struggling economy.

During the severe nationwide recession of 2008, Houston endured not only economic challenges but the historic destruction of Hurricane Ike, which cost the Gulf Coast seventy lives and $70 billion in damage. Even so, in 2011 Houston became the first major city to recover its pre-recession employment levels.

By any metric, Houston is a budget-friendly place to live and work. Living expenses are 18 percent lower than average for large metropolitan areas in the country, while San Francisco costs more than twice the average and New York City is almost four times the average. In the first quarter of 2023, office rents in New York and San Francisco were more than $55 per square foot, while the average in Houston was $29.

Race politics have never had the impact on Houston that they have on Detroit and some other cities. It has no racial majority and has been the most racially diverse big city in the U.S. for decades. At the end of 2022, the population was 38.5 percent Hispanic, 33.2 percent Anglo (non-Hispanic white), 16.8 percent African American, 8.0 percent Asian, and 3.5 percent Other.

Like cities of all sizes, Houston had individual communities struggling to keep residents safe and encourage the quality of life they expected. Responding to the situation, in 2005 Mayor Bill White announced Project Hope Houston, "a program designed to inject new life" into six neighborhoods. The aim, Mayor White told an audience of local stakeholders, was to "help create new jobs, improve and protect area schools and attract potential residents who would have previously written off the area."

The problems were the same as faced by neighborhoods across the country, including much of Detroit. While the Motor City was hamstrung by legal, financial, and practical difficulties, Houston focused on eliminating or working around the same issues. "You have these properties that aren't paying taxes to support the schools, and people don't want to move in next door. It's a downward cycle," the mayor said.

White explained that while commitments from the city to make improvements were important, the most effective catalyst for renewal was the people pitching in. "Stakeholders must take the initiative of helping out, instead of relying on government to do all the work. We can give you the instruments," White said, "but if there is no band to play, there won't be any music."

In February 2022, as violence jolted Portland, Minneapolis, Seattle, San Francisco, and other cities after the "defund the police" movement gathered steam, Houston mayor Sylvester Turner put down a marker: there would be no such lawlessness in this city.

Turner admitted the COVID-19 pandemic and a spike in violent crime produced "widespread social anxiety, economic uncertainty, mental health concerns," and other problems leading to "a strained court system plagued by criminal case backlogs that impact the pretrial release and prosecution of violent offenders."

Reminding residents, "we must collaborate as one community to combat our current crime challenge," Turner declared, "Houstonians, it is time to take our city back!" He then announced formation of One Safe Houston with four objectives: 1) violence reduction and crime prevention; 2) crisis intervention, response and recovery; 3) youth outreach opportunities; and 4) key community partnerships.

The key focus was on the city's most violent offenders in the most violent neighborhoods. The project emphasized traffic enforcement and prosecution in high-crime areas, since taking those violators off the streets could keep them from committing violent crimes later on.

The city set aside $5.7 million for overtime pay to put another 125 police officers on the street in these chronic crime hotspots. The program targeted specific nightclubs, convenience stores, and similar places where crime was common.

One Safe Houston included priority prosecution for the 200 most violent offenders currently awaiting trial and a $1.5 million grant to reduce criminal court backlogs. It also emphasized community inter-action with faith-based organizations, town hall discussions, and a long list of outreach programs to establish a comfortable rapport between citizens and the police. "We must . . . engage in the fight against violent crime and continue our legacy as one of the safest major cities in America," Mayor Turner concluded.

While crime reduction programs supported an already successful and respected police department, Houston had a substantial amount of remedial work to do in recent years on its school system. In 2020 the State of Texas filed an injunction to take over the Houston Inde-pendent School District (HISD) for poor performance. While the injunction was temporarily blocked by the district, a former board president, a chief operating officer, and four administrators either pled guilty or were indicted for bribery.

In the aftermath of the pandemic, Houston schools, like others across the country, recorded their worst academic performance scores in nearly two decades. Compared with the last pre-pandemic testing in 2019, Houston eighth-graders fell below 50 percent proficiency in 2022 in the math National Assessment of Educational Progress from nearly 61 percent; they declined from 59 to 56 percent in reading.

Many schools in the city improved their overall performance over the next year or two, with 78 percent earning A or B ratings from the Texas Education Agency, up from 50 percent in 2019. To help schools that still fell short, HISD instituted its RISE (Redesign Innovate Support Empower) program in twenty-four low-performing schools. This program, according to then-superintendent Millard House II, would give every child "access to great schools and programs." RISE put specially selected teachers and administrators in the most troubled classrooms; funded teacher incentives up to $10,000; supplied special materials and teacher coaching, additional staff, coaches, and counselors; and gave every student the chance to participate in after-school programs including transportation and an evening meal.

But the clock had run out for local leaders. The Texas Supreme Court overturned the injunction against a state takeover and on June 1, 2023, Texas Education Agency Commissioner Mike Morath officially announced the transition. Some of the city's minority advocates complained that the takeover would violate their rights to local control and dilute their influence. "We live in a democracy including elected school boards," Morath responded, "but if those boards fail, the commissioner of education is required" by state law to step in to operate the system serving 190,000 students (62 percent Hispanic, 22 percent black, 9.5 percent white, 4.5 percent Asian).

To find a head for the board of managers with the skill set to do the job, the Texas Education Agency reviewed 462 applications and interviewed 52 candidates. Their final choice was Dallas schools superintendent Mike Miles, a former army officer and State Department official with degrees from West Point, UC Berkeley, and Columbia who is half black and half Japanese.

In his first message to the Houston community, Miles wrote, "Schools don't fail on their own, and there is no such thing as a failing school inside a successful district. Most importantly, schools do not struggle because of the students they serve or the communities they are in. Schools fail because the district fails to support them." That point of view could revolutionize public education in far more places than Houston.

High-flying Houston does occasionally get a reality check. In January 2024, incoming mayor John Whitmire announced a $160 million budget shortfall despite his predecessor insisting the city had a surplus of $420 million. Federal Covid money apparently masked the financial crisis. Whitmire reluctantly proposed a five percent across-the-board pay cut for all city employees except police and firefighters.

Moving full circle from the city's founding, a final thought on Houston comes from writer and Texas transplant Erica Grieder: "No one moves to Houston because it's fun. Even residents would agree: it's ugly, the weather is horrible, and it's a pain having to drive everywhere. Its assets are entirely practical: lots of land, low cost of living, a couple of universities, a bustling port, lots of trade, and as ever, the economy. Everyone who's there is there for some practical reason. That makes it one of the country's least neurotic cities."

That also makes it a shining example of urban success. Houston and the other cities profiled here show an alternate path in the face of declining industries, criminal justice debates, tax policies, fiscal responsibility, school management, operational transparency, and the willingness to try something new when the old ways no longer work. These cities have visionary leaders willing to put some of their own skin in the game—such as buying a building site on three days' notice in Phoenix or building an opera house with private donations in the midst of a crippling recession in Houston. Another important characteristic they share is the ability to face problems honestly, admit something is wrong, and move ahead to a solution. Leaders in failing cities habitually point the finger at each other, at some outside situation, or at something that happened fifty years ago. It's always someone else's fault. Until a city is willing to own its problems and face them honestly, it can never start to solve them.

Detroit has paid a terrible price for its choices. In an encouraging turn of events, there are unmistakable signs that not only has the city learned its lesson at least in part, it is moving into the future with new energy and confidence. From the small business owners who refuse to say die to billionaire investors who are turning their vision of a new

Detroit into a reality of steel and glass and new job opportunities, Detroiters are rolling up their sleeves and bringing their city back.

Daunting challenges remain. Unlike the past, however, Detroiters seem ready to meet them head-on with whatever it takes. A look at the old problems and the new spirit for dealing with them puts the contest between these two forces in perspective. ▦

Chapter 14

Open for Business

"Detroit is my home. . . . Whenever anybody writes us off,
we come together, get to work, and write a new chapter."
—Bill Ford, Executive Chairman,
Ford Motor Company, 2018

■ ■ ■

FOLLOWING DETROIT'S historic bankruptcy in 2013, urban issues journalist Scott Beyer published an essay about the path the city took and its prospects for the future. He surveyed the often-quoted reasons for the city's problems including racial tension, loss of manufacturing jobs, and middle-class migration to the suburbs. Yet looking closer, he concluded Detroit's problems were "self-inflicted by half a century of government excess."

Beyer noted that Thomas Sowell labeled this excess "the Detroit Pattern," defined as a city's policy of "increasing taxes, harassing businesses, and pandering to unions." In 2013 Detroit had the highest property taxes in the nation, a "cobweb of protectionist regulations" hamstringing small business, and a powerful "union-controlled public bureaucracy" gobbling up tax revenues and squelching reform.

Legitimate condemnation of racial discrimination through the 1950s and '60s has been at least partly misdirected over time by ignoring or marginalizing the federally backed destruction of Black Bottom and Paradise Valley to build freeways and public housing which, instead of "modernizing" these areas, effectively ruined them. President Johnson's Model Cities program fragmented and displaced a black population that, again quoting Sowell, had 3.4 percent unemployment and "the highest rate of home-ownership of any black urban population in the country," as noted previously.

A silver lining in the bankruptcy cloud, Beyer concluded, was "the opportunity for structural change," which, at best could transform Detroit into "a reemerging economic star."

From the vantage point of the mid-2020s, Detroit shows unmistakable signs of economic re-emergence. Not only marquee names like Dan Gilbert and Mike Ilitch but thousands of small business owners and entrepreneurs are reinforcing an economic beachhead, staking their futures on the future of Detroit and its prospects for a comeback. Ford Motor Company, under Executive Chairman Bill Ford, has made a sweeping commitment to the city with its world-class Michigan Central project when it would have been easy to decamp to the tech-friendly world of nearby Ann Arbor or even the West Coast.

A ride on the QLINE tram downtown today takes a visitor by too many new buildings and renovation projects to count, sidewalks bustling with shoppers and workers, restaurants and coffee shops doing swift business, boutique hotels, spacious squares, and a beautiful vista of the Detroit River down the way. The Lions, the Tigers, and the Pistons all play within walking distance.

But heading out of downtown, away from Woodward Avenue and a few select neighborhoods, more and more windows are boarded up, more businesses keep their doors locked, more lots are empty, and more abandoned foyers smell like outhouses because they are.

Detroit's past and Detroit's future are duking it out. Though the glass is surely half full, some Detroiters learn from experience better than others.

People are still leaving the city. The good news is the pace of population decline is progressively slower. Between 2000 and 2010, Detroit lost one-fourth of its residents. The decline in the next decade was just over 10 percent and in the years since the 2020 census, the rate has stayed roughly comparable. Between 2020 and 2022, the Census Bureau estimates Detroit lost another 17,800 people.

People are likely leaving for the reasons Detroiters have left for three generations and which still stubbornly persist as part of the local landscape.

A primary challenge remains the city's troubled police department and Detroit's continuing reputation as a dangerous place. A 2019 internal investigation uncovered indications that officers planted evidence in narcotics cases, lied to prosecutors, robbed dope dealers, and took bribes from them, stole drugs confiscated from hospitalized suspects, and embezzled money from the department fund set up to pay informants.

Police officers are leaving the force at historic rates. By September 2022, more than 200 officers had left the force that year, nearly twice the number of departures as the year before. Some of them left for suburban forces, including nearby Warren where the annual salary for an officer with five years' experience was almost $30,000 more than the Detroit pay. Officers also tire of the anti-police attitude that has suspects taunting them, taking videos, and exposing them to legal action just for doing their jobs.

Historically Detroit has spent millions to train officers who then move to better-paying, less stressful jobs elsewhere. In some cases, recruiters from other police departments intercept Detroit officers at their police academy graduations and offer them jobs with suburban forces on the spot. Between 2020 and 2022, a thousand officers in Michigan left their jobs due to "the negative portrayal of police officers," according to Bob Stevenson, executive director of the Michigan Association of Chiefs of Police. Detroit lost 14 percent of its officers between 2021 and 2022, though at least some suburban departments with higher pay had no problem attracting new hires.

While specific crime statistics rise and fall over time, Detroit's overall reputation as a dangerous place continues. In a July 2022 report, the website Safe at Last advised travelers, "Historically, Detroit ranks as one of the most dangerous cities in the US." Quoting a range of comparisons, the piece concludes with the advice: "This is a city you might want to avoid. The total crime rates are 130% higher than the US average, and you should also be worried about the violent crime, which is 462% higher." Another travel site painted an even starker picture in the spring of 2023: "Detroit is dangerous. Locals may claim that the city is safe but on the whole, the city has some of the worst property and violent crime rates in the country." Downtown and Midtown "are generally safe from the horrific violent crime of the impoverished neighborhoods. . . . Unfortunately, there are more neighborhoods to avoid than visit."

Into the decade of the 2020s, Detroit still had one of the highest tax burdens in America, and the nation's highest effective rate for tax on commercial property valued at $1 million. Decades of falling demand have reduced the value of homes and their worth for taxation purposes, so although property tax rates are high, revenue remains relatively low. In March 2023, Mayor Mike Duggan proposed a reduction in residential property taxes of about 30 percent to stimulate the housing market, then ranked the most undervalued in the nation. The mayor's proposal would also reduce taxes on commercial buildings by 30 percent and triple the tax on land, targeting owners of vacant land, parking lots, and abandoned buildings, and encouraging landlords to renovate rather than abandon their property. The change would require approval of the state and also Detroit voters.

The proposal is a world away from city policies extending back before the bankruptcy that overtaxed thousands of Detroit homeowners and then foreclosed on them. Between 2010 and 2016, residents were overcharged by at least $600 million. Wayne County foreclosed on one in three Detroit homes between 2009 and 2018, illegally inflating the values of up to 83 percent of homes between 2009 and 2015, and around 33 percent of homes between 2016 and 2018. These illegal assessments caused 10 percent of all tax foreclosures and 25 percent of foreclosures on the lowest-valued homes.

Detroit's beleaguered schools still struggle. In 2009 then-governor Jennifer Granholm appointed Robert Bobb as emergency financial manager to improve the district's $219 million budget deficit and some of the lowest graduation rates and test scores in the country. By the end of the next school year the deficit was $327 million. In 2011 that emergency manager was replaced by a second, former GM executive Roy Roberts, who also lasted two years, battling the school board for control and struggling to reduce the deficit.

The third emergency manager, Jack Martin, made news at his retirement in 2015 by receiving a $50,000 bonus after eighteen months in office on top of his $225,000 annual salary. This reward came despite continued financial and academic performance problems, though to his credit Martin brokered an exchange of fifty-seven vacant schools and twenty vacant lots to the city for $11.6 million in unpaid electric bills.

By 2016 a cascade of bad news hit the district from every direction. Accrued debt was $515 million. Combined operating and capital liabilities totaled $3.5 billion, more than half of which was employee legacy costs and cash flow borrowings. Teacher and counselor Valerie Strauss wrote in the *Washington Post* of her once clean and functioning school, "any city would be proud to have in its district," now dangerously damaged by buckling floors, mold, a playground off-limits "because a geyser of searing hot steam explodes out of the ground," and missing ceiling tiles leaving exposed electrical wiring.

That same year, 2016, Detroit's fourth- and eighth-graders ranked last nationwide in educational assessments for the fourth year in a row. Later in 2016, Detroit U.S. Attorney Barbara McQuade announced the charges leveled at twelve Detroit school principals who took $2.5 million in kickbacks on supplies that were never delivered.

In the spring of 2018, Detroit Public Schools once again scored last in the nation on academic assessments, with 5 percent of fourth-graders proficient in reading and 4 percent in math. Superintendent Nikolai Vitti blamed the failure on state control of the school district.

"It's really evidence that emergency management didn't work—that state control did not work," he said.

Circumstances were still dire at the end of 2022 according to Dr. Alveda King, niece of Martin Luther King Jr., and chairman of the Center for the American Dream at the America First Policy Institute. Dr. King noted that for four years the Detroit school board debated the pros and cons of removing the name of former Secretary of Housing and Urban Development Dr. Ben Carson from the district's high school of medicine and science. King highlighted Carson's career as a world-famous pediatric neurosurgeon, founder of the Carson Scholars scholarship fund, and leader of the HUD Opportunity Zone Initiative that waived some capital gains taxes in thousands of districts across the country raising $75 billion in capital for underserved communities in two years.

Carson's critics on the Detroit school board said he "adversely affected the African American community" and "allied himself with a president that says he is a white nationalist." After the board voted to remove Carson's name in November 2022, Dr. King commented, "I would think they would focus their attention on the dismal education statistics they produce for our children." For the 2021–2022 academic year, Detroit students "lost ground" on the National Assessment of Educational Progress, "and scored below their peers in every other large city. . . . On every metric, the Detroit district's average scores fell below every other big city district." High rates of child poverty and absenteeism were cited as factors in the poor showing.

Corruption in the school district, the city government, and the police department over the years earned Detroit a bad reputation the city needs somehow to turn around. The *Detroit News* has estimated more than a hundred "labor leaders, police officers, politicians, and others have been caught up in investigations that simply keep mounting," including council members arrested by the FBI, two former United Auto Workers Union presidents sentenced to federal prison for embezzling millions of dollars set aside for retraining laid-off members in new careers, and a host of other wrongdoers.

As former U.S. district attorney Matthew Schneider noted, "The bankruptcy fixed the problems it could fix, but one of the problems it couldn't fix [was] the greedy, evil nature of some human beings." Urban specialist Richard Florida adds that if Detroit wants new investment, leaders must "double down to beat back any semblance of corruption." Auto industry historian and columnist Micheline Maynard agrees: "The city has come too far since 2013 to let all that progress slip away."

Yet old habits die hard and the far corners of corruption resist a clean sweep, as a sample of stories ten years after the bankruptcy reveals. In 2023 email hackers stole more than $685,000 from the Detroit Public Library by sending fraudulent wiring instructions to the city and transferring library funds to a private bank account. About 40 percent of the money was eventually recovered. The library is struggling even without the indignity of an inside heist. Its magnificent Beaux Arts main campus limps along with a failing climate control system, broken and unrepairable elevator, understaffing, and a $3 million deficit. Following a too-familiar pattern, a proposal for the city to take over the library drew a sharp rebuke from former Library Commission president Franklin Jackson. "The city is the threat to our continued financial success and they will castigate us as a profligate while they help destroy us," he said. "You wouldn't trust them with your house cat, let alone the library system."

Also in 2023, a group including two former Detroit police officers was charged with accepting bribes from tow truck drivers to direct business their way. Even the Detroit Lions made their mark, with a spring 2023 announcement about four players being suspended for violating the NFL's gambling policy.

Though longstanding problems continue, Detroit has taken definite, measurable steps to break with its troubled past and prove to the world where it is willing to do things differently. This is the case especially in the all-important areas of public safety and business climate.

The city initiated a raft of programs to target high-crime neighborhoods and respond quickly to criminal activity in those areas.

Mayor Mike Duggan introduced the Shot Stoppers program that would pay community groups up to $700,000 per year to help the police prevent crime in any of a handful of chronic trouble spots. Deputy mayor and former police officer Todd Bettison explained, "What makes our program unique is the fact that it's going to be performance-based." If crime goes down in the area, the partnering community group gets more money.

The One Detroit Partnership is a coalition of the police department, U.S. Attorney's Office, FBI, DEA, ATF, and a long list of community groups focused on reducing violent crime. Not only does it have the impact of multiple organizations and the input of local citizens, it wields the strength of federal penalties for lawbreakers. For example, suspects charged with carjacking, certain gun-related crimes, and drug trafficking will face higher mandatory sentences that come with conviction in federal court.

As Dawn Ison, U.S. Attorney for the Eastern District of Michigan, explained, "If you are a felon in possession in the federal system, you could potentially get 25 years." The likelihood of a conviction and a longer sentence, Ison said, would make wrongdoers think twice about committing a crime.

Mayor Mike Duggan added, "If you're committing gun crimes in this area, you're going to have the full force of federal law enforcement." Billboards announcing the program are designed to warn potential criminals of the new setup. The city also sent letters to 200 repeat offenders out on probation or parole to inform them of the new penalties.

A second vital component of the One Detroit Partnership besides the combination of law enforcement partners is a series of community picnics called "peacenics." These neighborhood cookouts in targeted areas give residents a chance to interact with law enforcement in a positive way and also get information on educational and vocational opportunities, medical screenings, and help applying for criminal record expungement. Mayor Duggan said the cookouts show residents law enforcement authorities "care about the quality of life. We don't want to lock anybody up." Attorney Ison added, "Every kid at risk that we show a different way of life to make a different choice makes our community better."

Two similar programs over the longer term have concentrated on public-private cooperation to reduce violent crime and a support system for citizens who have stepped outside the law. Project Green Light is a joint effort between police and business owners. It began in 2016 when eight gas stations in high-crime areas purchased camera equipment and bright green lights that signaled their presence, with video feeds going directly in real time to the police department. Seven years later more than 800 businesses had installed cameras sending high-definition video to a dedicated crime center at police headquarters. The flashing green lights notify customers and potential criminals alike of the video feed. Carjackings were down 44 percent after five years, and suspects were more likely to plead guilty when their crimes were recorded on video. Arrests and convictions were up, with suspects sometimes detained in minutes even without the crime being reported. Police Chief James White called it "a game changer."

In tandem with Project Green Light, Mayor Duggan opened an office in the city's legal department in 2016 to help convicted felons navigate the process of applying to expunge convictions from their records. Christened Project Clean Slate, the program reflects research by the University of Michigan that those who had convictions expunged had a recidivism rate of only 2.6 percent. According to Shayla McElroy, community outreach manager for the project, a second chance leads to better job opportunities, higher wages, and reduced chances of being re-arrested. The average former convict who successfully expunges a conviction sees a 22 percent increase in wages after the first year. To naysayers who claim Project Clean Slate is "soft on crime," McElroy counters, "When you have misdemeanors or felonies on your record, you come across a host of barriers . . . as it comes to employment, housing and educational opportunities. . . . It's not soft on crime to set somebody up for success, so they don't have to return back to a life of crime."

In its first year, Project Clean Slate processed eight applications; in 2022 the number was 1,723 with thousands more in the pipeline. The result has been more job opportunities for people whose prospects were once severely limited. As one participant said, "After I got my record clean, the sky's the limit. I can do anything." With a clean slate, this former two-time felon opened his own trucking company hauling goods between Michigan and Canada.

And the good news keeps on coming. Detroit's $2.6 billion fiscal 2024 budget proposed by Mayor Duggan and approved by the city council is a historic document. It marks the city's tenth consecutive balanced budget, putting Detroit only one step away from investment grade status. The budget allots $79.5 million to capital projects including demolition of blighted buildings, new sidewalks, park renovations, and tree removal; $60 million to a risk management fund for workman's comp and other legal expenses; $18 million for fire department overtime; and funds toward a program to compensate homeowners who were overtaxed by hundreds of millions of dollars between 2010 and 2016.

The budget also includes an "unprecedented" $230 million surplus, $74 million of which is earmarked for the 2025 budget. A balance sheet which seemed impossible a dozen years ago is now reality thanks to a host of Detroit visionaries who refused to give up.

■ ■ ■

The most consequential improvement in Detroit's business climate has been through cultivating partnerships with entrepreneurs who were predisposed to invest in Detroit in the first place. With all its longstanding and exhaustively documented problems, Detroit has not historically been on the shortlist of many business investors. What has given Detroit new hope and encouraging signs of life are a handful of visionaries who see untapped potential and are willing to underwrite developments in the community. These changes are not without controversy—some locals think the city is giving away the store to secure new projects—but they have brought Detroit a steady smattering of good news after decades of unrelieved misery. One common bond the major dealmakers share is they all have a personal connection with the city going beyond business projects and return on investment.

Mike Ilitch was born to Macedonian immigrants in Detroit in 1929. After a hitch in the Marine Corps, he played minor league baseball for four years in the Detroit Tigers organization. He worked as a door-to-door salesman until 1959, when he used his savings to open a pizza restaurant he called Little Caesars. By the time Ilitch died in 2017, Little Caesars had locations around the world and the company was worth more than $3 billion, with Ilitch's personal wealth estimated at double that amount.

Throughout his long and successful career, Ilitch remained loyal to his hometown, pouring hundreds of millions into investments and philanthropic work. In 1982, when Detroit had little to recommend itself to the world of business, he bought the Detroit Red Wings hockey team, which hadn't won the Stanley Cup in forty-two years. Under his ownership they won the Cup four times. They also moved from Joe Louis Arena, later demolished, to new Little Caesars Arena, which became the nucleus of a revitalized downtown neighborhood. In 1988 Ilitch bought the derelict Fox Theater and restored it to its 1928 glory, moving Caesars headquarters to his nearby Fox Office Center. In 1992 he bought his old baseball team, the Detroit Tigers, and installed them in the new Comerica Park. Between 2000 and his death, Ilitch and his wife donated $220 million to local causes, including nearly $50 million to Wayne State University.

In 2012 he wrote, "Develop a love for all people, be humble; work hard. I guarantee you will be successful in life." Following his death the world learned that after civil rights icon and Detroit resident Rosa Parks was robbed and beaten in her own home in 1994, Ilitch quietly paid her rent to live in a better neighborhood until her death eleven years later.

Mike Ilitch was an incredibly successful and generous man who gave back to his community on a colossal scale. He was also a shrewd businessman who capitalized on Detroit's depressed property values to buy and hold land, and who negotiated generous tax abatements for his ventures. Ilitch was the vanguard of investment at a time when many businessmen had written Detroit off completely. His confidence and highly public projects encouraged others to re-examine long-held assumptions about the city.

Directly and indirectly he brought thousands of new jobs, new workers, and new residents downtown. Even so, he had his critics, including one who wrote less than a week after his death, "The truth is, Mike Ilitch was a rich old man who owned a bunch of stuff and never saw a tax break he didn't like." In a more measured assessment, the *Detroit News* commented that Ilitch had "a demonstrated knack for buying low, holding on and building value." On balance, the facts indicate Mike Ilitch loved his hometown, invested in it when almost no one else would, and single-handedly slowed the economic freefall that plagued it for decades.

Dan Gilbert is another Detroit native son who has used his phenomenal business success to boost the city's fortunes, delivering thousands of jobs and dozens of building renovations while negotiating generous tax breaks in return. In sheer volume of money invested, projects undertaken, and results achieved, Dan Gilbert has uplifted and improved Detroit more than anyone else in history.

Gilbert was born in 1962 and grew up in the Southfield neighborhood. His father's bar was destroyed during the 1967 riots. At age twenty-two Gilbert co-founded Quicken Loans, which grew to become the largest mortgage lender in America with a portfolio totaling $320 billion when it went public in 2020. Early in his career he decided "if he ever did something big, he wanted to do it in Detroit."

With downtown occupancy rates less than 50 percent, depressed commercial real estate prices, and the enormous cash-generating power of Quicken Loans, Dan had "the perfect storm of opportunity" according to Detroit businessman and investor Bryan Waldron. For example, Gilbert's investment partnership bought the First National

Building in 2011. Built in 1922 and expanded in 1927, it was Detroit's tallest building when it opened. It was proud but faded when Gilbert acquired it for $7 million. Ten years after he spent $100 million renovating it, the building was worth an estimated $300 million.

The scale of Gilbert's investment in his hometown is hard to fathom. According to Waldron, by the mid-2020s Gilbert controlled more than 100 properties in Detroit with a total of 15 million square feet. He moved the headquarters of his own Quicken Loans downtown in 2007, bringing thousands of workers, shoppers, and potential homeowners to the area.

One of his crown jewels is the development complex on the site of the old Hudson's Department Store. Vacant for nearly twenty years, the midtown location was a constant reminder of Detroit's storied past and its troubled present. Gilbert envisioned a million-square-foot combination of office, retail, hotel, and residential space and an investment of $900 million.

By 2022 the Hudson's site project had become a $1.4 billion investment and the city council was determined to get concessions they deemed fair to offset a $60 million municipal tax abatement. That summer the Gilbert team agreed to a series of conditions including: setting aside twenty percent of ground floor retail for Detroit-based small business, donating $5 million for neighborhood improvement projects, and increasing the amount of affordable housing in a future project. While the council passed the agreement, some members complained that the proposal was considered without public notice and Gilbert could still do more for the city.

One of Gilbert's latest ventures is the restoration of the classic Book Building as a luxury residential tower. Overall, Gilbert's companies have invested more than $5 billion buying and renovating Detroit properties. Four of the biggest projects in his portfolio garnered a total of $618 million in tax incentives from the Michigan Strategic Fund, which was set up by the state in 1984 to promote economic development and create jobs. Gilbert's estimated personal net worth in 2023 was $19.5 billion.

Though Tom Kartsotis is a Texan by birth, he has not only embraced the gritty underdog persona of Detroit, he made it central to the branding of his business. Kartsotis has not invested billions in the city like other super-rich businessmen, but he has arguably done more than anyone to put Detroit front and center in the world of popular culture and retail fashion.

Tom made so much money as a ticket scalper in college that he dropped out of Texas A&M to launch his business career. With $200,000 in scalping profits, he opened Overseas Products International to make watches. Inspired by mid-century designs, he built his Fossil brand into a trendsetting powerhouse, took the company public in 1993, and stepped down as head of the company in 2009 with annual sales of more than $3 billion.

The Detroit connection started with a vacation to a tourist attraction near Williams, Arizona, that was definitely past its prime. Bedrock City was modeled after the Flintstones cartoon show, with the family's hometown replicated in life-sized rocks of battered, sun-faded fiberglass. Kartsotis, a lifelong Flintstones fan, considered buying Bedrock to develop it as a model for sustainable living, with proceeds going to support local Native Americans. When he floated the idea to a friend he was vacationing with, the friend answered, "If you want to do something to help, you should go to Detroit."

Kartsotis made a scouting trip to the Motor City. During his research there, he met Dan Gilbert and the two of them soon became friends and business partners. Gilbert appreciated the fact Kartsotis was looking more for challenge and adventure than for yet another business deal.

As Kartsotis later explained, "This was half about creating jobs and the rest, pure sport. I wanted to see if I could do it. I don't need more money." He loved the idea of re-starting America's watch industry, which disappeared over the previous fifty years, in "a city that was long ago left for dead." For Tom it was "an irresistible marketing proposition. From the beginning he planned to build Detroit's story into his brand. "A city's struggle is its greatest asset."

He wanted to bring 100 skilled jobs to Detroit. By 2022 he employed 400 craftsmen—some of whom he sent to Switzerland to observe the fine points of watchmaking—and had annual revenues of $10 million. His Shinola products, named after a defunct brand of shoe polish, were according to *Adweek*, "the coolest brand in America."

Shinola's factory was in the old General Motors research building where the first automatic transmission was built. In 2012 Tom added the Filson line of clothes and leather goods to his Detroit products portfolio. He also added a line of high-end audio equipment and restored a group of old buildings including a former Singer sewing machine store to make the Shinola Hotel as trendy and fashionable as the brand itself.

When Detroit declared bankruptcy, Shinola ran a full-page ad in the *New York Times* with the headline, "To those who've written off Detroit, we give you the Birdy," a reference to a line of the company's $500 watches. If native sons brought passion and commitment to the rebirth of Detroit, Tom Kartsotis brought a healthy dose of Texas swagger.

The history of Ford Motor Company has been intertwined with the history of Detroit for more than 120 years. The two have such a close and constant relationship that an observer may overlook it in light of high-profile partnerships with relative newcomers like Mike Ilitch, Dan Gilbert, and Tom Kartsotis. The company and the Ford family have been relentless Detroit boosters generation after generation. The NFL Detroit Lions—which the family owns—play football at Ford Field. They have given millions in artwork and other contributions to the Detroit Institute of Art, and many millions to philanthropic, religious, and civic causes. As the city defines its new way forward in the twenty-first century, Ford Executive Chairman William Clay "Bill" Ford Jr., has made it clear he and his company are all-in as investors and supporters of their hometown. The company's latest major move is one of the most visible, most consequential steps on Detroit's long path to recovery.

When Michigan Central Station opened in 1913, it was a wonder of steam's golden age. Soaring eighteen stories above the Corktown neighborhood where Ford's Irish immigrant ancestors once lived, the building reflected Detroit's position as a national transportation hub. By the time it closed in 1988, Detroit was already shorthand for urban failure. Vandals stripped the station of marble cladding and copper wire, covered it with graffiti, and broke hundreds of windows, opening the once-elegant interior to the elements. In 2009 it was scheduled for demolition but those plans were shelved. For nearly thirty years it towered above the neighborhood, an abandoned, hopeless symbol of the Detroit that was and would never be again. It was one of the most popular stops on urban blight tours of the city.

Then in 2018, Bill Ford announced that Ford Motor Company had bought the building and planned to make it the "crown jewel" of the Michigan Central project, a thirty-acre campus dedicated to transportation solutions for the future. Other nearby buildings became part of the program, including the adjacent Albert Kahn–designed post office that sat empty for thirty-five years after a 1987 fire. Ford envisioned it as a home to hundreds of Ford employees plus a boutique hotel, shops, and restaurants. Plans for the 270,000-square-foot building included space for dozens of companies developing drones, automated vehicles, electric vehicle recharging systems, and more.

As Ford explained, "If we made this a Ford-only thing, it wasn't going to reach its full potential. This space will be where young companies really can start."

The Central Station project was necessary, Ford said, because his company wanted the best engineers and other workers. "We should reinvent mobility here [in Detroit], not in Silicon Valley," he explained. "We're in a war for talent," fighting technology companies on the West Coast with pristine, state-of-the-art campuses for the best minds in the business.

Detroit Mayor Mike Duggan encouraged the company to develop their new technology center in Detroit rather than out of state or the pre-existing technology corridor in nearby Ann Arbor. "I said, 'Look, we'll move heaven and earth for you.' It's flipping our image around the world." The city offered $104 million in tax breaks, part of a $250 million total from local, state, and federal tax incentives.

For its part, Ford budgeted $740 million for a complex to house 2,500 Ford workers, 2,500 entrepreneurs, tech companies, and partners. The old Michigan Central Station will showcase markets and retail on the lower levels and offices and apartments in the tower, a total of 500,000 square feet. Ford noted, "It's not just a building. . . . It's all about the connection to Detroit, to the suburbs, and the vision around developing the next generation of transportation."

"One thing that's very important to me," Ford said of the project, "is that this is not seen as a corporate takeover of Corktown. . . . It's really important that we become part of the community and that we're not isolated or insulated from it."

Ford—both family and business empire—have stayed with Detroit through the lean years and are not about to abandon it now. "This isn't just where we do business. This is my home," Bill Ford notes. "We stayed here when others were leaving. . . . Whenever anybody writes us off, we come together, get to work, and write a new chapter."

Big names and big projects grab the headlines as Detroit travels its emerging path toward long-term renewal. These visionaries set the pace for others to follow. True, they have attractive tax incentives and other perks to encourage them on, and they have negotiated real estate bargains on a historic scale. They claimed these because they are going where others have feared to tread. They acquired property on the cheap because no one else would take the risk; they look for tax considerations because these breaks are economically essential in a market that has been depressed for generations.

For Detroit truly to catch fire as a new American business and social hotspot, two more conditions must take place. First, a critical mass of long-term residents and their (sometimes self-appointed) spokesmen have to join the party. Too many Detroiters who have had the opportunity to make their city better either did nothing or were part of the problem. They are too content to stew about the slights and conflicts of sixty years ago instead of looking for opportunities and answers based on today's realities and opportunities. Rather than their first question being, "What's in it for me?" they would serve their city better by asking, "How can I contribute? What of my knowledge and experience can make these projects more successful? What can I bring to the table developers will not have otherwise? How soon can we sit down together and exchange ideas?" There are encouraging pockets of these attitudes all over town. They must be nurtured and expanded.

The second essential condition for success is thousands of other entrepreneurs, investors, dreamers, and business developers must follow the corporate giants in staking a claim on the future of Detroit. Walking around downtown, a visitor feels an unmistakable sense that this is happening. And from these many points of economic light, Detroit's new believers have the chance to spread their energy and resolve to the whole city.

Spending an hour with one of the most energetic and successful of these dynamos of renewal gives a visitor some idea of what is unfolding today and what is possible tomorrow. ▪

Chapter 15

Resurget Cineribus

*"What we need is to convince 250,000
more people to be a part of the energy here."*
—Christos Moisides, Detroit developer
and civic leader, 2023

■ ■ ■

ANYONE WHO believes Detroit is dead needs to spend an hour
with Christos Moisides. Christos is a major player in town, a developer and entrepreneur who, if he doesn't have billions at stake like
Dan Gilbert, is extremely accessible to a visitor and conducts a whirl-
wind tour of the city with contagious enthusiasm.

Moisides grew up in Detroit. His father-in-law, Ted Gatzaros,
arrived penniless from Greece in 1967, started as a dishwasher, and
worked his way up the business and political ladder in town. The ambitious young immigrant attracted the atten-
tion of Mayor Coleman Young, who admired
his attitude. "Young gave my father-in-law
opportunities, and Ted always delivered,"
Moisides explains. "Coleman is demonized by
a lot of people but he was passionate about
Detroit and supported people he believed in.
Ted called him 'Pop.'"

*"Keep sound
wisdom and
discretion . . .
and your
feet will not
stumble."*
—Proverbs 3:21, 23

211

Gatzaros led the charge for casino gambling and in 1999 was awarded one of the three casino licenses for Detroit. His Greektown Casino, says Moisides, "brought incredible tax revenues and jobs" to the community. Gatzaros invested in restoring historic buildings and would eventually become Moisides's mentor in the business of urban development.

As a young man, Moisides left Detroit for film school in Los Angeles where he built a career making music videos and TV commercials. After eleven years on the West Coast, he returned to Detroit to start his own film studio. Today he is a senior member of the family business, buying up old abandoned or struggling buildings and converting them into showpieces. He is also on the board of the Downtown Development Authority, which works with developers to bring projects to completion, offering loans, tax breaks, infrastructure improvements, and other inducements in turn for project commitments under terms that support local communities with affordable housing and other benefits.

He picks up a guest at the Hotel St. Regis, which Moisides is currently renovating. When it opened in 1966 across the street from General Motors world headquarters, the St. Regis boasted Italian marble, French molding, 23k gold leaf, and the most expensive rooms in America. Only a few years later this showpiece began a long decline toward bankruptcy and decay. Today it is a rising star in the New Center neighborhood, welcoming visitors even as its dining room and other amenities are still emerging from the construction dust.

For the next hour Moisides and his guest zip around town to various projects, parking in one loading zone after another, dashing inside where everybody from manager to janitor knows Christos and he knows everybody by name. First on the tour is the historic Ferry Seed building, a huge, dilapidated warehouse his father-in-law bought in 1985. Today it is the elegant, European-style Atheneum Suite Hotel. Part of the structure is a restaurant near an area of the building that once had dangerously rotted floors. The solution: remove the damaged flooring to open a six-story atrium with the tallest indoor waterfall in the world. The result is breathtaking.

The next stop is the London Chop House, its dark wood paneling, leather banquettes, and caricature-lined walls looking like a movie set from Hollywood's golden age. Opened shortly after Prohibition ended, the Chop House became the go-to choice of visiting celebrities. Frank Sinatra, Jerry Lewis, Elvis Presley, and Muhammed Ali were among the stars who held court in booth number one, a prime corner spot strictly reserved for VIPs. In 1961 celebrity chef James Beard ranked it one of the top ten restaurants in America. As Detroit faded so did the Chop House, finally closing in 1991. Christos took it over after a twenty-year hibernation and has restored it to its former glory, with booth number one still reserved for distinguished guests. One-upping the original, the reborn Chop House has a large and elegant cigar bar upstairs and a nightclub and event space on the roof.

On to the next project, the old Detroit Brewing Company, built in 1864, a labyrinth of former processing, storage, and shipping spaces on several floors. An army of workers scurries around in the midst of transforming the building into headquarters for the six Detroit-area iHeartMedia radio stations, including studios, offices, and production facilities. Christos greets the concrete finishers going off their shift. "You guys are doing a great job."

Then to the Cass Corridor neighborhood for a quick look at the former Kresge Corporation world headquarters, designed by Albert Kahn and slated for conversion to 200 residential units within walking distance of Little Caesar's Arena. After that, it's a few minutes journey to a massive abandoned factory known as Fisher 23. Christos drives through the parking lot, up a ramp, and inside without a pause. The mammoth building, 415,000 square feet, is where General Motors built busses and, during the war, Sherman tanks. Massive steel beams rise six stories. He is negotiating an agreement to bring in green transportation technology companies, including hydrogen power and battery production. Where twentieth-century technology once ruled, twenty-first-century innovation will soon be turning out practical solutions for the future.

How does he decide what to do with the various spaces? "The building speaks to you," he explains. "The building tells you what to do. All the time I tell the architects, 'Quit looking at your computer, get in your car, and come down here!'"

There are other buildings, other plans, including ten acres in Corktown near the new Ford Michigan Central project that used to house halal and kosher slaughterhouses.

"You can buy a building in Detroit for ten percent of what it would cost in New York," Christos says. "The challenge is getting it renovated and repurposed for the right price. We use union labor in Detroit. I'm not complaining—they're good at what they do—but that means building costs are the same here as Chicago. It's an uphill battle you can't win because you can't charge Chicago rents. You need help from the city to pencil it out." There are also state and federal dollars to bring into the mix.

To residents who say developers get too much help from the city, or who complain about "gentrification" of their neighborhoods, Christos invites them to join in building their own future. "They don't get it," he says. "They can stay and take advantage of all the new facilities and opportunity, or they can sell at a big profit." From this developer's perspective, there's something for everyone in Detroit's forward progress.

What will it take to make Detroit click? What will turn the corner for a city on the way back up? "We need people," he says. "Not a lot of people, not as many as before. But we need 250,000 new people to come here and be a part of the energy.

"Before Covid we were on a tremendous trajectory. Dan Gilbert and others had taken development to an all-time high. Momentum was shifting in our favor but that stopped with the lockdown. Covid brought a deeper pain to this city than many others because we lacked the density of people and businesses to bounce back.

"Now we're finally emerging from that cloud. You can see the spirit of Detroit rising. New jobs and the economic boom are propelling Detroit back into the conversation. We've got a great technological base, with start-ups popping up for EVs, hydrogen, biodiesel, alternative fuels, and other new technologies.

"Cities fall by the wayside because they become obsolete. Every day Detroit is becoming more relevant and more essential, more a city for the future. We still have the auto industry legacy but also healthcare, insurance, the startups I mentioned. We now have multiple spokes in this wheel of commerce and energy that give us great diversity in our economy and our culture.

"There's a rich history in Detroit of strength and determination. No matter what happens, Detroiters will always prevail. They have the ability continually to reinvent themselves, to lead the way in manufacturing, technology, and culture. There's an undeniable energy in this city, which is why we've produced some of the greatest technological minds of the twentieth and twenty-first centuries.

"Don't ever count Detroit out."

Though they never make the national news, thousands of other business owners in Detroit demonstrate by their actions that they have never counted their city out. A visitor staying in the New Center neighborhood will find plenty of them. Some are new on the scene, such as Promenade Artisan Foods in the Fisher Building. The Fisher Building has traced the familiar arc from early brilliance as one of the most expensive and beautiful office buildings in America, to shabby decline, to current facelifting and renewal. Carved out of one ground-floor retail space is Promenade, opened at this location in 2021. They have to keep the street door locked for safety, but the pastries and other delicacies are world-class, the service is excellent, and the business appears steady. May they thrive and prosper as New Center is renewed again.

Down Woodward Avenue toward downtown is another locked door at the entrance to London Luggage Shop. A passer-by is first surprised by window displays full of high-end luggage and accessories, including famous British brands. A hesitant knock brings a quick response and an open door. Inside is a large selection of fine merchandise. On the wall is a framed 1980s-era letter from Lee Iacocca, former Ford executive and later chairman of Chrysler, thanking the store for its quick service in providing some gifts on short notice. The clerk is professionally turned out in a stylish dress and proves to be a genuine expert on luggage for every situation. The store has been open since 1946. Having survived from the highest times to the lowest, it has a head start on Detroit's renaissance.

A few blocks in the other direction is a store rooted in the earliest history of Detroit. Dittrich Furs started out buying pelts directly from Detroit trappers, continuing a trade that built the city from a small pioneer outpost to a major commercial center. Walking into their salon today, a customer could imagine being in an exclusive shop in Manhattan or Milan, only this one is bigger.

When the business opened in 1893, Dittrich had more than a hundred competitors in town. Now there are only a handful. So, though the population has shrunk over the years, business is good. "Detroit has always had a cool factor," notes fifth-generation owner Jason Dittrich. "We have a whole new demographic than we had a generation ago." Over the years, classic formal coats have given way to a kaleidoscope of options from pink and purple to silver lamé. There are high-fashion jackets and accessories aplenty lining the room as well as traditional styles.

Today Dittrich is the oldest family-owned business in Detroit. "The best thing about Detroit is the community," Jason says. "They support us. To them I say thank you for sticking with us for 130 years."

Whether Detroit and Christos Moisides get the extra people and energy they need is yet to be determined. Signs are promising, and a balanced review of the situation indicates 1) Detroit can be saved and 2) Detroit is worth saving. Nonetheless, it is not out of the woods yet. Population is still declining, schools are still a disaster, and corruption is still a major force to be dealt with. The 2013 bankruptcy gave Detroit a once-in-a-lifetime opportunity to get its house in order. Municipal budgets are now balanced, businesses feel welcome, people are building up some neighborhoods, and the city has an encouraging share of good press. Mike Duggan, assuming office as the bankruptcy crisis reached its peak, was elected to his third term as mayor in 2021. (Jason Dittrich declares, "Mayor Duggan has made the difference. He said he was cleaning this place up, and he did.")

It may be the city's hardest days are behind it. Its challenge now is to keep making good decisions, get the word out about recent successes, keep looking forward, and not allow itself to fall back into old practices with their predictable results. The key to the future is to continue doing what works and turn that newfound positive energy to improving schools and tending to the other problems yet to be solved, both large and small.

Detroit in the twenty-first century has a historic opportunity. For sixty years it has showed America how not to run a city. Now it can show America how to recover, how to rescue and renew a city, how to shake off the baggage and bad decisions of the past and set off in a new direction. The city that showed us all how to do things wrong is poised to show us how to do things right.

Resurget Cineribus: "They will arise from the ashes." When a fire destroyed the young frontier town, its people, led by the visionary Lewis Cass, built it back. When cast iron stoves became outmoded and killed the city's largest business, workers put their metalworking know-how into cars and became the transportation center of the world. When the city struggled to survive in harsh economic times, Hazen Pingree and Frank Murphy led the way back to solvency. In recent times Dan Gilbert and Bill Ford have headed an army of twenty-first century pioneers ready to take on whatever challenges lie ahead. When faced with seemingly impossible difficulties throughout its history, Detroit looked at the road ahead and saw not the ashes of despair but the shining light of hope and opportunity.

Detroit did it before. Detroit can do it again.

May other American cities soon follow. ■

Acknowledgments

■ ■ ■

EVERY YEAR writing a book like this one becomes harder. As archives are thrown out, trimmed from the budget, sent to storage, and otherwise marginalized, as paper files deteriorate and microfilm readers break down with no one available to repair them, history is disappearing before our eyes. The remnant left online is a pale representation of the whole: there, someone else has already decided what a researcher will see and what he will not, how it is catalogued, and how it is presented. The most surprising and newsworthy research discoveries are accidental. Browsing at random through an old newspaper, idly flipping through a box of unpublished notes—that's where the real gems are.

Random browsing of old newspaper microfilm led me to the astonishing story of Louis Lomax and to his papers at the University of Nevada, Reno. Special thanks to Elspeth Olson there for help in meeting this remarkable, history-making journalist. Thanks also to Jacque Sundstrand, who helped me make the original connection.

I'm grateful to James Smith, now retired, of the Detroit Public Library who, in addition to being the best-dressed public servant in town, was generous with his time and assistance even as the inconveniences of Covid faced us seemingly at every turn. At the library's Burton Historical Collection (mercifully old-school with a real card catalogue in addition to its digital database), special thanks to Kat Emrich, Carla Reczek, and the head of Special Collections, Mark Bowden.

I am grateful as well to Allison Bauer of the Detroit Historical Society; Gavin Strassel and Kristen Chinery of the Walter P. Reuther Library, Archives of Labor and Urban Affairs at Wayne State University; Jim Orr of the Henry Ford Museum; and Dan Austin of the Michigan Central Project.

Several new friends helped bring this story to life, particularly the essence of New Detroit and its prospects for the future. Thanks to Christos Moisides for a crash course in Detroit real estate and an exciting tour of some up-and-coming projects; to Bryan Waldron, who was always generous with his time and willing to answer questions about his exciting role in rebuilding the city; to Jason Dittrich, who took time from a busy day to speak with a stranger who literally walked in off the street; and to Sal at the Hotel St. Regis who, hearing a conversation about this project at the lobby bar, introduced me to Bryan, who introduced me to Christos.

I owe a great debt to Gary Terashita and the production team at Fidelis Publishing, Miko Griffin and Erin Ashley. They have been true partners in this remarkable and rewarding project, and I appreciate their passion, encouragement, and energy in bringing this story to completion. Thank you, my friends. May our message fall on fertile soil.

Soli Deo Gloria
John Perry
Memorial Day, 2024
Nashville, Tennessee ▪

Note on Sources

■ ■ ■

BECAUSE THE Detroiting of America is an ongoing phenomenon, its story continues evolving every day and its history is a moving target. Statistics and other information about various cities were accurate at the time of writing. Yet experience proved that, try as a writer might, it has been impossible to ensure every example and notation reflected the latest, most accurate data. Realizing that up-to-the-minute corrections were impossible in a book—facts and figures changed even as the book was being researched and written—your correspondent resigned himself to producing a snapshot, as it were, of the situation at the beginning of 2024. Fortunately for the reader, updates are as accessible as today's headlines.

Of the hundreds of sources cited in the footnotes, a few merit special acknowledgment for their scholarship and relevance to this project.

For the history and background of Detroit:
Woodford, Arthur W., *This is Detroit: 1702-2001*. Detroit: Wayne State University Press, 2001.

For enlightening and detailed information about the Detroit bankruptcy:

Bomey, Nathan, *Detroit Resurrected: To Bankruptcy and Back.* New York: W. W. Norton & Company, Inc., 2017; also numerous news articles (as cited) by the same author related to the bankruptcy proceedings.

For analysis and insights regarding Detroit's failure and its continued struggles:

Beyer, Scott, "Root Causes of Detroit's Decline Should Not Be Ignored," NewGeography.com, August 26, 2013.

Beyer, Scott, "Why Has Detroit Continued to Decline?" *Forbes,* July 31, 2018, forbes.com.

For a comprehensive study of Detroit's school system:

Mirel, Jeffrey, *The Rise and Fall of an Urban School System: Detroit, 1907–81.* Ann Arbor: The University of Michigan Press, 1993.

For information about the history of the Detroit auto industry:

Ingrassia, Paul, *Crash Course: The Automobile Industry's Road from Glory to Disaster.* New York: Random House, 2010.

Maynard, Micheline, *The End of Detroit: How the Big Three Lost Their Grip on the American Market.* New York: Currency Doubleday, 2003.

Key additional news sources:

Associated Press

The *Detroit Free Press*

The *Detroit News*

Michigan Chronicle

North American Newspaper Alliance

U.S. Census Bureau

United Press International

Exhibits and collections:

Burton Historical Collection, Detroit Public Library

Detroit Historical Museum—Exhibit on 1967 Riots

Louis Lomax Papers, Special Collections, University of Nevada Library and Archives, Reno

Walter Reuther Papers, Walter P. Reuther Library, United Auto Workers Archives, Wayne State University, Detroit ▦

Citations

PROLOGUE

1 Churchill quote: "Quotes falsely attributed to Winston Churchill," International Churchill Society, winstonchurchill.org. There are various other versions of this quotation, but this is the accurate wording.

2-4 Population figures and other population figures not otherwise cited: "The 200 Largest Cities in the United States by Population," worldpopulationreview.com.

CHAPTER 1 – COMING OF AGE

7 Surveyors' quote: Arthur W. Woodford, *This Is Detroit: 1702–2001* (Detroit: Wayne State University Press, 2001), 48.

7-9 History of French fashion and the founding and settlement of Detroit: Woodford, 15 ff.

9-10 History of British rule over Detroit and conflict with Native Americans: Woodford, 25 ff.

10 ". . . a cosmopolitan flavor": Woodford, 36.

10-11 1805 fire and rebuilding: Woodford, 37 ff.

10 "*Speramus meliora . . .*": Woodford, 39.

11 Detroit and the War of 1812: Woodford, 43 ff.

12 Early growth and development under Lewis Cass: Woodford, 47 ff.

13 1830 and 1840 census figures: Woodford, 54.

13 Cholera epidemics: Woodford, 59 ff.

14 Elijah McCoy invention: Woodford, 79.

14 Elijah McCoy biographical information: "Elijah McCoy," *The Canadian Encyclopedia*, thecanadianeneyclopedia.ca.

15 1850 census figures: Woodford, 61.

15 The Civil War and postwar growth: Woodford, 63 ff.

15 1860, 1870, 1880 census figures: Woodford, *This Is Detroit*, 87.

15 Stove industry: Woodford, 80.

16 Black businesses: Woodford, 87.

16 Turn-of-the-century prosperity: Woodford, 82–83.

16 1900 census and ranking figures: "Biggest US Cities in 1900," Historical Population Data, biggestuscities.com/1900.

CHAPTER 2 – SETTING THE TEMPLATE

17 "The first horseless carriage . . .": *Detroit Free Press*, March 7, 1896, quoted in Arthur W. Woodford, *This Is Detroit: 1702–2001* (Detroit: Wayne State University Press, 2001), 89–90.

17-18 Background history of the first automobile: "Who Invented the Auto-mobile," Library of Congress, oc.gov/everyday-mysteries/motor-vehicles-aeronautics-astronautics/item/who-invented-the-automobile/#:~:text=There%20are%20many%20different%20types,true%20automobile%20in%201885%2F1886

18-19 Early history of the automobile in Detroit: Woodford, *This Is Detroit*, 89 ff.

18 "The darn thing ran": Woodford, 90.

19 Packard plant information: Maureen McDonald, Packard Plant Guided Tour Information, thehubdetroit.com/peek-inside-packard-plant-guided-tours, September 25, 2017. [This plant has since been demolished.]

19 Early Ford history: corporate.ford.com/articles/history/highland-park.html and corporate.ford.com/articles/history/the-model-t.html.

19-20 Ford production, pay scale, and payroll: Woodford, *This Is Detroit*, 92 ff.

20 Pre-war and WWI industrial production: Woodford, 98 ff.

20-23 Hazen Pingree history: Bill Loomis, "Hazen Pingree: Quite possibly Detroit's finest mayor," *Detroit News*, February 8, 2020, https://www.detroitnews.com/story/news/local/michigan-history/2020/02/08/hazen-pingree-quite-possibly-detroits-finest-mayor/4686854002/.

23 John C. Lodge history: Dan Austin, "Meet the 5 best mayors in Detroit history," *Detroit Free Press*, March 13, 2015, https://www.freep.com/story/news/local/2014/08/28/meet-the-5-best-mayors-in-detroit-history/14748731/.

24 Ford and Chevrolet sales figures: "The Year in Cars," Mac's Motor City Garage, https://www.macsmotorcitygarage.com/category/the-year-in-cars/.

24-25 Illegal liquor trade and Depression-era economy: Woodford, *This Is Detroit*, 118 ff.

25 Charles Bowles history: Dan Austin, "Meet the 5 worst mayors in Detroit history," *Detroit Free Press*, February 20, 2019, https://www.freep.com/story/news/local/2014/08/29/5-worst-mayors-in-detroit-history/14799541/.

25 Frank Murphy history: Dan Austin, "Why Frank Murphy was one of Detroit's best mayors ever," *Detroit Free Press*, July 20, 2015, https://www.freep.com/story/news/local/michigan/detroit/2015/07/19/frank-murphy-detroit-history/30381049/.

25-26 History and development of Detroit schools: Jeffrey Mirel, *The Rise and Fall of an Urban School System: Detroit, 1907–81* (Ann Arbor: The University of Michigan Press, 1993).

26 New at-large school board: Mirel, *The Rise and Fall*, 27–29.

26 "one of the preeminent school systems in the nation": Mirel, 79.

26-28 Depression-era school district struggles: Mirel, 89 ff.

28 Student achievement and changes in curriculum: Mirel, 132.

29 History of IQ test and tracking: Mirel, 68–69.

29 "By 1940, high schools in Detroit . . .": Mirel, 134.

CHAPTER 3 – CRUCIBLE OF CONFLICT

31 Ford River Rouge size and employment: "The History of the Ford Rouge Factory," thehenryford.org; Austin Weber, "Special Section: The Rouge an industrial icon," assemblymag.com.

31 Population figures: Historical Population Data, Biggest US Cities, biggestus cities.com/1900 and biggestuscities.com/1930.

32 Detroit Federation of Teachers formation and public announcement: Jeffrey Mirel, *The Rise and Fall of an Urban School System: Detroit, 1907–81* (Ann Arbor: The University of Michigan Press, 1993) 112, 117.

32 Challenges to forming an auto workers' union and union formation: Arthur W. Woodford, *This Is Detroit: 1702–2001* (Detroit: Wayne State University Press, 2001), 142–44.

33 Fisher Body strike and eventual agreement between UAW and Detroit car makers: Woodford, 147–49.

33 200,000 UAW members in Detroit: Woodford, 145.

34 "a new era in human rights": Walter Reuther Papers, Reuther Library, Wayne State University, Detroit, Michigan: United Auto Workers Archives, President's Papers – Accession #261, Walter Reuther, Box 3, Folder 2 (hereafter Reuther Papers).

34 Percentage of national income going to wages: Congress of Industrial Organizations report, Reuther Library UAW President's Papers, Accession #261, Reuther Papers, Box 3, Folder 2.

34 National Defense Council and transition to war production: Woodford, *This Is Detroit*, 153.

34 In-migration of whites and blacks to work in wartime factories: "Detroit Is Dynamite," *Life*, August 17, 1942, Vol. 13, No. 7, p. 15 (hereafter "Dynamite").

35 Quotations "Detroit workers, led by the lusty U. A. W., . . ." through ". . . willing to fight Hitler": "Dynamite," 15–16.

35 "Detroit's politicians have shamelessly plundered . . .": "Dynamite," 19 (photo caption).

35 Mayor Reading's crime and sentence: "Ex-Mayor Reading of Detroit Is Dead," *New York Times*, December 10, 1952, p. 43.

35 "They have no great love for their city . . .": "Dynamite," 19.

35 "influence and control": "Dynamite," 19.

36 "impossible to rent a decent house": "Dynamite," 20.

36 "8000 B-24 bombers": Woodford, *This Is Detroit*, 156.

36 "hundreds of tents . . ." and description of workers' quarters: "Dynamite," 20.

36 Black participation at Ford: Wilbur C. Rich, *Coleman Young and Detroit Politics: From Social Activist to Power Broker* (Detroit: Wayne State University Press, 1989), 44.

36 "No Jim Crow in the CIO" and "regardless of race . . .": CIO newsletter, Reuther Papers, Box 2, Folder 23.

36-37 Sojourner Truth Homes history: "Prelude to 1967: Detroit's Racial Clashes of 1942–43," *Detroit News*, July 10, 2017, https://www.detroitnews.com/story/news/local/michigan-history/2017/07/07/detroit-riots-1942-43/103482496/.

37 National Workers League "heavily involved in agitating for violence,": "Prelude to 1967."

37-38 Detroit Housing Commission quotations: "Statement from Director-Secretary of Detroit Housing Commission," April 13, 1943, Reuther Papers, Box 6.

38 "I have tried to safeguard your neighborhoods . . .": "Mayor Jeffries Is Against Mixed Housing" campaign flyer, Reuther Papers, Box 8, Folder 12.

38-39 Black population growth and background on Black Bottom and Paradise Valley: Woodford, *This Is Detroit*, 109 ff.

39-40 Ossian Sweet history: Woodford, *This Is Detroit*, 109 and "Sweet, Ossian," *Encyclopedia of Detroit*, detroithistorical.org.

40 Summer heat on Belle Isle: Woodford, 157.

40 Fight with sailors: Woodford, 157.

40 Five thousand people fighting: Woodford, 157.

41 Death and arrest figures, "Many of those killed . . ." and Horatiis beating: "Prelude to 1967: Detroit's racial clashes of 1942–43," *Detroit News*, July 10, 2017, https://www.detroitnews.com/story/news/local/michigan-history/2017/07/07/detroit-riots-1942-43/103482496/.

41 "No one knows . . .": Woodford, *This Is Detroit*, 157.

41 Rumors of whites throwing blacks off a bridge and of a white woman being raped: Woodford, 157.

41 Adler quotations: Philip A. Adler, "Planning Seen in Race Riots," *Detroit News,* June 24, 1943, p.1.

42 "torn by social injustice . . .": "Detroit Disorders Hailed by Nazi Radio," *Detroit News*, June 24, 1943, p.1.

Chapter 4 – Shifting Gears

43 Population figures: Historical Population Data, biggeestuscities.com and Arthur W. Woodford, *This Is Detroit: 1702–2001* (Detroit: Wayne State University Press, 2001),160, 164.

44 UAW 113-day strike: Woodford, *This Is Detroit*, 147.

44 GM first company to earn $1 billion: Paul Ingrassia, *Crash Course: The Automobile Industry's Road from Glory to Disaster* (New York: Random House, 2010).

44 Demise of Packard and loss of jobs: Woodford, *This Is Detroit*, 162. See also Dennis Adler, *Packard* (St. Paul, MN: MBI Publishing Company, 1998), 135 ff.

44-46 Urban renewal history: Woodford, 163 ff.

47 Complaints about high school graduates: Jeffrey Mirel, *The Rise and Fall of an Urban School System: Detroit, 1907–81* (Ann Arbor: The University of Michigan Press, 1993), 237.

47 "simple arithmetic, arithmetical reasoning . . .": Mirel, 238.

48 State law requiring retirement funding: Mirel, 247.

48 Cavanaugh election and income tax: Woodford, *This Is Detroit*, 165.

49 Frank Murphy quotations: Nathan Bomey and John Gallagher, "How Detroit went broke: The answer may surprise you – and don't blame Coleman Young," *Detroit Free Press*, September 15, 2013, freep.com.

49 Detroit 70% white in 1960: "Race and Hispanic Origin for Selected Large Cities and Other Places: Earliest Census to 1990 Table 23 – Michigan," U.S. Census Bureau.

49 School board election and advisory committee: Mirel, *The Rise and Fall*, 253.

50 Alfred Pelham appointed comptroller: Woodford, *This Is Detroit*, 165.

CHAPTER 5 – INFERNO

51 "There's no real benefit . . .": Detroit Historical Museum exhibit on 1967 riots.

51 Cities with racial unrest in the summer of 1967: Sid Moody, "Ordeal in Detroit: Costliest Riot in U.S. History," *Tennessean*, July 30, 1967, pp. 1-B ff.

51-53 Detroit expecting to avoid riots, black representation and wages: "Rioting Blasts Detroit Boast of Race Peace," *Tennessean*, July 24, 1967, p. 4.

52 Black workers' salary and economic health: Bureau of Labor Statistics notes, Reuther Papers, Accession #261, Box 578, Folder 9.

53 Gallup poll predicting no more riots – George Gallup, "1 in 7 Expects More Riots," *Tennessean*, July 23, 1967, p. 5-B.

53 Detroit Historical Society account of riot: "Uprising of 1967," *Encyclopedia of Detroit*, https://detroithistorical.org/learn/encyclopedia-of-detroit/uprising-1967.

53-54 *Encyclopedia Britannica* account of riot: Traqina Quarks Emeka, "Detroit Riot of 1967," *Encyclopedia Britannica*, https://www.britannica.com/event/Detroit-Riot-of-1967.

54 History.com account of riot: "1967 Detroit Riots," March 23, 2021, https://www.history.com/topics/1960s/1967-detroit-riots.

54 *Time* magazine description of riots: "The Fire This Time," *Time*, August 4, 1967, p. 13.

54 *Time* 50-year retrospective: Lily Rothman, "What We Still Got Wrong About What Happened in Detroit in 1967," *Time*, August 3, 2017, https://time.com/4879062/detroit-1967-real-history/.

54 Detroit Free Press 50-year review: Rochelle Riley, "The rebellion that almost killed Detroit will some day make it stronger," *Detroit Free Press*, July 29, 2017, https://www.freep.com/story/news/columnists/rochelle-riley/2017/07/30/detroit-riot-uprising-rebellion/517735001/,

55 Temperature information: National Weather Service archives.

55 "Of the question of why . . ." and other Walker quotations: George Walker, "The Riot: A Quick Look at What It Is," *Detroit Free Press*, Wednesday, July 26, 1967, p. 5-A.

57 "relatively light street crowds . . .": This and other police report quotations and information from "Summary of the Report of Sgt. Arthur Howison on raid 3:45–4:45 a.m., July 23, 1967," Detroit Historical Museum exhibit. Despite inaccuracies and subjectivity in its *Encyclopedia*, the Historical Society's museum exhibit gives a thorough, balanced, entertaining, expertly researched and curated account of the riots.

57 "Youths began smashing store windows . . .": "Detroit Asks Federal Troops," *Nashville Banner*, July 24, 1967, p. 2.

58 "They say they need more protection . . .": "Rioters Turn Detroit Area into Wasteland," *Tennessean*, July 24, 1967, p. 12.

58 Looters give firemen beer: "Rioters Turn Detroit Area into Wasteland."

58 "carnival spirit . . ." and tour by Romney and Cavanaugh: "Detroit Asks Federal Troops," *Nashville Banner*, July 24, 1967, pp. 1–2.

58 "The riot was very good . . ." Detroit Historical Museum exhibit.

59 Romney requests National Guard: "Detroit Asks Federal Troops."

59 Romney-Johnson conflict: "Detroit Riot to Rights Lack," *Nashville Banner*, July 31, 1967, p. 6; "Romney Accuses Johnson of Using Riot for Politics: Curfew Locks Milwaukee," *Commercial Appeal* (Memphis), August 1, 1967, p. 1; "Romney Claim of Troop Delay Is Contradicted," *Commercial Appeal* (Memphis), August 2, 1967, p. 1.

59 President Johnson comments: "101st Troopers Charge into Riot-Lashed Detroit," *Tennessean*, July 25, 1967, p. 4.

59 "Thousands of rampaging Negroes . . .": "Rioters Turn Detroit Area into Wasteland," *Tennessean*, July 24, 1967, p. 1.

59 "Negro sniper squads . . .": "Death Toll Rises to 33," *Nashville Banner*, July 26, 1967, p. 1.

59 "Negro outlaws engage federal paratroopers . . .": "Racial Situation at a Glance," *Nashville Banner*, July 25, 1967, p. 1.

59 "the nation's worst racial explosion . . .": "Detroit Toll Tops Watts; Troops Implore Calm," *Tennessean*, July 27, 1967, p. 1.

59 Detroit disturbance not a "race riot," blacks and whites looted together: George Walker, "The Riot: A Quick Look at What It Is," *Detroit Free Press*, Wednesday, July 26, 1967, p. 5-A.

60 "hoodlums with a total disregard for the law": Walker, "The Riot."

60 James Del Rio effort to calm the mob: "Detroit Asks Federal Troops," *Nashville Banner*, July 24, 1967, p. 2.

60 Congressman Conyers efforts to quiet mob: "Rioters Turn Detroit Area into Wasteland," *Tennessean*, July 24, 1967, p. 12.

60 Reverend Nicholas hood threatened: "Detroit Asks Federal Troops."

60 "trying to discourage young people from looting . . .": Detroit Historical Museum exhibit.

60 "There was no harm done to me and my family . . .": Detroit Historical Museum exhibit.

60 "We're going to get you rich niggers next!": "The Fire This Time," *Time*, August 4, 1967, p. 13.

61 Death toll at 33, including girl; continued sniper action: "Sniper War Rocks Detroit," *Nashville Banner*, July 26, 1967, pp. 1–2.

61 Three white snipers charged: "Sniper War Rocks Detroit."

61 Seasoned troopers outperform National Guard: "Sniper War Rocks Detroit."

61 "I had no intention of having innocent women and children killed . . .": "Empty Gun Order in Detroit Rapped," *Nashville Banner*, August 23, 1967, p. 15.

Churches distribute food and clothing, lack of grocery stores and other services: "'War' Rages in 200 Blocks as Detroit Toll Reaches 33," *Tennessean*, July 26, 1967, p. 8.

62 "all-out war": "'War' Rages in 200 Blocks," p. 1.

62 Death toll surpasses Watts: "Detroit Toll Tops Watts; Troops Impose Calm," *Tennessean*, July 27, 1967, p. 1.

62 Firemen get a break; firefighter casualties: Karl Mantyla, "Detroit Firemen Get 6-Hour Break," *Nashville Banner*, July 27, 1967, p. 4.

62 Lindberg birthplace guarded: "Famous Birthplace Guarded," *Nashville Banner*, July 28, 1967 (photo caption).

62 "Now Girardin's compassion is bringing him criticism . . ." Gene Roberts, "Detroit Riot 'Not Plotted,'" *Nashville Tennessean*, July 28, 1967, p. 4.

62 Fears of charges of police brutality: Jerry M. Flint, "Police Laxity Ires Negroes," *Tennessean*, July 26, 1967, p. 8.

63 "half-drunken young Negroes . . .": Roberts, "Detroit Riot."

63 Black residents saying police should have stopped riots early on: Jerry M. Flint, "Police Laxity Ires Negroes," *Tennessean*, July 26, 1967, p. 8.

63-64 Charles Tindal, Longworth Quinn, *Michigan Chronicle*, and William Greene quotations: Flint, "Police Laxity Ires Negroes."

63 Police anxious not to "inflame" crowd but "little attempt was made . . .": "Police Laxity."

CHAPTER 6 – MINORITY REPORT

65 Lomax first black journalist hired by Hearst and other biographical information: Thomas Aiello, *The Life & Times of Louis Lomax: The Art of Deliberate Disunity* (Durham: Duke University Press, 2021), 19.

65 *The Hate That Hate Produced* documentary: Louis Lomax Papers, University of Nevada Library and Archives, Reno (hereafter Lomax Papers), Box 3, folder 82-30/2/1/2; the program first appeared over the course of a week in five nightly segments, then was rebroadcast as a single program on July 22, 1959.

66 Movie about Malcolm X: "20th Inks Lomax For Malcolm X Script," *Hollywood Reporter*, November 29, 1967, p. 1.

66 Lomax and Ho Chi Minh, trip to Cambodia: telegram from Minh representatives, Lomax Papers, Box 3, folder 82-30/4/16.

66 Lomax mention of civilian task force: Louis E. Lomax, "'Operation Detroit' Outsiders Laid Groundwork for Riot," *Nashville Banner*, August 14, 1967, pp. 1–2 (hereafter Lomax #1).

66 Marquis Childs mention of civilian task force: Marquis Childs, "Detroit Tried Hard to Avoid Race Clash," *Tennessean*, July 27, 1967, p. 17; Childs went on to win a Pulitzer Prize in 1970.

67 The closest thing to a black ghetto in Detroit: Sid Moody, "Ordeal in Detroit: Costliest Riot in U.S. History," *Tennessean*, July 30, 1967, p. 1-B.

67 "because it overlooked the fact . . ." and "highly organized and well trained . . .": Lomax #1.

67 "Operation Detroit": Lomax #1.

67 "I thought I was helping a worthy Negro . . ." and story of magazine salesmen: Lomax #1.

68 Failed efforts to instigate riot: Lomax #1.

68 "They called us niggers!": Lomax #1.

68 "I was standing on the street . . .": Lomax #1.

69 "At this point the professionals moved in": Lomax #1.

69 "Come on, baby, help yourself" and other looter quotes: Lomax #1.

69 "The professionals wanted hundreds of people running . . .": Lomax #1.

69 Preference for color TVs, stealing refrigerator: Sandra A. West, "West Side Called 'Nice Neighborhood,'" United Press International, *Nashville Banner*, July 24, 1967, p. 2 (hereafter West #1).

69 Out-of-town license plates and "The feeling is growing in my neighborhood . . .": Sandra A. West, "Gunshots Surpass 2-Day Entrapment," *Nashville Banner*, July 26, 1967, p. 6 (hereafter West #2).

70 "saw sights I never dreamed possible" and preparation to evacuate: West #1.

70 Locals spotting out-of-town cars and "a man who seemed to be the leader . . .": West #2.

70 "Methodically breaking store windows . . ." and "They are not thieves . . .": Louis E. Lomax, "Fate, Human Weakness Aided Detroit Agitators," *Nashville Banner*, August 15, 1967, p. 2. (hereafter Lomax #2).

70 Looters evade police: Lomax #2.

71 "I burned that damn Jew store down!" and story of furniture store arson: Lomax #2.

71 Stories of liquor store arson, grocery store arson: Lomax #2.

71 "A weary but happy arsonist . . .": Lomax #2.

71 Riot spreads to Seven-Mile Road: Lomax #2.

71 "burning, choking . . . heavy smoke . . .": West #2.

72 "It's fun": Louis E. Lomax, "'Unorganized' Snipers Joined Detroit Rioting," *Nashville Banner*, August 16, 1967, p. 12 (hereafter Lomax #3).

72 ". . . on the whole were Detroit's own sons . . .": Lomax #3.

72 "Responsible Negroes" account of six suspected instigators, their connections, and meetings at Vaughn's Bookstore: Lomax #3.

73 "Several factors about the involvement of white people are clear . . ." and discussion of white snipers and participation: Louis E. Lomax, "Detroit Soon Became City of Fright, Suspicion," *Nashville Banner*, August 17, 1967, p. 17 (hereafter Lomax #4).

74 "irrefutably evident that a Black Power revolutionary organization . . .": Louis E. Lomax, "Revolutionary Group Directed Detroit Riot," *Nashville Banner*, August 26, 1967, p. 3 (hereafter Lomax #5).

74 "Detroit, like every other American city . . .": Undated handwritten notes, Lomax Papers, Box 3, folder 82-30/3/10.

74 Civil rights changes for "the Negro with training, brains, and talent": Lomax #5.

75 "as articulated by Dr. Martin Luther King": Lomax #5.

75 "They were the same old crowd . . .": Lomax #5.

75 "You told them . . .": Lomax #5.

75 "God forbid, the only thing they will hear . . .": Lomax #5.

75-76 Lomax field notes from riots: Lomax Papers, Box 3.

76 "one of the agitators": Field notes, Lomax Papers, Box 3.

76 "hub for black revolutionaries": Louis E. Lomax, "Newark called hub for 'black revolutionaries,'" *Newark Star-Ledger*, August 27, 1967, p. 1.

76 Willie Wright history: Lomax, "Newark called hub."

76 "When assigned to do a series of articles . . .": Louis E. Lomax, "Newark Riot Was Planned: New Riots Up to Johnson," The Lomax Column, Bell-McClure Syndicate, February 24/25, 1968, Lomax papers, Box 3, folder 82-30/3/7.

76 "Newark's revolutionaries were congratulating themselves . . .": Louis E. Lomax, "Voices of dissent remain muffled," *Newark Star-Ledger*, August 29, 1967, p. 1.

77 "unerringly points to one of the nationally known . . .": Bob Hull, "Lomax Claims 'Plot' Behind Recent Disorder," TV Talk, *Los Angeles Herald-Examiner*, August 1, 1967, p. A-12.

77 "How in the hell can you build a bridge . . .": Louis E. Lomax, "The bone of contention: How to get the 'goodies,'" *Newark Star-Ledger*, August 30, 1067, p. 1.

77 Louis Lomax death: *New York Times* obituary: "Louis Lomax, 47, Dies in Car Crash," *New York Times*, August 1, 1970, p. 23.

77-79 Schuyler quotations from "that the government, by pandering to the least responsible . . ." to "The more handouts they are given, the louder they clamor for more. . . .": George S. Schuyler, "Writer Says Negroes Hurt; Sees Whitewash," *Nashville Banner*, August 21, 1967, p. 3.

79-80 Schuyler quotations from "onset ten years ago of the campaign of agitation . . ." to ". . . after the cities have burnt to ashes": George S. Schuyler, "Anti-Riot Bill Said 'Too Little, Too Late,'" *Nashville Banner*, August 22, 1967, p. 10.

80-81 Commissioner Girardin and Governor Romney comments: Gene Roberts, New York Times News Service, "Detroit Riot 'Not Plotted,'" *Tennessean,* July 28, 1967, p. 4.

81 Congressman Ford and Senator Baker quotations: Edmund Willingham, "Must Investigate for Riots' 'Master Plan' Says Baker," *Tennessean*, July 30, 1967, p. 1.

81 Senator Dirksen and Governor Reagan comments: "Congress Pressured to Halt Violence," *Nashville Banner*, July 26, 1967, pp. 1–2.

81 *Barron's* article: excerpt published as "The Riots Are Subsidized as Well as Organized," from *Barron's*, July 31, 1967; reprinted in *Nashville Banner*, August 7, 1967, pp. 1–2.

82 Governor Romney lifts state of emergency: "Detroit Is Out of Emergency," *Commercial Appeal*, August 7, 1967.

82-83 "Most important of all, it is not a race riot..." [same as when this quote was used previously] George Walker, "The Riot: A Quick Look at What It Is," *Detroit Free Press*, Wednesday, July 26, 1967, p. 5-A.

83 Origins of the New Detroit Committee: "Detroit Under Fire," New Detroit Committee, University of Michigan History Labs, https://policing.umhistorylabs.lsa .umich.edu/s/detroitunderfire/page/home.

83 New Detroit Committee report, quotations, and commentary: "New Detroit Committee Is Not Representative," *Michigan Chronicle*, August 12, 1967, https://policing .umhistorylabs.lsa.umich.edu/s/detroitunderfire/item/1301.

CHAPTER 7 – SHORTHAND FOR HOPELESS

85 Kerner Commission report, quotations, and commentary: Fred Siegel, Stephan Thernstrom, and Robert Woodson, Sr., "The Kerner Commission Report," The Heritage Foundation, June 24, 1998, https://www.heritage.org/poverty-and-inequality/report/ the-kerner-commission-report.

86 Siegel quotations: "The Kerner Commission Report."

87 "Everybody thinks it was the riots . . .": Mike Alberti, "Squandered Opportunities Leave Detroit Isolated," January 11, 2012, https://www.remappingdebate.org/article/squandered-opportunities-leave-detroit-isolated.

87 1971–72 school year attendance compared with aftermath of riots: Jeffrey Mirel, *The Rise and Fall of an Urban School System: Detroit, 1907–81* (Ann Arbor: The University of Michigan Press, 1993), 359.

87 Detroit Public Schools enrollment 1966: John Grover and Yvette van der Velde, *A School District in Crisis: Detroit Public Schools 1842–2015* (Detroit: Loveland Technologies, 2015).

88 School conflicts redrawn on basis of race: Mirel, *Rise and Fall*, 308–9.

88 "the virtual end of white working-class support . . .": Mirel, 322.

88 *Michigan Chronicle* publishes test results: Mirel, 344.

89 "decentralization" process: Mirel, 336.

89 School board meeting April 7, 1970: Mirel, 340–41.

89 "these black organizations are unalterably opposed . . .": Mirel, 341.

90 *Milliken v. Bradley* case: Mirel, 345–46.

90 Projected budget deficit of $40 million: Mirel, 351.

90 Teacher strike 1973–74: Mirel, 363.

90 "Detroit schools are filled to overflowing . . .": Mirel, 363.

90 "rightful perks of their office": Mirel, 355 (see footnote 220).

90 Black families turn to Catholic schools: Mirel, 367.

90 Standardized test results 1972, 1979: Mirel, 366.

91 "Now hear us out on this . . .": Dan Austin, "Meet the 5 best mayors in Detroit history," *Detroit Free Press*, August 28, 2014, https://www.freep.com/story/news/local/2014/08/28/meet-the-5-best-mayors-in-detroit-history/14748731/.

91 "Under Young, Detroit has become . . .": Zev Chafets, *Devil's Night Out and Other True Tales of Detroit* (New York: Vintage Books, 1991), 177.

91 Budget surpluses and trimming city workforce: Joe Swickard, "Young Felt Targeted: Federal authorities prosecuted his associates," *Detroit Free Press* December 5, 1997, pp. 6C-8C.

91 Young's focus on the future: Detroit Historical Museum display.

91 Loss of $600 million transportation grant: Kathy Warbelow and William Mitchell, "Rapid Transit in Detroit: A $600 Million Question," *Detroit Free Press*, November 24, 1976, pp. 1C, 4C. See also Mike Alberti, "Squandered opportunities leave Detroit isolated," January 11, 2012, https://www.remappingdebate.org/article/squandered-opportunities-leave-detroit-isolated.

91 Young managed a political machine and other criticism: Detroit Historical Museum display.

91 Increase in number of Detroit residents on welfare: Wilbur C. Rich, *Coleman Young and Detroit Politics: From Social Activist to Power Broker* (Detroit: Wayne State University Press, 1989), 137.

92 "Despite intense competition . . .": Rich, 14, 29.

92 "Since blacks have few economic penalties . . ." Rich, 28.

92 "This is the Coleman Young of *Hardstuff* . . .": Joe Swickard, "Young Felt Targeted: Federal authorities prosecuted his associates," *Detroit Free Press* December 5, 1997, p. 8C.

92-93 Young biographical information: Coleman Young, *Encyclopedia of Detroit*, Detroit Historical Society, detroithistorical.org.

93 *Daily Worker* photo: *Daily Worker*, loose clipping in Reuther Library Accession #261

93 National Negro Labor Council information: Coleman Young, *Encyclopedia Britannica*, https://www.britannica.com/topic/National-Negro-Labor-Council.

93 "I consider the activities of this committee . . .": *Encyclopedia of Detroit*, https://detroithistorical.org/learn/encyclopedia-of-detroit/young-coleman.

93 "You have mixed me up . . .": Bill McGraw, "Coleman Young: The 10 greatest myths" *Detroit Free Press*, May 26, 2018, https://www.freep.com/story/opinion/2018/05/26/coleman-young-myths/638105002/.

93 Disbanding the National Negro Labor Council: *Encyclopedia Britannica*.

93 1969 and 1973 mayoral elections: Edward L. Glaeser and Andrei Shleifer, "The Curley Effect: The Economics of Shaping the Electorate," *The Journal of Law, Economics, & Organization* 21, no. 1 (April 2005): 1–19.

94 Bad relations between Young and federal agencies: Swickard, "Young Felt Targeted."

95 "Construction has yet to begin . . .": David Kushma, "Young makes pitch for transit system," *Detroit Free Press*, February 7, 1984, p. A3.

95 "equally opposed by suburban and outstate politicians . . .": David Kushma, "Overruns on People Mover Kill Rail Plans," *Detroit Free Press*, November 14, 1984, p. A3.

96 Problems with People Mover construction: David Kushma, "SEMTA finds cracks in more Mover beams," *Detroit Free Press*, August 22, 1985, p. 1.

96 Control of People Mover turned over to city of Detroit: David Kushma, "SEMTA OKs giving control of People Mover project to city," *Detroit Free Press*, October 2, 1985, p. A3.

96 "having survived bungled management . . .": David Everett, "Glitches didn't detail People Mover," *Detroit Free Press*, July 31, 1987, p. 1.

96 Fitzgerald comments on riding People Mover: Jim Fitzgerald, "East ride, west ride, all around downtown: It's different," *Detroit Free Press*, July 26, 1987, p. G1.

96-97 History of Joe Louis Arena: M. L. Elrick, "How Coleman Young got Joe Louis Arena built, and kept the Red Wings in Detroit," Fox 2 Detroit, April 17, 2017, https://www.fox2detroit.com/news/how-coleman-young-got-joe-louis-arena-built-and-kept-the-red-wings-in-detroit.

97 Exit problems and steps at Joe Louis Arena: Carey English, "Architect has doubts about Louis Arena," *Detroit Free Press*, December 12, 1979, p. 1.

97 Fans loved Joe Louis Arena; plans for the site: "Our Joe Louis Arena Memories: Games, players, more," *Detroit Free Press* April 9, 2017, https://www.freep.com/story/sports/nhl/red-wings/2017/04/09/detroit-red-wings-joe-louis-arena-free-press-memories/100189508/; Carlos Monarrez, "Thank you, Joe Louis Arena; It has been a sweet, smelly ride," *Detroit Free Press*, April 9, 2017, https://www.freep.com/story/sports/nhl/red-wings/2017/04/05/joe-louis-arena-farewell/100089172/.

98 "Are we willing to do what is necessary . . .": Swickard, "Young Felt Targeted."

98-99 Scandals during Young's administration: Swickard, "Young Felt Targeted."

99-102 Glaeser and Shleifer study including quotations: Edward L. Glaeser and Andrei Shleifer, "The Curley Effect: The Economics of Shaping the Electorate, *The Journal of Law, Economics, & Organization*, April 1, 2005."

CHAPTER 8 – STALLED

104 "To blame the union alone for what happened to the Detroit companies . . .": Micheline Maynard, *The End of Detroit: How the Big Three Lost Their Grip on the American Market* (New York: Currency Doubleday, 2003), 299.

105 "Mr. Ford, I don't think what we're doing . . .": Paul Ingrassia, *Crash Course: The American Automobile Industry's Road from Glory to Disaster* (New York: Random House, 2011), 28.

105 Union strike at GM: Ingrassia, *Crash Course*, 45.

105 Union strike at Chrysler: Ingrassia, 55.

105 Blue collar/white collar income spread: Ingrassia, 57.

106 Toyota/GM Fremont joint venture: Maynard, *The End of Detroit*, 82–85.

106 "level the playing field": Ingrassia, *Crash Course*, 72–73.

106 Honda plant in Lincoln, Alabama: Maynard, *The End of Detroit*, 212.

107 Detroit factory absenteeism and delays: Ingrassia, *Crash Course*, 48.

107 Modular car production: Maynard, 164.

107 Jobs bank: Ingrassia, 87, 96.

107 Detroit auto makers legacy costs: Ingrassia, 136

108 Furloughed Delphi workers: Ingrassia, 169.

108 GM retirees and liabilities: Ingrassia, 258.

108 Big Three spend $20 billion while Mercedes-Benz builds: Ingrassia, 90.

108 U.S. Camrys made in Kentucky: Maynard, *The End of Detroit*, 117.

108 Nashville Nissan efficiency: Maynard, 163.

108-109 "The ultimate irony of Detroit's demise . . .": Maynard, 10.

109 "the epicenter of the American automotive universe": Maynard, 308.

109 Auto industry bailout a "moral imperative": Ingrassia, *Crash Course*, 222.

109 "We're in Crisis": Ingrassia, 237.

109 "I find it very difficult to believe . . .": Ingrassia, 219.

109 "the worst-managed company": Ingrassia, 238.

109 General Motors bankruptcy filing: Ingrassia, 270.

110 Background on Dennis Archer: Peter Gavrilovich, "Mayors of Detroit, 1950–2013," *Detroit Free Press*, September 15, 2013, https://www.freep.com/story/news/local/michigan/detroit/2013/09/15/mayors-of-detroit-19502013/77154478/.

110 Detroit casinos 2022 revenue: "Detroit casinos produce $1.276 billion in aggregate revenue during 2022," Michigan Gaming Control Board, January 10, 2023, Michigan.gov.

110 Background on Kwame Kilpatrick: Dan Austin, "Meet the 5 worst mayors in Detroit history," *Detroit Free Press*, February 20, 2019, https://www.freep.com/story/news/local/2014/08/29/5-worst-mayors-in-detroit-history/14799541/.

111 Kilpatrick financial dealings: Tresa Baldas, "How corruption deepened Detroit's crisis," *USA Today*, October 6, 2013, https://www.usatoday.com/story/news/nation/2013/10/06/how-corruption-deepened-detroits-crisis/2929137/.

111-112 Background on/quotations from Dave Bing: Chanel Stitt, "New book 'Attacking the Rim' details Dave Bing's triumph over obstacles," *Detroit Free Press*, November 14, 2020, https://www.freep.com/story/money/business/michigan/2020/11/13/dave-bing-attacking-the-rim/6070306002/.

Chapter 9 – Hope to the People

113 ff. Detroit Bankruptcy perspective and historical context: Nathan Bomey, *Detroit Resurrected: To Bankruptcy and Back* (New York: W. W. Norton & Company, Inc., 2017).

115 Mayor Bing's efforts to stave off city bankruptcy: Sarah Cwiek, "In Detroit, Drastic Steps to Avoid Bankruptcy," *Morning Edition*, NPR, December 9, 2011, https://www.npr.org/2011/12/09/143429357/in-detroit-drastic-steps-to-avoid-bankruptcy.

115 "It could have worked . . .": Nathan Bomey and John Gallagher, "How Detroit went broke: The answers may surprise you—and don't blame Coleman Young," *Detroit Free Press*, September 15, 2013, https://www.freep.com/story/news/local/michigan/detroit/2013/09/15/how-detroit-went-broke-the-answers-may-surprise-you-and/77152028/.

116 Judge Ferguson indictments and "This is the greatest injustice . . .": David Ashenfelter, "Detroit Had a Corruption Scandal in 1930s That Was Bigger Than Today's, *Deadline Detroit*, February 21, 2013, https://www.deadlinedetroit.com/articles/3835/detroit_had_a_corruption_scandal_in_1930s_that_was_bigger_than_today_s.

116 Detroit higher taxes and falling revenue: Bomey and Gallagher, "How Detroit went broke."

116-117 Thirteenth check bonus: Bomey, *Detroit Resurrected*, 52–54 and Bomey and Gallagher, "How Detroit went broke."

118 Size of Detroit workforce verses other cities: Bomey and Gallagher, "How Detroit went broke."

118-119 "heads-in-the-sand" obstructionists: Bomey and Gallagher, "How Detroit went broke."

118-119 Mayor Kilpatrick's unsuccessful financial scheme: Tresa Baldas, "How corruption deepened Detroit's crisis," *USA Today*, October 6, 2013, https://www.usatoday.com/story/news/nation/2013/10/06/how-corruption-deepened-detroits-crisis/2929137/.

119 Detroit's financial picture at the time of bankruptcy: "Legacy Costs and Indebtedness of the City of Detroit," Citizens Research Council of Michigan, Report 373, December 2011, https://crcmich.org/PUBLICAT/2010s/2011/rpt373.pdf.

119-120 Detroit Symphony financial troubles and strike: Stephanie Gallman, "Detroit symphony goes on strike," CNN, October 5, 2010, https://www.cnn.com/2010/US/10/05/michigan.symphony.strike/index.html.

120 Detroit teacher salary in 2010: Tom Gantert, "Up and Down: The Story of Teacher Salaries in Detroit," *Capcon*, August 5, 2016, https://www.michigancapitolconfidential.com/22673.

121 "You've got to be kidding me!": Bomey, *Detroit Resurrected*, 35.

122 "Burn down the city of Detroit . . .": Bomey, 34.

122 "a plantocracy . . .": Bomey, 39.

122 "an elitist outsider": Bomey, 41.

123 Crime statistics: Bomey, 45.

123 "Things were . . . probably bleaker than people thought . . .": Bomey, 47.

123-124 Figures and quotations from meeting on June 14, 2013: Bomey, 47–48.

124 Public pensions protected by state constitution: Bomey, 69.

124 "If the City of Detroit were to cease to exist . . .": Bomey, 83.

124-125 Size of creditor list: Bomey, 87.

125 Art "shall become in its broadest sense democratic . . .": Bomey, 115.

125-126 "If it came down to selling a Van Gogh . . .": Bomey, 128.

126 Value of top artworks: Bomey, 127.

126 Meeting of top nonprofits: Bomey, 138.

126 "What you're asking us to do . . .": Bomey, 143.

127 "I think this is wonderful . . .": Bomey, 147.

127 Other foundation contributions and the Grand Bargain: Bomey, 148.

127 "completely unfeasible": Bomey, 150.

127 Other donations to the Grand Bargain: Bomey, 153.

127-128 Total pledges for the Grand Bargain: Bomey, 167.

128 Estimated value of the collection: Bomey, 171.

128 Agreement on settlement terms: Bomey, 158.

129 Proposed sale of Belle Isle park: Bomey, 176.

129 Water main breaks and bond issue, agreement with regional authority: Bomey, 181, 189, 191.

130 "scrubbed its balance sheet of the legacy costs...": Bomey, 216.

130 "What emerged from the city's bankruptcy . . .": Bomey, 235–36.

130 "I urge you now not to forget your anger . . .": Bomey, 239.

CHAPTER 10 – HARD LESSONS

133 Regional population figures: Detroit Metro Area Population 1950–2023, macrotrends.net.

133 Detroit population decline: Kim Kozlowski, "Detroit's 70-year population decline continues; Duggan says city was undercounted," *Detroit News*, August 12, 2021, https://www.detroitnews.com/story/news/local/detroit-city/2021/08/12/census-detroit -population-decline-u-s-census-bureau/5567639001/.

133-134 Education issues remain after bankruptcy: Nathan Bomey, *Detroit Resur- rected: To Bankruptcy and Back* (New York: W.W. Norton & Company, Inc., 2017), 244.

134 Dan Gilbert and Mike Ilitch investments: Bomey, *Detroit Resurrected*, 245.

134 "There's a real roadmap . . .": Bomey, 247.

134-135 Hawaii trip, ambulance, streetlight, and emergency response times: Eric Boehm, "Top 10 reasons Detroit went bankrupt," *Washington Examiner*, July 20, 2013, https://www.washingtonexaminer.com/news/378029/top-10-reasons-detroit-went -bankrupt/.

135-138 "Why has Detroit continued to decline . . ." and following related questions: Scott Beyer, "Why Has Detroit Continued to Decline?" *Forbes,* July 31, 2018, https://www.forbes.com/sites/scottbeyer/2018/07/31/why-has-detroit-continued-to -decline/?sh=2f4609123fbe.

136 "aggressive courtship of business investment . . .": John Wisely, "L. Brooks Patterson dies after leading Oakland County for a generation," *Detroit Free Press*, August 5, 2019, https://www.freep.com/story/news/local/michigan/2019/08/03/l-brooks-patterson -death-obituary/3497059002/.

136-138 "invoke the events from long ago . . ." and following quotes comparing Detroit with other cities: Beyer, "Why Has Detroit Continued to Decline?"

138-139 Detroit schools post-bankruptcy information and quotations: Chad Livengood, "DPS debt payments mount to unsustainable levels," *Detroit News*, January 4, 2016, https://www.detroitnews.com/story/news/education/2016/01/04/detroit-schools -debt-payments/78240726/.

139 District ranked last in national progress: Valerie Strauss, "How bad are conditions in Detroit public schools?" *Washington Post*, January 20, 2016, https://www .washingtonpost.com/news/answer-sheet/wp/2016/01/20/how-appalling-are-conditions -in-detroit-public-schools-this-appalling/.

139 2016 principal kickbacks: Sarah Cwiek, "(The Latest) Corruption Charges In Detroit's Struggling Schools," NPR, April 22, 2016, https://www.npr.org/sections/ ed/2016/04/22/474737468/-the-latest-corruption-charges-in-detroits-struggling-schools.

139 StoryTown curriculum: Cwiek, "(The Latest) Corruption."

139-140 Civil rights lawsuit on behalf of DPS students: Erin Einhorn, "Eighth grader taught classes and 23 more startling allegations in schools lawsuit," *Chalkbeat Detroit*, September 14, 2016, https://www.dailydetroit.com/eighth-grader -taught-classes-23-startling-allegations-schools-lawsuit/.

Chapter 11 – History Repeats

144 Recent Chicago crime: "Crime in Chicago: What Does Research Tell Us?" Institute for Policy Research, Northwestern University, May 28, 2018, https://www.ipr .northwestern.edu/news/2018/crime-in-chicago-research.html.

144 Chicago Crime Lab figures: "What's behind Chicago's surge in violence?" Editorial, *Chicago Tribune*, January 17, 2017, https://www.chicagotribune.com/2017/01/17/ whats-behind-chicagos-surge-in-violence/.

144 Laquin McDonald killing: Jason Johnson, "Why violent crime surged after police across America retreated," *USA Today*, April 9, 2021, https://www.usatoday.com/ story/opinion/policing/2021/04/09/violent-crime-surged-across-america-after-police -retreated-column/7137565002/.

144-145 2021 Chicago shootings and homicides: "2021 ends as Chicago's deadliest year in a quarter century," January 1, 2022, https://www.foxnews.com/ us/2021-chicagos-deadliest-year-quarter-century.

145 Chicago arrests decline, murders increase: Johnson, "Why violent crime surged."

145 Kim Foxx charging decisions: Johnson, "Why violent crime surged."

145 Court approval of ending cash bail in Michigan: https://news.wttw.com /2024/03/28/cook-county-courts-have-seen-mostly-smooth-transition-after-elimination -cash-bail-new.

145 Mayor Lori Lightfoot criticized: Ashley Carnahan, "Lori Lightfoot torpedoed over re-election campaign: 'Worst mayor in America, worst mayor Chicago has ever had,'" Fox News, January 13, 2023, https://www.foxnews.com/media/lori-lightfoot-torpedoed -re-election-campaign-worst-mayor-america-worst-mayor-chicago-has-ever-had.

145 "I'm a Black woman . . .": Taylor Penley, "Lori Lightfoot slammed for suggest-ing voters oppose her because she's a Black woman in power: her 'time is up,'" Fox News, February 27, 2023, https://www.foxnews.com/media/lori-lightfoot-slammed-suggesting-voters-oppose-because-shes-black-woman-power-time.

145-146 April 2023 teen rampage: Aubrie Spady, "Illinois state senator defends Chicago teens' rioting, looting: 'It's a mass protest'" Fox News April 17, 2023, https://www .foxnews.com/politics/illinois-state-senator-defends-chicago-teens-rioting-looting -mass-protest.

146 Mayor Brandon Johnson "the police's worst nightmare": Khaleda Rahman, "Brandon Johnson's Chicago Election Win Is the Police's Worst Nightmare," *Newsweek*, April 5, 2023, https://www.newsweek.com/brandon-johnson-chicago-election-win-police -worst-nightmare-1792609.

146 2023 increase in Chicago crime: Chicago Police Department, quoted in Ashley Carnahan, "Gianno Caldwell slams Chicago's mayor-elect . . ." Fox News, April 18, 2023, https://www.foxnews.com/media/gianno-caldwell-slams-chicagos-mayor-elect-response-rioting-always-blaming-something-else.

146 "more crime, violence and blood on the streets": Rahman, "Brandon Johnson's Chicago Election Win."

146-147 Assessment of Mayor Johnson's first 100 days: "Mayor Brandon John-son's First 100 Days in Review," August 25, 2023, Illinois Policy Institute press release, illinoispolicy.org.

147 Chicago school closings: Margaret Littman, "A decade after nearly 50 schools closed . . ." *Crain's Chicago Business*, April 24, 2023, https://www.chicagobusiness.com/ crains-forum-cps-crossroads/chicago-school-closures-2013-decade-later.

147 Chicago Public Schools enrollment decline and other CPS data and informa-tion: Ted Dabrowski and John Klingner, "New CPS data: Mayor Lightfoot, Chicago Teach-ers Union continue to keep dozens of empty, failing schools open," Wirepoints, December 29, 2022, https://wirepoints.org/new-cps-data-mayor-lightfoot-chicago-teachers-union -continue-to-keep-dozens-of-empty-failing-schools-open-wirepoints/.

147 No students able to read at grade level: Reagan Reese, "Not A Single Student is Proficient in Reading Or Math At 55 Chicago Schools: REPORT," *Daily Caller*, February 14, 2023, https://dailycaller.com/2023/02/14/math-reading-chicago-schools-report/.

147-148 Black and Hispanic literacy figures: Dabrowski and Klingner, "New CPS data."

148 Barbara Byrd-Bennett corruption case: Lauren FitzPatrick and Nader Issa, "Bar-bara Byrd-Bennett steered another $10 million . . ." *Chicago Sun-Times*, January 6, 2021, https://chicago.suntimes.com/education/2021/1/6/22216111/cps-ceo-barbara-byrd -bennett-contract-fraud-inspector-general.

148 History of Chicago corruption: Mauricio Peña, "Chicago Is Once Again the Most Corrupt City in the US," Block Club Chicago, https://blockclubchicago .org/2021/02/23/chicago-is-once-against-the-most-corrupt-city-in-the-u-s-according -to-new-study/; Heather Cherone, "Chicago ranks No. 1—Again—in Corruption,"

WTTW News, February 22, 2021, https://news.wttw.com/2021/02/22/chicago-ranks -no-1-again-corruption-report.

148 Operation Greylord: Operation Greylord, https://www.fbi.gov/history/ famous-cases/operation-greylord.

148-149 Theory why Chicago is so corrupt: Daniel Engber, "Why Is Chicago So Corrupt?" Slate, December 9, 2008, https://slate.com/news-and-politics/2008/12/why- is-chicago-so-corrupt.html.

149 High Chicago taxes: Alex Carlucci, "Chicago Ranks as Highest Taxed City in the Nation," Gustan Cho Associates mortgage brokers report, June 23, 2021, https:// gustancho.com/chicago-ranks-as-highest-taxed-city/.

149 High Chicago property taxes and debts: Matt Paprocki, "High property taxes on business owners hurt more than pocketbooks," *Daily Herald*, April 16, 2023, https://www.dailyherald.com/20230416/business/high-property-taxes-on-business -owners-hurt-more-than-pocketbooks/.

149-150 Chicago out-migration and black resident decline: Shia Kapos et al., "Black People Are Leaving Chicago En Masse," December 7, 2021, Politico, https://www .politico.com/news/magazine/2021/12/07/chicago-black-population-decline-523563.

150 Consequences of Mayor John Lindsay's policies in New York: "Former NY Mayor Lindsay Dead at 79, CBS News, December 20, 2000, https://www.cbsnews.com/ news/former-ny-mayor-lindsay-dead-at-79/.

150 "Broken windows" policing: Heather Mac Donald, "The criminologist who saved New York," *New York Post*, May 17, 2019, https://nypost.com/2019/05/17/ the-criminologist-who-saved-new-york/.

151 Claims of "broken windows" racism: Michael Goodwin, "How NYC used, then tore up broken windows policing," *New York Post*, August 15, 2020, https://nypost. com/2020/08/15/how-nyc-used-then-tore-up-broken-windows-policing-goodwin/.

151 Heather McDonald comments on "broken window" policing: Heather Mac Donald, Heather, "'Broken windows' policing doesn't target minorities, it saves them," *New York Post*, June 19, 2016, https://nypost.com/2016/06/19/broken-windows -policing-doesnt-target-minorities-it-saves-them/.

152 "we have twice proven that broken-windows policing works": Goodwin, "How NYC used, then tore up broken windows policing."

152 "impact on public safety and the NYPD . . .": Goodwin, "How NYC used, then tore up broken windows policing."

152 de Blasio missteps: Julia Marsh et al., "Bill de Blasio leaves City Hall with broken promises and dashed dreams," *New York Post*, December 30, 2021, https://nypost. com/2021/12/30/bill-de-blasio-leaves-nyc-city-hall-with-broken-promises/.

152 Mayor Eric Adams crime statistics: Gregory P. Mango, "A year into Eric Adams mayoralty . . ." *New York Post*, February 12, 2023, https://nypost.com/2023 /02/12/a-year-into-eric-adams-mayoralty-nyc-is-still-losing-ground-on-crime/.

152-153 Mayor Adams budget cuts and legislative changes: Hannah E. Meyers, "New York Must Recognize the New Realities of Crime," *City Journal*, April 26, 2023, https://www.city-journal.org/article/new-york-must-recognize-the-new-realities-of- crime.

153 George Floyd death and autopsy: Scott Neuman, "Medical Examiner's Autopsy Reveals George Floyd Had Positive Test for Coronavirus," NPR, June 4, 2020, https://

www.npr.org/sections/live-updates-protests-for-racial-justice/2020/06/04/869278494/
medical-examiners-autopsy-reveals-george-floyd-had-positive-test-for-coronavirus.

154 Greg Goodman comments about Portland: David Aaro, "Businesses leaving downtown Portland over 'lawlessness': report," Fox News, August 25, 2020, https://www .foxbusiness.com/business-leaders/businesses-leaving-downtown-portland-riots-unrest -report.

154 PDX store closing and 2020-21 homicide statistics in Portland: Emma Colton, "Portland store shuts down . . ." Fox News, November 27, 2022, https://www .foxbusiness.com/retail/portland-store-shuts-down-posts-blistering-note-front-door-slamming-rampant-crime-city-peril.

155 "if authorities don't crack down . . .": Emma Colton, "Walmart to shutter Portland locations . . ." Fox News, March 4, 2023, https://www.foxbusiness.com/retail/ walmart-shutter-portland-locations-just-months-after-ceos-warnings-crime.

155 Cracker Barrel closes Portland stores, 2,600 businesses leave: Andrew Miller, "Cracker Barrel becomes latest company to flee Portland . . ." Fox News, March 26, 2023, https://www.foxbusiness.com/retail/cracker-barrel-becomes-latest-company-flee -portland-amid-rising-crime-retail-theft.

155 REI closes Portland store: Jon Brown, "REI to shutter downtown Portland store . . ." Fox News, April 18, 2023, https://www.foxbusiness.com/retail/rei-shutter-downtown-portland-store-amid-20-year-high-break-ins-overwhelming-systems-place.

155-156 CHOP movement in Seattle: Emma Colton, "Seattle to pay millions to settle lawsuit over damages . . ." Fox News, February 25, 2023, https://www.foxbusiness .com/lifestyle/seattle-to-pay-millions-to-settle-lawsuit-over-damages-from-george-floyd-inspired-autonomous-zone-protests.

156 Seattle schools enrollment decline and layoffs: Joshua Nelson, "Seattle school district forced to do layoffs . . ." Fox News, March 2, 2023, https://www.foxnews.com/ media/seattle-school-district-forced-layoffs-amid-plummeting-student-enrollments.

156 Reasons for Seattle parents abandoning public schools: Dori Monson, "What's behind Seattle schools big enrollment drop?" KIRO News Radio, July 7, 2022, https://mynorthwest.com/3553116/dori-whats-behind-seattle-schools-big-enrollment -drop/#:~:text=While%20there%20are%20no%20exact,out%20of%20Seattle's%20 public%20schools.

156 San Francisco Farmer's Market overrun: Elizabeth Heckman, "Vendors abandon popular San Francisco farmers market . . ." Fox News, March 7, 2023, https:// www.foxnews.com/media/vendors-abandon-popular-san-francisco-farmers-market-drug -addicts-overtake-streets.

157 Nordstrom closes San Francisco locations: Louis Casiano, "Nordstrom closing 2 San Francisco stores . . ." Fox News, May 2, 2023, https://www.foxbusiness.com/retail/ norsdtrom-closing-2-san-francisco-stores-dynamics-downtown-area.

157 San Francisco District Attorney Chesa Boudin recalled: Musadiq Bidar, "San Francisco votes overwhelmingly to recall progressive DA Chesa Boudin," CBS News, June 8, 2022, https://www.cbsnews.com/news/chesa-boudin-san-francisco-da-recalled/.

157 "We can't arrest and prosecute our way . . .": Benjamin Wallace-Wells, "Why San Francisco Fired Chesa Boudin," *New Yorker*, June 8, 2022, https://www.newyorker .com/news/the-political-scene/why-san-francisco-fired-chesa-boudin.

157 "knee-jerk" reaction to drug dealer prosecution: Nicole Gelinas, "Chesa Boudin's recall is great for San Francisco . . ." *New York Post*, June 8, 2022, https://nypost .com/2022/06/08/chesa-boudins-recall-is-great-for-all-crime-plagued-cities/.

157 "Cities only work when people behave . . .": Gelinas, "Chesa Boudin's recall."

158 "share books and knowledge with neighbors": Jeffrey Clark, "San Francisco hits family with $1,402 fee..." Fox News, March 27, 2023, https://www.foxnews.com/ media/san-francisco-hits-family-1402-fee-built-free-library-neighbors-report.

158 Jackson Mayor Chokwe Antar Lumumba narrative: Laurel Duggan, "Jackson's Mayor Wanted to Create the 'Most Radical' City on Earth . . ." *Daily Caller*, August 31, 2022, https://dailycaller.com/2022/08/31/jackson-mississippi-chokwe-lumumba-water/.

158-159 Jackson trash crisis: Bracey Harris and Deon J. Hampton, "Jackson, Mississippi, reels from sudden end to trash collection," NBC News, April 6, 2023, https://www .nbcnews.com/news/us-news/jackson-mississippi-trash-collection-contract-rcna78174.

159 Prospect of legal takeover by Mississippi legislature: Omar Jimenez and Devon M. Sayers, "Democratic elected officials in Jackson, Mississippi . . ." CNN, April 26, 2023, https://www.cnn.com/2023/04/25/us/jackson-mississippi-law-enforcement -judicial-system/index.html.

159 "a slap in the face of our city," NAACP lawsuit: Jimenez and Sayers, "Democratic elected official in Jackson."

160 "ruthlessly racist," "The people I hear from . . .": Tammy Estwick, "Jackson, Miss., faces multiple challenges from multiple directions," Scripps News, April 24, 2023, https://scrippsnews.com/stories/jackson-miss-faces-challenges-from-multiple-directions/.

160 Judge allows new patrol area for capitol police: Emily Wagster Pettus, "Judge allows new court in Mississippi's majority-Black capital . . ." AP News, December 3, 2023.

160 New water utility manager: Michael Goldberg, "What's changed – and what hasn't – a year after Jackson, Mississippi's water crisis?" *Clarion Ledger*, October 18, 2023, clarionledger.com.

CHAPTER 12 – ALTERED STATES

161 New York State tax rate and wealthy payers: Thomas Barrabi, "New York's income sinks nearly $16B . . ." *New York Post*, May 1, 2023, https://nypost.com/2023/05/01/ new-yorks-income-sinks-nearly-16b-compared-to-pre-covid-as-residents-flee/.

161-162 New York State 2023 budget: Laura Nahmias and Donna Borak, "Hochul's $229 Billion New York Budget deal . . ." Bloomberg, April 28, 2023, https://www .bloomberg.com/news/articles/2023-04-28/hochul-s-229-billion-new-york-budget-deal-boosts-wages-taxes?embedded-checkout=true.

161-162 Florida state budget: John Kennedy, "After culture clashes, Florida Legislature's latest . . ." *Tallahassee Democrat*, May 4, 2023, https://www.tallahassee.com/ story/news/politics/2023/05/05/florida-legislative-session-ends-deep-cultural-divides /70177035007/.

162 Mayor Suarez commentary: Francis Suarez, "Miami's simple solution to America's crime surge," Fox News, April 27, 2023, https://www.foxnews.com/opinion/ miami-simple-solution-america-crime-surge.

162 New York and Florida education expenses per student: publicschoolreview
.com.

162 New York and Florida high school rankings: Robert Morse and Eric Brooks,
"How States Compare in the 2022 Best High School Rankings," *U.S. News & World
Report*, April 25, 2022.

163 New York and Florida changes to gross adjusted income: Barrabi, "New York's
income sinks."

**163 Governor Kathy Hochul tells residents to "jump on a bus," later wants to
"reverse the trend":** Gabriel Hays, "Hochul flamed for asking people to stop 'leaving'
New York . . ." Fox News, January 3, 2023, https://www.foxnews.com/media/hochul-
flamed-asking-people-stop-leaving-new-york-after-telling-republicans-get-out-months-
prior.

164 Karol Markowicz story and commentary: Karol Markowicz, "It's been a year
since we left New York for Florida . . ." Fox News, January 4, 2023, https://www.foxnews
.com/opinion/been-year-since-left-new-york-florida-what-learned.

165 California and Texas population changes 2021–22: Paul Best, "Texas and
Florida remain top destinations . . ." Fox News, January 3, 2023, https://www.foxbusi-
ness.com/economy/texas-florida-remain-top-destinations-movers-2022-uhaul-says.

165 California Proposition 47 and its consequences: Louis Casiano, "California
lawmakers want to reverse Prop 47 . . ." Fox News, February 16, 2022, https://www
.foxnews.com/us/california-prop-47-crime.

166 San Francisco crime: Zachary B. Wolf, "What's really going on with crime
in San Francisco?" CNN, May 3, 2023, https://www.cnn.com/2023/05/03/politics/san-
francisco-crime-rate-what-matters/index.html.

166 Consequences of Sacramento homelessness: Lee Brown, "Sacramento
sees record rise in homelessness...." *New York Post*, July 19, 2022, https://nypost
.com/2022/07/19/sacramento-facing-record-homeless-crisis-crime-wave/.

166 California homeless crisis and mental illness: Andrew Noh, "New Data Reveals
Link Between Homelessness and Crime Wave in California," 600 KOGO News Radio,
March 29, 2022, https://kogo.iheart.com/featured/the-california-report-with-carl-demaio
/content/2022-03-29-new-data-reveals-link-between-homelessness-and-crime-wave-in-
california/.

167 "make crime illegal again": Casiano, "California lawmakers want to reverse
Prop 47."

167 Massive increase in California prostitution: Emma Colton, "California
cities rattled by prostitution . . ." Fox News, February 9, 2023, https://www.foxnews
.com/us/california-cities-rattled-prostitution-human-trafficking-broad-daylight
-cops-pin-blame-new-law.

**168 Texas state law bans homeless camping, Austin residents reinstate camping
ban:** Andrew Weber, "Gov. Abbott signs bill banning homeless encampments . . ."
KUT 90.5/NPR, June 15, 2021, https://www.kut.org/crime-justice/2021-06-15/gov
-abbott-signs-bill-banning-homeless-encampments-in-texas.

168 Buying sex in Texas becomes a felony: Safia Samee Ali, "Texas is the first state to
make buying sex a felony . . ." NBC News, August 12, 2021, https://www.nbcnews.com/
news/us-news/texas-first-state-make-buying-sex-felony-will-help-trafficking-n1276617.

168 California income taxes: "California income tax brackets . . . 2023," *Business Insider*, businessinsider.com.

169 Average price of houses in California and Texas: Median Home Price by State 2023, World Population Review, worldpopulationreview.com.

169 California and Texas motor fuels taxes: State Motor Fuels Tax, Tax Policy Center, Jan 1, 2023, https://www.taxpolicycenter.org/statistics/state-motor-fuels-tax-rates.

169 trifecta of success: "Texas Dominates Nation in Annual Job Creation" press release, Office of the Texas Governor, July 21, 2023, https://gov.texas.gov/news/post/ texas-dominates-nation-in-annual-job-creation.

169 Texas budget surplus: Karen Brooks Harper, Yuriko Schumacher and Alex Ford, "How could Texas spend its record $32.7 billion surplus?" *Texas Tribune*, March 13, 2023, https://www.texastribune.org/2023/03/13/texas-budget-surplus/#:~:text=The%20 %2432.7%20billion%20budget%20surplus%20would%20cover%20school%20 lunches%20for,kindergarten%20to%20high%20school%20graduation.

169 Texas state biennial budget: Karen Brooks Harper, "Texas comptroller certifies new $321.3 billion state spending plan, sends to Abbott's desk," *Texas Tribune*, June 7, 2023, https://www.texastribune.org/2023/06/07/Texas-budget-balanced.

169 California budget deficit: Dan Walters, "California's budget deficit may be even larger than predicted," Cal Matters, February 20, 2023, https://calmatters.org/ commentary/2023/02/budget-deficit-may-be-larger/.

169-170 California population decline: Ben Christopher, "California's persistently shrinking population . . ." Cal Matters, February 17, 2023, https://calmatters.org/ newsletters/whatmatters/2023/02/california-population-exodus-housing/.

170 "there are more opportunities in California's relative youth . . .": Irene Bloem-raad and Ethan Roubenoff, "Opinion: No, California doesn't have a population crisis," *Los Angeles Times*, February 26, 2023, https://www.latimes.com/opinion/story/2023-02-26/ california-population-exodus-2022-texas-florida.

170 "For years we denied that . . .": George Skelton, "Want to stop California desertion? . . ." *Los Angeles Times*, May 4, 2023, https://www.latimes.com/california/story /2023-05-04/column-want-to-stop-california-desertion-lower-housing-costs-and-taxes.

170 "California is not a high-tax state . . .": Skelton, "Want to stop California desertion?"

170-171 Mississippi Center for Public Policy report on population decline: Aaron Rice, "Mississippi population decline continues . . ." Mississippi Center for Public Policy, January 3, 2020, https://mspolicy.org/mississippi-population-decline-continues -what-can-we-do-to-break-the-cycle/.

Chapter 13 – Success Cities

174 Coronado, California homelessness solution: Bailee Hill, "California city nearly eliminates homeless population . . ." Fox News, March 2, 2023, https://www .foxnews.com/media/california-city-nearly-eliminates-homeless-population-zero -tolerance-policy-encampments.

174-175 Miami Mayor Francis Suarez commentary: Francis Suarez, "Miami's simple solution to America's crime surge," Fox News, April 27, 2023, https://www .foxnews.com/opinion/miami-simple-solution-america-crime-surge.

175 Charlotte, North Carolina, as a banking hub and other rankings: Alaya Linton, "North Carolina Home to Top 3 Places to Start a Small Business," Lending Tree, November 13, 2023, https://www.lendingtree.com/business/small/best-places-for-new-small-businesses/.

176 Charlotte's twentieth century growth through "thoughtful and light" regulation: "The rise of banking builds a globally connected region," UNC Charlotte Urban Institute, August 28, 2019, https://ui.charlotte.edu/story/historical-overview-part-3-rise-banking-builds-globally-connected-region.

176 International companies attracted to Charlotte: "The rise of banking."

176-177 Jeremy Markovich commentary: Jeremy Markovich, "From Rust Belt to Bible Belt," *Charlotte Magazine*, August 26, 2014, https://www.charlottemagazine.com/from-rust-belt-to-bible-belt/.

177 Phoenix growth rate 2010–20: Phoenix, britannica.com

177-178 Early Phoenix history: City of Phoenix History, https://www.phoenix.gov/pio/city-publications/city-history.

178 Development of Luke Field: Thomas E. Sheridan, *Arizona: A History* (Tucson: The University of Arizona Press, 1995), 271.

178 Wartime development and round-the-clock operation: Sheridan, *Arizona*, 272.

178 Dell Webb real estate developments: Sheridan, 268–69.

178-179 Phoenix wartime corruption, prostitution, reforms: Sheridan, 273.

179 Phoenix postwar politics and reorganization: Sheridan, 273–74.

179 Open shop laws, sales tax repeal: Sheridan, 275.

179 Copper industry unionized, but overall wages lower: Sheridan, 276–77.

180 "We can run an ad in the trade magazines . . .": Sheridan, 279.

180 "refrigeration cooling has transformed Phoenix": Sheridan, 279.

180 Businessmen raise $650,000, Phoenix continues to grow: Sheridan, 280.

180-182 GPEC, The Connective, and modern-day success of Phoenix: Daisy Gonzalez-Perez, "Arizona cities continued booming growth . . ." Cronkite News, Arizona PBS, May 27, 2022, https://cronkitenews.azpbs.org/2022/05/27/arizona-cities-continued-booming-growth-last-year-census-bureau-says/; Savannah King, "Why people and companies are moving to Greater Phoenix," May 26, 2020, Greater Phoenix Economic Council, https://www.gpec.org/blog/why-people-and-companies-are-moving-to-greater-phoenix/.

182 Early history and impressions of Houston: Randolph B. Campbell, *Gone to Texas: A History of the Lone Star State* (New York: Oxford University Press, 2003), 165.

183 Businessmen build road to first Texas railroad line: T. R. Fehrenbach, *Lone Star: A History of Texas and the Texans* (New York: Da Capo Press, 2000), 319.

183 Houston builds one of America's first electric plants: "Exploring the History of Houston," (the year 1882), Greater Houston Partnership, https://houston.org/timeline.

183 Galveston hurricane: "Exploring the History of Houston" (the year 1900).

183 Spindletop gusher: "Exploring the History of Houston" (the year 1901).

183-184 Houston Ship Channel: "Exploring the History of Houston" (the year 1914).

184 "scant support" for zoning: "Exploring the History of Houston," (the year 1929).

184-185 Houston avoided racial upheavals; Texans opposed integration but obeyed the law: Fehrenbach, *Lone Star*, 683–84.

185 Houston home to more African-American millionaires: Fehrenbach, 685.

185 "Southern social ethos . . .": Fehrenbach, 685.

185 "instances in which Negroes from outside Texas . . .": Fehrenbach, 686.

185 "This is not a city . . .": Campbell, *Gone to Texas*, 445.

186 1982 energy recession and recovery: https://houston.org/timeline.

186 Lack of race politics in Houston: Erica Grieder, *Big, Hot, Cheap, and Right: What America Can Learn from the Strange Genius of Texas* (New York: Public Affairs, 2013).

186 2022 population breakdown: Greater Houston Partnership, Demographics—Race/Ethnicity, Data, Insights & Analysis, 10/12/22 (report uses 2021 data), houston .org.

187 Mayor Bill White and Project Hope Houston: Barrett Goldsmith, "Mayor outlines his vision for Project Houston Hope," *Houston Chronicle*, August 11, 2005, https://www.chron.com/news/article/Mayor-outlines-his-vision-for-Project-Houston-Hope-1479795.php.

188 One Safe Houston narrative and statistics: "One Safe Houston," Mayor's Public Safety Initiative to Combat Violent Crime, February 2022, https://www.houston tx.gov/onesafehouston/.

188 Injunction filed against HISD: Daniela Hurtado, "'Ultimately, this intervention is necessary' . . ." ABC13 Eyewitness News, March 15, 2023, https://abc13 .com/houston-isd-state-takeover-official-what-is-next-for-hisd-board-of-managers -commissioner-mike-morath-interview/12956975/.

188 Sharp decline in HISD student performance: "Houston ISD sees sharp declines in math and reading performance . . ." October 24, 2022, https://www .houstonpublicmedia.org/articles/education/2022/10/24/435786/houston-isd-sees- sharp-declines-in-math-and-reading-performance-along-with-rest-of-country-in-first- national-assessment-test-since-pandemic/.

188-189 HISD student performance improved: "HISD makes significant gains in student achievement outcomes," August 15, 2022, blogs.houstonisd.org/news.

189 RISE: "What Is RISE?" houstonisd.org/rise.

189 Texas Education Agency takes over HISD, appoints new superintendent: Pooja Lodhia and Charly Edsitty, "Former superintendent from Dallas gets the job at Houston . . ." ABC13 Eyewitness News, June 1, 2023, https://abc13.com/houston- isd-state-takeover-of-school-district-largest-in-texas-names-new-hisd-superintendent /13327538/.

190 High-flying Houston reality check: Maryann Martinez, "Houston Mayor John Whitmire says city is 'broke'. . ." *Houston Chronicle*, March 28, 2024, quoted on dailymail.co.uk.

190 "No one moves to Houston because it's fun . . .": Grieder, *Big, Hot, Cheap, and Right*, 166.

CHAPTER 14 – OPEN FOR BUSINESS

193 Scott Beyer commentary and Thomas Sowell quotes: Scott Beyer, "Root Causes of Detroit's Decline Shout Not Go Ignored," NewGeography, August 26, 2013, https://www.newgeography.com/content/003897-root-causes-detroit-s-decline-should-not-go-ignored.

194-195 Detroit population decline slowing: Quick facts, Detroit city, Michigan, https://www.census.gov/quickfacts/fact/table/detroitcitymichigan/PST045223.

195 2019 internal police investigation: George Hunter, "Detroit police probe yields allegations of widespread corruption in drug unit," *Detroit News,* December 12, 2019, https://www.detroitnews.com/story/news/local/detroit-city/2019/12/11/detroit-police-probe-uncovers-widespread-alleged-corruption-drug-unit/4398321002/.

195 Detroit police officers leaving the force a historic rate: Charlie Langton and Amber Ainsworth, "The Detroit police department has lost 223 officers this year . . ." September 1, 2022, Fox 2 Detroit, https://www.fox2detroit.com/news/the-detroit-police-department-has-lost-223-officers-this-year-why-they-are-leaving.

195 Detroit officers offered suburban jobs at graduation: Chastity Pratt, "Facing police shortage, Detroit seeks to stop new cops from jumping ship," Bridge Michigan, April 10, 2018, https://www.bridgemi.com/urban-affairs/facing-police-shortage-detroit-seeks-stop-new-cops-jumping-ship.

195 A thousand Michigan police officers left the force: "'It's just unprecedented': Michigan law enforcement agencies impacted by nationwide officer shortage," August 25, 2022, CBS Detroit, https://www.cbsnews.com/detroit/news/its-just-unprecedented-michigan-law-enforcement-agencies-impacted-by-nationwide-officer-shortage/#:~:text=shortage%20%2D%20CBS%20Detroit-,%22It's%20just%20unprecedented%22%3A%20Michigan%20law%20enforcement%20agencies,impacted%20by%20nationwide%20officer%20shortage&text=(CBS%20DETROIT)%20%2D%20The%20labor,the%20country%20and%20in%20Michigan.

195 Detroit lost 14% of its officers: Briana Rice, "More than 200 officers have quit the Detroit Police Department this year…" Michigan Radio, September 2, 2022, https://www.michiganpublic.org/public-safety/2022-09-02/more-than-200-officers-have-quit-the-detroit-police-department-this-year-twice-as-many-as-all-of-2021.

195-196 "Historically, Detroit ranks as one of the most dangerous cities . . .": "Detroit Crime Rate: The Freshest 2023 Data," July 12, 2022, Safe at Last, safeatlast.com.

196 "Detroit is dangerous . . .": Andrew Helling, "Is Detroit Safe to Visit in 2023?" March 14, 2023, Travellers Worldwide, travellersworldwide.com.

196 Detroit's high tax burden: "Detroit's High Property Tax Burden Stands as on Obstacle to Economic Growth," September 2, 2021, Citizens Research Council of Michigan, https://crcmich.org/detroits-high-property-tax-burden-stands-as-an-obstacle-to-economic-growth.

196 Proposed residential and commercial tax reduction: Caitlin Delohery, "What Is Happening to Property Taxes in Detroit?" Mansion Global, April 23, 2023, https://www.mansionglobal.com/articles/what-is-happening-to-property-taxes-in-detroit-a23084b6; Samuel Robinson, "Duggan's tax reform plan would target speculators, parking lot owners," Axios Detroit, June 1, 2023, https://www.axios.com/local/detroit/2023/06/01/duggan-tax-reform-speculators-parking-lot-detroit.

196 $600 million property tax overcharge and restitution: Jon Brown, "Detroit reveals tentative compensation plan . . ." Fox Business News, January 23, 2022, https://www.foxbusiness.com/politics/detroit-reveals-tentative-compensation-plan-overtaxed-foreclosed-homeowners.

196-197 Robert Bobb and Roy Roberts as school emergency managers: Nina Kampfer, "Detroit Public Schools: Who's Failing?" n.d., Against the Current, https://againstthecurrent.org/atc154/p3354/; "DPS Emergency Manager Roy Roberts Retires," Chicago Defender, May 2, 2013, https://chicagodefender.com/dps-emergency-manager-roy-roberts-retires/; Rebecca Klein, "Roy Roberts, Detroit Public Schools Emergency Manager, Announces Retirement," HuffPost, May 13, 2013, https://www.huffpost.com/entry/roy-roberts-retirement-detroit-public-schools-emergency-manager_n_3206014.

197 Jack Martin $50,000 bonus: Ann Zaniewski, "Former DPS emergency manager got $50,000 in bonus pay," *Detroit Free Press*, March 8, 2015, freep.com.

197 School district trades property to the city for electricity: Zaniewski, "Former DPS."

197 DPS accrued debt reaches $515 million: Chad Livengood, "DPS debt payments mount to unsustainable levels," *Detroit News*, January 4, 2016, https://www.detroitnews.com/story/news/education/2016/01/04/detroit-schools-debt-payments/78240726/.

197 DPS liabilities and legacy costs: Esmat Ishag-Osman, "Detroit Public Schools' Legacy Costs and Indebtedness," Citizens Research Council of Michigan, January 6, 2016, https://crcmich.org/publications/detroit_schools_legacy_costs_indebtedness.

197 Valerie Strauss commentary: Valerie Strauss, "How bad are conditions in Detroit public schools?" *Washington Post*, January 20, 2016, https://www.washingtonpost.com/news/answer-sheet/wp/2016/01/20/how-appalling-are-conditions-in-detroit-public-schools-this-appalling/.

197 Twelve Detroit principals took kickbacks: Sarah Cwiek, "(The Latest) Corruption Charges in Detroit's Struggling Schools," NPR, April 22, 2016, https://www.npr.org/sections/ed/2016/04/22/474737468/-the-latest-corruption-charges-in-detroits-struggling-schools.

197 "It's really evidence that emergency management didn't work . . .": "Detroit schools scores are lowest in the country in reading, math," Fox 2 Detroit, April 10, 2018, https://www.fox2detroit.com/news/detroit-schools-score-are-lowest-in-the-country-in-reading-math.

198 Dr. Alveda King commentary on renaming Ben Carson school: Dr. Alveda King, "Failing Detroit school board cancels Ben Carson . . ." Fox News, December 28, 2022, https://www.foxnews.com/opinion/failing-detroit-school-board-cancels-ben-carson-instead-doing-whats-right-students.

198 Detroit students scored below peers 2021–22: Ethan Bakuli and Koby Levin, "Detroit NAEP scores put an exclamation point on the pandemic's academic toll," Chalkbeat Detroit, October 23, 2022, https://www.bridgedetroit.com/detroit-naep-scores/.

198-199 Matthew Schneider and Richard Florida comments on corruption: Micheline Maynard, "Corruption threatens the Detroit comeback story," *Washington Post*, September 16, 2021, https://www.washingtonpost.com/opinions/2021/09/16/corruption-threatens-detroit-comeback-story/.

199 "The city has come too far since 2013 . . .": Maynard, "Corruption threatens."

199 Library system fraud: Malachi Barrett, "Fraud, tax captures and distrust define Detroit Public Library battle," Bridge Detroit, January 20, 2023, https://www.bridgedetroit.com/etroit-public-library/.

199 Police accept bribes from tow truck drivers: "Ex-Cop Sentenced for Bribery," *American Towman*, June 2023, p. 11, https://issuu.com/dortiz-towman/docs/06.2023_24 b5708dd25216.

199 Detroit Lions players suspended for gambling: Emmanuel Morgan, "The N.F.L. Broadens Its Broadcast Ambitions," *New York Times*, May 12, 2023, p. B9

199-200 Shot Stoppers program: Charlie Langton, "Detroit's new plan to fight crime pays citizens, communities up to $700K," Fox 2 Detroit, March 8, 2023, https://www.fox2detroit.com/news/detroits-new-plan-to-fight-crime-pays-citizens-communities-up-to-700k.

200 One Detroit Partnership: Russ McNamara, "Detroit police, feds announce new summer crime reduction program . . ." WDET 101.9 FM, May 26, 2023, https://wdet.org/2023/05/26/detroit-police-feds-announce-new-summer-crime-reduction-program-contains-familiar-elements/#:~:text=Detroit%20police%2C%20feds%20announce%20summer%20crime%20reduction%20program%20containing%20familiar%20elements&text=The%20initiative%20will%20target%20high,city%20on%20May%2024%2C%202023.

201-202 Project Green Light and Project Clean Slate: Mark Maxwell, "Searching for Solutions: Detroit's crime plan paves path to progress," KSDK-TV, May 18, 2023, https://www.ksdk.com/article/news/local/searching-for-solutions-detroits-crime-plan-path-progress/63-d2545110-9c9b-407a-8d9a-3dd9d11c8520.

202 2024 budget surplus and related data: Dana Afana, "Detroit City Council Approves $2.6B Budget," *Detroit Free Press*, April 10, 2023, quoted in Chamber of Commerce press release detroitchamber.com and Malachi Barrett, "Detroit has a $230M surplus. Here's how it might be spent." February 16, 2023, bridgedetroit.com. https://www.bridgedetroit.com/detroit-230m-surplus-heres-how-it-might-be-spent/.

203 Mike Ilitch biography and business history: Matt Rehbein, "Little Caesars founder Mike Ilitch dies at 87," CNN, February 11, 2017, https://www.cnn.com/2017/02/11/us/mike-ilitch-little-caesars-founder-obit/index.html.

203 Ilitch paid Rosa Parks's rent: Jim Axelrod, "After a Detroit icon dies a hidden good deed comes to light," CBS News, February 16, 2017, https://www.cbsnews.com/news/after-mike-ilitich-detroit-icon-dies-a-hidden-good-deed-comes-to-light-rosa-parks/.

204 "The truth is, Mike Ilitch was a rich old man . . .": Bill Bradley, "Mike Ilitch was no saint," Deadspin, February 17, 2017, https://deadspin.com/mike-ilitch-was-no-saint-1792480558.

204 "a demonstrated knack for buying low": quoted in Bradley, "Mike Ilitch was no saint."

204-205 Dan Gilbert background, First National Building project: Author interview with Bryan Waldron, Detroit, April 13, 2023.

205 Complaints that Gilbert's companies could do more: Annalise Frank, "Hudson's tax break gets green light," Axios Detroit, July 27, 2022, https://www.axios.com/local/detroit/2022/07/27/hudsons-tax-break-approved-detroit.

205 Gilbert's companies have invested $5 billion in Detroit including Hudson's site and Book Building: David Wysong, "Cavaliers Owner Dan Gilbert . . ." Sports Casting, April 22, 2020, sportscasting.com.

205-207 Biography and business history of Tom Kartsotis: Stacy Perman, "The Real History of America's Most Authentic Fake Brand," *Inc. Magazine*, April 2016, https://www.inc.com/magazine/201604/stacy-perman/shinola-watch-history-manufacturing-heritage-brand.html.

207-208 Ford plans for Central Station and surrounding neighborhood: Greg Migliore, "Bill Ford's dream takes shape: Historic Detroit building turns tech incubator," Autoblog, April 26, 2023, https://www.autoblog.com/2023/04/26/michigan-central-ford-detroit/.

209 Ford budgeted $740 million, other data about train station renewal: Ian Thibodeau, "Train station a necessary risk, Bill Ford says," *Detroit News*, September 12, 2018, https://www.detroitnews.com/story/business/autos/ford/2018/09/12/train-station-necessary-risk-bill-ford-says/1282287002/; Steve Friess, "The Grand reopening of Michigan Central Station," *Hour Detroit Magazine*, October 12, 2022, https://www.hourdetroit.com/community/the-grand-reopening-of-michigan-central-station/.

209 "One thing that's very important to me . . ." and following quotes: "Transcript: Bill Ford on automaker's way forward in Detroit," *Automotive News*, June 17, 2018, https://www.autonews.com/article/20180617/OEM02/180619774/transcript-bill-ford-on-automaker-s-way-forward-in-detroit; "Bill Ford, Jr., speaks at Ford celebration at Detroit train station," WXYZ-TV Detroit | Channel 7, YouTube, June 19, 2018, https://www.youtube.com/watch?v=mDsuQ67iHR.

Chapter 15 – *Resurgent Cineribus*

211-215 Christos Moisides information and quotations come from author interviews, April 15 and July 18, 2023

216 Jason Dittrich information and quotations come from author interview, April 14, 2023.

Photographs

Detroit Historical Society

Page 1: Zeppelin over Detroit
Page 2: Cars coming off assembly line

Burton Historical Collection, Detroit Public Library

Page 1: Detroit, looking up Woodward Avenue (Library of Congress Prints and Photographs Division, Washington, DC)
Page 2: Army tank being assembled
Page 3: Aerial view of highway construction; Concerned people around maps
Page 4: National Guardsmen with bayonets; Soldier protects electrical worker; Aerial view of burned-out blocks
Page 5: Boys on bikes at looted store; Line of people on a sidewalk
Page 6: Broadcast of *Meet the Press*

Christos Moisides

Page 8: New interior of Ford's Michigan Central Project

Historic Detroit

Page 8: Old exterior of Michigan Central Station, Archives, the *Detroit Free Press*, retouching by Helmut Ziewers, HistoricDetroit.org, https://historicdetroit.org/galleries/michigan-central-station-old-photos; Vandalized interior of Michigan Central: Lou Peeples, photographer (© 2010, all rights reserved, www.pointephotography.net), Historic Detroit.org, https://historicdetroit.org/galleries/michigan-central-station-photos

Joe Louis Arena

Page 7: Entrance photo by Michael Barera, https://en.wikipedia.org/wiki/Joe_Louis_Arena#/media/File:Detroit_December_2015_59_(Joe_Louis_Arena).jpg

Louis Lomax headshot

Page 6: Courtesy of the Afro-American Newspapers Archives and Research Center, Baltimore, MD; https://www.researchgate.net/figure/Louis-Lomax-author-photo-taken-for-one-of-his-later-books-Photo-courtesy-of-the_fig1_336270780

People Mover

Page 7: https://www.thepeoplemover.com/about

Reuther and Frankensteen

Page 2: Walter P. Reuther Library, Archives of Labor and Urban Affairs, Wayne State University

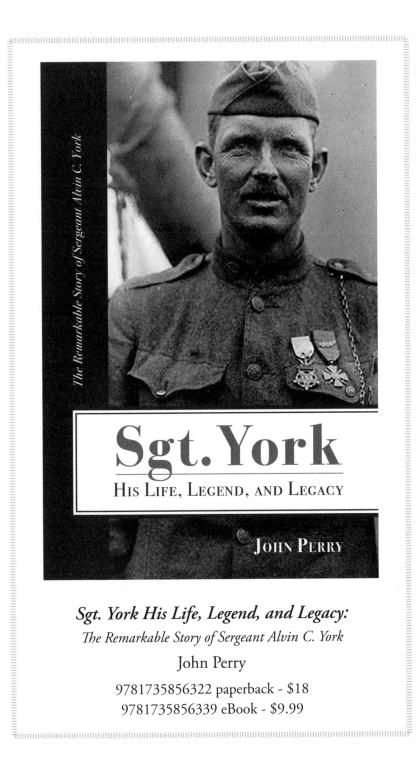

Sgt. York His Life, Legend, and Legacy:
The Remarkable Story of Sergeant Alvin C. York

John Perry

9781735856322 paperback - $18
9781735856339 eBook - $9.99

Other Great Fidelis Publishing Nonfiction

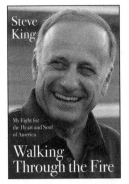

Walking Through the Fire: My Fight for the Heart and Soul of America – Steve King
9781736620649 hardcover - $28
9781736620656 eBook - $12.99

The Shadow of Death: From My Battles in Fallujah to the Battle for My Soul – Fernando Arroyo
9781737176329 paperback - $17
9781737176336 eBook - $9.99

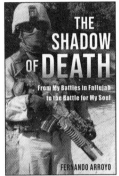

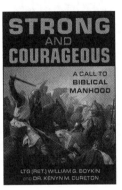

Strong and Courageous: A Call to Biblical Manhood – William G. Boykin
9781736620687 paperback - $17
9781736620694 eBook - $9.99

From Bluegrass to Blue Water: Lessons in Farm Philosophy and Navy Leadership – John Palmer
9781956454154 hardcover - $2
9781956454161 eBook - $12.99

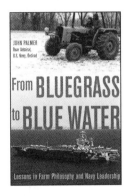

Be Bold: How a Marine Corps Hero Broke Barriers for Women at War – Tom Sileo
9781736620663 hardcover - $28
9781736620670 eBook - $12.99

Sweet Land of Liberty: Reflections of a Patriot Descended from Slaves – E. W. Jackson
9781956454208 hardcover - $29
9781956454192 eBook - $12.99

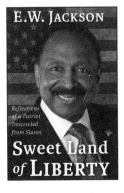